FIFTH EDITION

MAJORING

IN THE
REST OF
YOUR LIFE

career secrets for college students

Dedication

For my parents, John and Mary, and my brothers, David, Scott, Craig, and Kent, who have always provided the balance between being demanding and being supportive.

President/Publisher: Carol J. Carter—LifeBound, LLC
Managing Student Editor: Chelsey Emmelhainz
Developmental Editor: Cynthia Nordberg
Assistant Editors: Kristen Fenwick, Kara Kiehl, Amy Piazza and Heather Brown
Contributor: Tiffany Yore
Cover and Interior Design: John Wincek, Aerocraft Charter Art Service
Design Intern: Lisabeth Rea
Printing and Binding: Data Reproductions

LifeBound
1530 High Street
Denver, Colorado 80218
www.lifebound.com

Copyright © 2010 by LifeBound, LLC

ISBN-13: 978-0-9820588-0-0
ISBN-10: 0–9820588-0-2

10   9   8   7   6   5   4   3   2   1

Printed in the United States of America.

FIFTH EDITION

MAJORING

IN THE
REST OF
YOUR LIFE

career secrets for college students

Carol Carter

LifeBound

DENVER, COLORADO

contents

CHAPTER FIVE

finances for college students   84

YOUR MONEY—HOW TO GET IT AND WHAT TO DO WITH IT

CHAPTER SIX

the technology age   104

GIZMOS YOU USE

CHAPTER SEVEN

being on your own   118

BALANCING THE DEMANDS OF YOUR WORLD

CHAPTER EIGHT

stand up and be counted   134

EXTRACURRICULAR ACTIVITIES

foreword

As you embark on your college career, think about the most you can learn from this experience, not the least you can learn or the most you can do to "get by." Find your edge. Stretch yourself. Go outside of your comfort zone. Try things you have never tried. Assert yourself and your ideas. Connect with people who are different from you. Ask yourself what you have in common with people from all walks of life, not just people who see the world the way you do. Find the professors who will really challenge you, not the ones who are most likely to "give" you an A. You are your own scorekeeper now, so be sure you measure up to your own highest level of integrity, self-worth, and self-respect.

When you can, lead. Lead in class with your questions. Lead outside of class in the organizations you join. Lead with your ideas. Lead with your heart as well as your head. Lead with your convictions. Vote. Speak up. Play a role. Get an internship. Make a difference. Pay attention to your passions and your interests; work as hard as you can to develop them to the fullest. Pay attention to your weaknesses. They need not become your strengths, but you don't want them to be liabilities. So persist with the things that are hard for you and you will see that, over time, you can manage them and integrate them with the things that you do best.

Finally, connect with people who motivate and inspire you. Find role models whom you value in your friends, peer leaders, professors, and business contacts. Ask yourself how you can be of service to others and how you can use your unique abilities to help others learn and grow through your everyday actions, not just your service work.

You are creating your life. College is the chance to plant the seeds. Your life is your garden and this is your chance to get the tools and skills to tend it well for the rest of your life.

Stephen E. Loflin
EXECUTIVE DIRECTOR, NATIONAL SOCIETY OF COLLEGIATE SCHOLARS

acknowledgments

Many people have contributed their instincts, time and talents to completing my vision for the fifth edition of this book. Notably, Chelsey Emmelhainz worked as the managing student editor and masterfully composed the different featured elements. Former intern, Brittany Henning, who lives and works in San Francisco, used her journalism skills to help formulate everything from the appendices to the finance worksheet. Miriam Evangelista updated and reworked the corresponding curriculum and I greatly appreciate Heather Brown contributing her savvy editing skills and helping us organize the various stages of the manuscript process. Many thanks to Cynthia Nordberg for drafting the profile stories on each of our former LifeBound interns.

Additionally, I extend my thanks to the following former LifeBound interns for sharing their insights and strategies for personal success in each chapter: Jordan Austin, Vijali Brown, Erika Bergstrom, Josh Carter, Kelly Carson, Athena Dodd, Amanda Larghe, Jeremy Hawn, David Horn, Stephen Hosea DeMarco Kelsey, Kati Pope, and Leslie Ruybal. Their own personal successes are testimonies to the results that can be achieved when you consider what's possible and then determine to be your best. My thanks also go out to all the educators around the world that I've had the privilege of meeting and working with over the years, and to the devoted staff and academic coaches, which have inspired me to make the book relevant for today's college students and graduates.

Gratefully yours,

Carol Carter

MAJORING IN THE

CHAPTER ONE

I find that the harder I work the more luck I seem to have.

We have an extraordinary leverage in influence—individually, professionally, and institutionally—if we can only get a clear sense, a clear conception, a clear vision of the road ahead.

Who am I to talk to high school graduates and college freshmen about planning? As a high school student in Tucson, Arizona, I never planned. I just coasted along, letting things happen to me. Sure, I was spontaneous. I spent weeknights talking on the phone and studied only when I felt like it—that is, seldom. On weekends, my friends and I roamed shopping malls and partied in the mountains. I was the typical irresponsible high school student. And then, BOOM. The ax fell. The ax was not some accident, scandal, or divine intervention. It was simply a conversation with my older brother Craig during the first week of my senior year in high school. Our talk changed the course of my life.

write your own success story

PLANNING AHEAD

At seventeen, I was intimidated by my four older brothers. I saw them as bright, motivated, and respected achievers—the opposite of me. Whenever one of them asked me about what I was doing or thinking, I'd answer with a one-liner and hope he'd soon leave me alone.

This conversation with Craig was different. He didn't give up after five minutes, despite my curt, vague responses.

"Carol, what are you interested in?"

"I dunno."

"What do you think about all day?"

"I dunno."

"What do you want to do with your life?"

"I'll just let things happen."

Craig persisted. His voice grew indignant. He criticized me for talking on the phone, for spending too much time at pep rallies and rock concerts, for not studying, for not challenging myself. He pointed out that I hadn't read an unassigned book in three years. He asked if I intended to approach college in the same way I approached high school—as one continuous party. If so, he warned, I'd better start thinking of a career flipping burgers because no respectable employer would ever take me seriously. He asked me if that was what I wanted to do with my life. He cautioned that out of laziness and lack of planning I would limit my options so narrowly that I would never be able to get a real job. I had wasted three years of high school, he said. College was a new start, since employers and graduate schools seldom check as far back as high school for records. He advised me to quit making excuses, decide what I wanted, and plan how to achieve it. My only limitations would be self-imposed.

Craig left my room, sermon completed. I didn't speak to him before he flew back to New York that afternoon to finish his senior year at Columbia. I hated him for interfering in my life. He made me dissatisfied with myself. I was scared he was right. For the first time, I realized that "typical" was not necessarily what I wanted to be.

The next day, still outraged but determined to do something, I went to the library and checked out six classics: *Pride and Prejudice* by Jane Austen, *The Great Gatsby* by F. Scott Fitzgerald, *A Farewell to Arms* and *For Whom the Bell Tolls* by Ernest Hemingway, *A Portrait of the Artist as a Young Man* by James Joyce, and *Sister Carrie* by Theodore Dreiser. Then I wrote down in a notebook a few goals that I wanted to accomplish. They all seemed boldly unattainable: Earn straight A's (previously I had made B's and C's); study every week including one weekend night; keep reading classics on my own. If I couldn't make it in my senior year of high school, why should I waste time and money on college? If that was the case, I'd beat fate to the door and begin my career at the hamburger stand immediately.

Three weeks later, I got a letter from Craig. He knew how angry I was with him. He told me our conversation hadn't been easy for him either, but that if he hadn't cared he wouldn't have bothered to say anything. He was right. I needed that sermon. If I didn't come to terms with my problems, I would never be able to move from making excuses to making things happen.

I worked hard and got results. The second semester of my senior year, I made all A's (except for a B in physics). I finished the six classics and others as well. I started reading newspapers and magazines. I had to move the *Vogue* on my nightstand to make room for *Time, Harper's,* and *Fortune.* I found I could set goals and attain them, and I started to realize that I wasn't so different from my brothers, after all.

To my utter astonishment, I discovered for the first time that I enjoyed learning. My world seemed to open up just because I knew more about different kinds of people, ways of thinking, and ways of interpreting things that I had previously assumed to be black-and-white. If you are a shy person, joining a club and getting to know—and actually like—a few people whom you had originally perceived as unfriendly or uninteresting may astonish you as much as my newfound appreciation for learning astonished me.

The summer before college, I thought about what I wanted to do with my life. But I couldn't decide on a direction. I had no notion of what I wanted to major in. What to do . . . what to do?

I turned to Craig, a phone call away in New York City, who told me not to spend my first year of college worrying about what I wanted to do. The main priority was to learn as much as I could. College, he told me, was my golden opportunity to investigate all kinds of things—biology, psychology, accounting, and philosophy. He told me I'd become good at writing and critical thinking techniques—skills that would help me learn any job after graduation. And though I could continue to expand my educational horizons throughout life, college was the best opportunity to expose myself to the greatest minds and movements of our civilization.

Craig also warned me that being a scholar, though important, wouldn't be enough. He had just graduated from Columbia as a Phi Beta Kappa, but since he hadn't gained any real-world experience in college, it took him several months to find his first job. To maximize my options upon graduation, I would have to do three things:

1. Learn as much as possible from classes, books, professors and other people.
2. Participate in extracurricular activities.
3. Gain real-world experience by working part-time and landing summer internships.

If I did these three things reasonably well, Craig assured me, I could choose from a number of career opportunities at the end of my senior year. And even if I only did two of the three full-force and one half-speed, I'd still be in good shape. Making an effort in each area and having a modest outcome were attainable goals. That way I could balance my college experience and open options for the future.

Craig advised me to look ahead and develop a plan of action for each of my four years of college. He told me that foresight—the ability to consider the bigger picture beyond short-term challenges and intermittent goals—is invaluable in most jobs; it distinguishes outstanding people from the rest of the pack.

This book is designed to be for you what Craig was for me: my adviser during college. The following chapters will provide you with guidelines for success by asking you to examine yourself, set goals, and believe in your ability to achieve them. It will give you specific examples of how to get things done. It will also introduce you to all kinds of people, all of whom followed diverse paths toward their goals. Most important, you'll learn that everyone—including YOU—has his or her own set of skills, abilities, passions, and unique talents to tap. Finding the career and lifestyle that allow you to cultivate and nurture them is one of the most important secrets of success.

Additionally, you will uncover ideas to structure your college years and beyond. These ideas will no longer be secrets of success; they will become tools for building a rewarding future. Use this book to your advantage but also enjoy it. While you explore this book, you will discover new things about your world and your life. The stories are written to help you understand the achievements and experiences of other students just like you! Take advantage of these stories, they'll help you mold life's decisions. In addition, the activities and questions at the end of each chapter are designed to help you grow into adult life while you learn more about yourself. The future is in your hands and the world full of opportunities. Only you can take the steps needed for your success, and these lessons will point you in the right direction.

so take action!

 good way to start is to assess your shortcomings and strengths. As I've already told you, one of my short-comings in high school was not learning all I could from my classes and teachers. Your shortcoming may have been that you focused entirely on your studies without developing many outside interests or activities. Someone else may feel that he concentrated so much on an outside activity (such as training for a particular sport) that he had no time for studies or friends. What was your major shortcoming in high school?

Now think about three things:

1. What pleased you in high school?
2. What could you have done better?
3. What do you want to improve on in the future?

Identifying these areas will help you balance your past experiences and future goals during college. You will have a clearer notion of what you do and don't want in the future. That's important.

Whether you are a high school senior, a college freshman or a college senior, the next thing you must do is decide to take action. Don't worry if you don't know what you want to do. Just commit yourself to the process. If you do, you'll eventually find out which careers might be best for you and how you could best prepare for them.

To recap, here are the priorities:

1. Gain knowledge.
2. Participate in activities.
3. Get real-world experience.

making it happen

"Luck is the residue of design," said Branch Rickey, known as The Mahatma for his strategic methods as a team owner and general manager in baseball. He developed the farm system in which the minor leagues are organized. His plans of action took a handful of disjointed teams in faraway cities and banded them into an organization that left its mark on American culture.

Nothing happens magically. If you want to be a success, you are going to have to take personal responsibility for your life. Why do some graduates get twenty job offers and others receive none? Although successful people may appear lucky, they actually illustrate the maxim "Luck favors the prepared mind."

Joe Cirulli agrees. He is the owner of the successful Gainesville Health and Fitness Center in Florida. Early in his life, exercise was a priority and an essential part of his day. So he followed his interests and put his talents to work by starting his own health club. While many other clubs folded around him, he experienced enormous success. His membership continues to grow, and he is able to keep his club filled with the best equipment and the most knowledgeable professionals.

When Joe was twenty, he worked as an assistant manager and a sales representative for a health club. One of his responsibilities there was to train new sales representatives. He worked hard to prepare them for their jobs only to have to compete with them once they were trained.

He remembers talking with the vice president of the company about his frustration. The vice president, a person Joe respected, advised him to keep on putting his best efforts into his work. "Right now you may not see the benefit of your hard work but one day you will."

Joe followed his advice. Less than five years later, his skills at training people in the health-club industry paid off—he was able to put his expertise to work at his own club. "Knowing how to motivate employees to do their best, to care about the quality of their work, and to care about our customers has had an enormous impact on the success of my own company."

Joe believes the secret to his success is giving 100 percent of himself in everything he does. "Success is the culmination of all your efforts. There are thousands of opportunities for people who give their all."

How do you arrange to have the most options when you leave college? Plan, develop foresight, and take charge of your life, and you will become one of the lucky ones. Most important, decide that you want to succeed—and believe it.

Charles Garfield, a clinical psychologist who has spent his career studying what motivates people to superior effort, says that the drive to excel comes primarily from within. Can "peak performances" be learned? Yes, says Garfield. High achievers are not extraordinarily gifted superhumans. What they have in common is the ability to cultivate what the German writer Johann Wolfgang von Goethe termed, "the genius, power, and magic" that exists in all of us. These achievers increase the odds in their favor through simple techniques that anyone can cultivate:

1. Envision a mission.
2. Be result-oriented.
3. Tap your internal resources.
4. Enlist team spirit.
5. Treat setbacks as stepping-stones.

These are skills that this book is going to teach you.

who will you meet in this book?

s you read through these chapters, you will meet people who have stretched themselves, tried, strived, and thrived. Some of the people realized dreams they held since childhood. Their path was straight and deliberate. Others embraced unique opportunities and discovered passions they never knew existed. Regardless of their start, they all remained open to possibility along the way.

In "Insights from an Intern" you will meet former LifeBound interns. LifeBound, in addition to publishing this book, provides seminars, coaching, tutoring, and resources for students, teachers, parents and professionals at all levels. With a mission to promote professional excellence and lifelong learning, LifeBound is selective when hiring interns. Some of those featured are still students, while others have graduated and launched careers. It's interesting to note that although they all interned at LifeBound, their aspirations and accomplishments vary greatly. They will share what they learned through interning and its application in the working world.

In "Real Work in the Real World" you will meet established professionals. These professionals share their advice, lessons they learned the hard way, and their keys to success. At one point they, too, looked into the future, anticipating what lay ahead. May their stories inspire you!

To get you started, here is the profile of one of LifeBound's first interns. As her story indicates, her dedication to growth and her future, along with an awesome internship, aided in the development of her professional confidence and poise.

Kelly S. Carson, web developer

K elly Carson began working with LifeBound after her freshman year of college as a "general purpose" intern and branched out into website and technology responsibilities. She soon assumed a three-year role as the organization's paid director of technology and website development.

Upon initially working with the organization, she recalls feeling as if she didn't necessarily have the "chops" to work with what she considered to be such an amazingly professional and accomplished group of people. "I think the biggest thing that I learned from working with LifeBound is the vital importance of professional confidence," Kelly says. "As I eventually learned, my age didn't have to factor into the equation—if I worked hard and came across as competent and driven, I would be successful."

Adaptability was another skill learned while working with LifeBound. She now understands that in the professional world, projects, staff, goals and ideas can all change without a moment's notice—and you need to be flexible in order to handle the challenge of change with grace and a high quality of work.

"I was both flattered and surprised when my current coworkers complimented me on how 'poised' I am when responding to change," Kelly says. "I credit that to my work with LifeBound and the incredible mentorship that Carol Carter provides."

Kelly says her internship with LifeBound planted a seed that has helped her to discover a desired path in life. "I enjoyed so much being in a professional atmosphere, especially when I had the opportunity to share my skills, knowledge and advice with others." This love of teaching and advising in a professional setting placed Kelly on a course to where she is today—about to enter business school at Harvard to obtain an MBA with a focus in consulting.

She believes that having an internship in college helped her to be successful quickly after obtaining an undergraduate degree. "The professional lessons I learned at LifeBound have been a great help to me in my work at El Pomar Foundation [Program Associate], and have served as an incredible asset as I applied to MBA programs." Kelly admits that she is a bit younger than the typical MBA candidate—but when she explained that her professional experience dates all the way back to her freshman year of college, she found that MBA programs respond very enthusiastically. In fact, she was recently offered a full-tuition scholarship to one of the top MBA programs in the country—what she considers to be an incredible repayment of the investment made by taking on an internship during college.

first things first

The first thing to keep in mind when planning: accept the world the way it is. Your plans should be based on a realistic assessment of how things are, not on some starry-eyed vision of how they should be. You can dream, but there's a happy medium between cold reality and the pie in the sky. That's why you must be open to opportunity. Indeed, you must create it. Although you can't change the hand you were dealt, you can play it wisely. That's what this book is about. So start today. Start now.

The more questions you ask now, the better prepared you'll be in four years. You don't want to be stuck in a boring job or wondering why you can't find work.

Are you going to make mistakes? I hope so, unless you're not human. Making mistakes is the process by which we learn. And whenever we're disappointed by the outcome, we need to maintain a positive attitude, log the information—and keep going. The key is to learn from your mistakes without letting them slow you down.

CHAPTER TWO

know thyself.

To thine own self be true.

WILLIAM SHAKESPEARE

Y ou've been told that it pays to find out everything you can about the colleges you're thinking of attending and the jobs they might lead to. But it's also worthwhile to do some serious research into the subject that can make or break your college experience: yourself.

Phil was a pre-law freshman. After spending six months talking to law students and attorneys, he made a great discovery. He realized that he didn't want to be a lawyer! No area of law intrigued him. He disliked spending hours in solitary research, and law didn't accommodate his strengths—working with groups and developing programs. So Phil switched his major to English and his minor to history. Today he's in business for himself as an international marketing consultant. And he loves his work.

discover who you are

DEFINING YOUR INTERESTS, ABILITIES, AND GOALS, AND UNDERSTANDING EMOTIONAL INTELLIGENCE

If you don't know yourself, you'll make uninformed decisions. My college friend Mary was an accounting major because she knew she'd be employable. She was right. But she soon discovered that she hated working with numbers, and after just two years, she quit accounting. So long, general ledger.

I recently had dinner with Mary. She's living in New York and writing for a food-and-wine magazine. We talked about the internal struggles that prompted her to make a career change. Now she's crazy about her job and regrets only that she didn't invest the time and energy in college to determine her interests. "College students shouldn't opt for a career because it will be easy to find a job," Mary says. "Easy can equal uninteresting and unfulfilling if you don't have a passion and interest for the work itself. Pursue what will be rewarding in the short term and the long term."

Cathy Hudnall agrees. After five years as a secretary at Wells Fargo Bank in San Francisco, she was invited to join the bank's junior officer training program. Realizing she had a true interest in and aptitude for banking, she enrolled in the American Graduate School of International Management. "Find out while you're in college what makes you tick," says Cathy, who is now a senior manager and vice president at the Bank of Canada.

"Nothing great was ever achieved without enthusiasm," said Ralph Waldo Emerson. You want to be enthusiastic about your job so that you will do it well and enjoy it. In order to do that, you must first take some time to analyze what it is you like to do.

An honest and complete self-appraisal is your first step toward choosing the right career. By asking yourself critical questions, you'll be way ahead of most of your classmates—leagues, fathoms, kilometers squared. Way ahead.

the three Ds

Which of the following describes you best?

1. **Drifter.** Life just happens to you, often in ways decidedly unfriendly or random.

2. **Dreamer.** You have wonderful plans for the future but can't always realize your dreams. Your favorite line is borrowed from Scarlett O'Hara, of *Gone with the Wind* fame: "I can't think about it now. I'll think about it tomorrow."

3. **Doer:** You have the confidence, the vision, and the persistence to make your goals come together. You plan, act, and achieve.

Most people are some combination of the above. Maybe you've been a Drifter. In this chapter, you'll be able to graduate to Dreamer as you explore your interests, abilities, and passions. The rest of this book is devoted to becoming a Doer.

Does this mean that drifting and dreaming are not important? On the contrary. One of my best friends, Madeline, aptly reminded me that a balance of drifting and dreaming is necessary. "All doing squashes the learning, pain, and growth that dreaming and drifting inspire," she wrote. "Success is balance. It is reading well, thinking deeply; having the wisdom to see the broader picture; knowing the importance of friends and family; taking the time to marvel at a sunset, a small child, or an older person."

finding a balance

A balance of drifting, dreaming, and doing will help you define and achieve what you determine is most important in college, in work, and in life. So how might you go about "discovering" yourself further? Here are four suggestions:

1. Keep a journal.
2. Survey yourself.
3. Keep asking questions.
4. Overcome obstacles.

1. KEEP A JOURNAL

Throughout college, keep track of your plans, deeds, fears, and dreams. Write down goals for yourself and then reread them after six months. Which have you achieved? Which do you want to pursue now?

Your journal is your secret companion. Write in it every day, through good times and bad. Share your expectations and aspirations, your disappointments and fears. Write about the world as you see it. Be blunt and honest. After a month, begin rereading your journal. It will reveal interesting patterns. You'll see a progression, too, and that's rewarding.

Pam Zemper, vice president and director of marketing at Security Pacific Executive Professional Services, says that she has always kept lists—they are her form of journal writing. Her lists remind her of activities she wants to try, subjects she wants to learn, and ways she wants to grow. "As I go back and review my lists over the years, I can see how certain dreams tie together. My lists give me a framework out of which I formulate my goals and then my plans."

2. SURVEY YOURSELF

Answer the following questions as honestly as you can. After all, no one else is going to see your answers unless you want them to.

These questions should help you evaluate your high school experience and define your college goals. They will also help you get a handle on your strengths and weaknesses, which will be the key elements to locate in your process of self-discovery. Throughout your life, you'll find it helpful to look back at what you've done periodically so that you can get perspective on what you want to do as you go forward. Later in the book you'll have a chance to look ahead and dream about what kinds of things you want to do. For now, look back and reflect for a moment.

how I see myself

1. In high school, I felt most proud that I

2. I feel most disappointed that I did not

3. The most important thing I learned in high school was

4. I developed confidence by

5. The teacher who had the greatest positive influence on me was

6. In high school, I was motivated by

7. The five things I enjoyed most were

8. The five things I enjoyed least were

9. The five things I found most interesting were _____

_____

10. My biggest disappointment was _____

_____

11. My greatest success was _____

_____

12. The most difficult thing I've had to do is _____

_____

13. In high school, I considered myself _____

_____

14. My friends would describe me as _____

_____

15. If I could change one thing in my life, it would be _____

_____

16. I am angered by _____

_____

17. I would describe myself as the kind of person who _____

_____

18. The thing I would most like to change about myself is _____

_____

19. My philosophy on life is _____

_____

20. One thing I would like to improve is _____

_____

myself among others

1. The kind of people I most like to be with are _____
   _____

2. I most admire my fellow students and teachers who _____
   _____

3. The kind of people I find it most difficult to be around are _____
   _____

4. The person who has had the most influence on my life has been ___
   _____

   because _____
   _____

5. The character traits I like most in people are _____
   _____

6. The ones I dislike most are _____
   _____

7. Given a choice between being with others or being by myself,
   I usually choose to _____
   because _____

Keep in mind that self-discovery requires reexamination. As your perspective and ideas change, you'll find yourself revising your earlier lists. With each revision you will move closer to your goals, both in the short and long term. Don't worry if you can't answer all of these questions now. You'll have plenty of time in the next few years to explore different areas that interest you. These answers will serve as your information base when the time comes to evaluate your career path.

3. KEEP ASKING QUESTIONS

Don't be complacent and accept everything you read and hear. Find out if things make sense. We've all heard the slogan, "Question authority." Let it serve as a gentle reminder.

Challenge friends, parents, and teachers in discussion. Learn opposing viewpoints and continually question your beliefs. Practice putting yourself in other people's shoes. Continue to develop your critical-thinking skills. Ask yourself what you're doing, why you're doing it, and how you can do it better.

Dick Christensen, a community psychiatrist and an assistant professor at the University of Florida, was torn between pursuing a career in medicine and working as a priest in the inner city. One of the strategies he used to help him make a decision was to talk with people and ask them questions.

"Perhaps the most valuable experiences of my college years were the opportunities I found to spend time with people who were doing what I was considering," he explains. "I spent time with people who had returned from the Peace Corps, I listened to physicians talk about their experiences in medicine and I saw firsthand what it was like for a person to live and work in the inner city as a priest. My college years afforded me the luxury of time, even in the midst of academic demands, to approach others with life questions that could only be answered by life experiences."

4. OVERCOME OBSTACLES

Everyone has insecurities and shortcomings. It's a fact of life. However, we don't like to explore our dark sides. We usually keep them locked up tightly inside. Left unattended, our insecurities are manifested as fear; and the more you try to run from fear, the more it will dominate your life. Think of the dilemma as an intellectual puzzle to be solved. Turn the puzzle around in your mind, looking at it from as many angles as possible. Be comforted by the fact that you do have a choice: you can be courageous and deal effectively with your fears.

The first step toward overcoming your fears is identifying them. Complete the following statements honestly.

what are you afraid of?

1. Very few people realize that I am afraid of _____
   _____

2. When I am alone the thing that frightens me most is _____
   _____

3. When I am with other people the thing that frightens me most is _____
   _____

4. I'm embarrassed when _____
   _____

5. My greatest fear about college is _____
   _____

The next step is to accept these fears. That's right. In order to over-come your fears, it helps to embrace them. Here's an exercise that will help. Imagine that each of the five situations above came true and that you were forced to confront your fear. Answer the following questions for each:

let go of your fears

1. Describe the scene in detail. _____
   _____
   _____
   _____
   _____

2. What happened?

_____

_____

_____

3. What does it feel like?

_____

_____

4. What were you thinking?

_____

_____

5. What could you have done to make the anxiety more tolerable?

_____

_____

_____

Aside from fears, other obstacles will surely get in your way. Maybe you think you're not smart enough because of that IQ test you took in fourth grade. You were having a bad day; it happens. Maybe you believe that you're incompetent because you didn't ace the SATs. Relax. Remember, even Einstein flunked at least one critical exam.

Einstein is not unique, at least not on that score. Robert Sternberg, a noted Yale psychologist, has done extensive research on IQ tests and intelligence. He has noted that intelligence is a composite of several factors. Many of these—including motivation and the capacity to adjust to change—are difficult to measure accurately using a written test. If you do score well on aptitude tests, don't rest on your laurels. Your brain is not a bank. It cannot pay the rent, nor can it pay for the Himalayan odyssey you're hoping will get you away from home for the summer. Stretch your natural talents by coupling your intellect with determination and a commitment to action.

Erika Bergstrom, *marketing coordinator*

*I*n college Erika started out majoring in natural resources with an emphasis on environmental conservation. Her long-term goal was to become a park ranger, but about halfway through her coursework, she changed her mind. Erika explains, "When I learned how much people had already marred the environment, I became discouraged and quit school for a while." After taking a semester off to reflect on a new career direction, Erika decided to pursue a degree in communications. "I always liked print communication, and when I heard about the publishing internship at LifeBound my senior year, it was a perfect fit."

While Erika enjoyed some aspects of the internship and felt a strong connection with its mission to make a difference in students' lives, she didn't feel her skills were a good match for the position. "The internship focused on sales, which wasn't my strength," says Erika. Rather than becoming discouraged and quitting, Erika talked with the president of LifeBound, Carol Carter, to voice her consternation and ideas. Together they created a new internship for Erika, one better suited to her abilities and interests. Reflecting on their conversation, Carol Carter says, "Erika's inner-determination and self-awareness helped us create an internship for her that met our company's needs and her expectations."

In the newfangled internship, Erika helped organize LifeBound's growing office by assigning space for the office supplies and products. "From the internship experience, I discovered that I like to see results at the end of the day. I like to bring order out of chaos and feel like I've contributed," Erika explains. Erika successfully completed two internships with LifeBound. In the second internship, she gained valuable experience developing marketing tools, which included presentation materials and PowerPoint presentations. "I really enjoy the entire production process."

Soon after graduating from college, Erika landed an amazing position as a marketing coordinator for Herry International, a construction management firm located on the Miracle Mile in Los Angeles, California. Describing her new work situation Erika says, "I can see the Pacific Ocean from our office building, and right next door is Beverly Hills. We're also near the La Brea Tar Pits archaeological site where they excavate dinosaur bones." In her latest project, Erika helped secure a $500-million contract for a new health center at the UCLA campus by making the exhibits for the proposal.

Erika credits the LifeBound internships for helping her get this job. She explains, "I could tell that the interviewers were impressed with the materials I had created for LifeBound and with LifeBound itself as a thriving new company. From my current vantage point, I really feel the sky's the limit."

winning against all odds

There are other obstacles much more formidable than genius or the lack of it. Jackie Fitzgerald, the national sales manager for Sunlover Clothing Products, supported her family while attending Villanova University in Pennsylvania. She had begun college as a pre-med student because her mother had always wanted her to be a doctor.

"I didn't have the financial support from my family that most students have," Jackie recalls. "After I decided I didn't want to be a doctor, I lost all emotional support from my mom." This, Jackie says, was the greatest obstacle she had to overcome.

She learned how to encourage herself when no one else was there to cheer her on. With her many commitments, Jackie learned time management and self-reliance. These skills enabled her to graduate with honors as a sociology major and psychology minor and to become enormously successful in business. "It's better to graduate with a solid education in a field you love than to pursue a career in an area you're not passionate about."

For Jill Goldfarb, things were worse. During the first week of her freshman year at the University of Michigan, her mother died of a stroke. Jill dropped out of school for the fall semester and worked at a department store before going back in the spring. In March, her father died suddenly of a heart attack.

"I survived because I had to," says Jill, who immersed herself in her studies and extracurricular activities. Her hard work and dedication were perhaps the greatest tributes she could pay to her parents. Remarkably, Jill graduated with a degree in management information systems with a 4.0 average.

If you're starting college under a difficult (or even tragic) circumstance, don't let a disadvantage deny you success. There is truth to the old adage that adversity breeds character. Learn the difference between situations that you can and can't control. Set your sights on a goal that you can achieve, and then go for it. Throughout life, each of us encounters obstacles and challenges on a regular basis. How we deal with these challenges, and what we make of them, determines our true success.

emotional intelligence

When you dare, your dreams, goals, and inspirations keep you looking ahead and moving forward. How you balance those ambitions with the setbacks and happenstance of everyday life shows how emotionally intelligent you are. Emotional intelligence also emerges from how gently you handle the dreams and hopes of others, as well as your own. By finding the strengths and weaknesses in your emotional intelligence, you discover whether you need to make sacrifices to achieve discipline in use of your time, without losing your underlying focus, to attend to spontaneous moments in your life. You never know.

WHAT IS EMOTIONAL INTELLIGENCE?

Feelings are a wonderful part of being alive. What would life be like without love, joy, and excitement? What if you could never enjoy the first snowfall of winter, a fun evening with your closest friends, or the welcome feeling of returning home on your breaks from school? Of course, there's the downside too—breaking up with your partner, failing a test, having your computer break down, and so on. But there's more to life than working, eating, and sleeping.

The way you handle your emotions is crucial to your success in life. Emotional intelligence is the ability to know what you and those around you are feeling—and to handle those feelings skillfully.

In 1995, Yale scholar Daniel Goleman released his groundbreaking book *Emotional Intelligence,* which brought this new thinking to light. Goleman contends that the mystique of a high IQ has led us to ignore emotional savvy, which can be as vital in determining the course of our lives. He argues that EQ (Emotional Intelligence Quotient) may be even more important for success in life than IQ (Intelligence Quotient.)

THE IMPACT OF EMOTIONS

Stress is everywhere—in our personal relationships, our jobs, our finances, our social standings. Do you cringe when you're expected to address a room full of people? How do you respond when you sense a friend is feeling nervous or lonely? These are the kinds of emotionally charged situations where a high IQ won't solve anything for you. Goleman explains that although you may be highly intelligent and studious, a lack of self-control or an impersonal demeanor can actually sabotage your career and personal relationships.

"The brightest among us," he writes, "can be emotional morons." Take the case of Jason Haffizulla, a Florida high school student who dreamed of entering Harvard Medical School. He had so many A1 grades in so many courses that his grade point average was 4.614, well above a straight A. But one day, when his physics teacher gave him a B on a quiz, Jason lost control and stabbed the teacher with a kitchen knife. The consequences of his impulsive actions will affect the rest of his life.

In addition to there being no insurance against acts of passion, a brainy IQ lends no warmth or social grace to a person's character. Emotional intelligence leads to greater drive, self-discipline, caring, and cooperation.

MANAGING STRESS

Stress is one of the most pressing concerns of our time. According to the American Medical Association, up to 90 percent of all visits to doctors are for stress-related ailments. A highly stressful life can lead to health problems as simple as tight muscles or as serious as heart disease and cancer. Learning to de-stress is an essential skill for maintaining your emotional equilibrium. Fortunately, there are a number of ways to manage our reactions to stressful events.

FACING INSECURITIES

Consciously or unconsciously, all of us have felt that we must meet certain arbitrary standards to attain self-worth. Failure to do so threatens our security and significance. This results in a fear of failure and can lead to obsessive behavior.

"The more insecure people are, the more desperate they are to have control," says Howard Rankin, clinical psychologist and director of the Carolina Wellness Retreat in Hilton Head, South Carolina. "If you can't get it in one area, you try to get it in another." Eating disorders like anorexia nervosa are another distorted form of control, he says—a way to compensate for feeling powerless.

You may feel overwhelmed and helpless. You may obsessively play over in your mind again and again how you could have performed better on a test or handled an argument better. Learning from your mistakes is certainly noble, but uncontrolled rumination only burns up precious emotional energy that could be used for other tasks. When you catch yourself obsessing, stop and remind yourself that while you could have done better, you've learned from that situation and it's time to move on. Say this to yourself several times a day, if necessary. This kind of positive self-talk will help you put things in perspective.

The key to the control teeter-totter is accepting that there are some things you simply cannot control. Diseases strike, your favorite team loses, and you can't be perfect at everything. Hard work does pay off, but in some cases it's best to let go. Remember, it's not all up to you.

Even though you can't control certain events, you can control your reaction to them, says psychologist Nancy Schlossberg, professor emeritus at the University of Maryland and author of *Overwhelmed: Coping with Life's Ups and Downs.* "Even if you can't control the earthquake, you can control how you deal with it," she says. "You have to acknowledge the loss, grieve, refocus the camera, and possibly reshape the dream." The ability to let go is a critical step toward fortifying your emotional intelligence.

MANAGING DIFFICULT EMOTIONS

Ruby Bridges, a shy little girl from New Orleans, accomplished an astonishing feat. In the fall of 1963, she became one of the first African Americans to integrate into an all-white school. It was a monumental task for anyone, especially for a six-year-old kindergarten student. Every day a federal marshal accompanied Ruby to school because she had to pass through a gauntlet of outraged citizens as she entered the building. The angry mob shouted abusive chants at her. One of the protesters even brought a black doll inside a baby's coffin and thrust it in Ruby's face in an effort to intimidate her.

Robert Coles, a child psychologist, came upon these harrowing incidents every day on his way to work and was deeply disturbed by the venom directed at this child. He had also studied the coping skills of children in stress, so he offered to help Ruby cope with her trauma. With her parents' permission, Dr. Coles began meeting regularly with Ruby to determine if she was emotionally holding up under the pressure, and if so, how.

He couldn't have been more surprised by his research. Ruby wasn't only coping; she was thriving in spite of the difficulties. At the close of his sessions with her, Dr. Coles noted, "Having something to believe in protected Ruby from psychiatric symptoms and gave her a dignity and a strength that is utterly remarkable."

The story of Ruby Bridges epitomizes what we mean by exercising emotional intelligence in the face of difficulties. Ruby's emotional resiliency helped to keep her strong. You too can face the stresses of college life, and beyond, when you channel your emotional energy toward a meaningful purpose.

THE GOOD NEWS ABOUT DIFFICULT EMOTIONS

Although emotional suffering feels like an unwelcome intruder, every difficult emotion has the potential for developing your emotional intelligence. Instead of denying or repressing negative emotions, realize that feelings like stress, anger, and sadness provide the training ground for developing healthy coping mechanisms.

Although you may find it hard to be content when you're confronted with a problem, a measure of contentment is possible as you learn to manage adverse emotions constructively instead of allowing them to control you. Consider Derik Baker, a sophomore at Columbia University in New York City. While playing football during his freshman year, he seriously injured his knee and could not return to the game. "All through high school I dreamed of playing football in college," he says. "Then everything was shattered."

Derik overcame his disappointment with the support of his family and friends. "I called my mom a lot, especially after rehab workouts, because I'd feel so discouraged," he says. "She listened and reminded me that even though I couldn't play football, I was at a top-notch school and that I had a lot to be thankful for." He also drew emotional strength from his friends. "Just being with my friends, even if we weren't talking about what happened to me, helped. They made me feel accepted."

Derik Baker also felt intellectually inferior to his peers. "Coming from a small public school in a small town, I wondered, 'Do I have the ability to go to school here?' I mean, the kids here are so amazing." Derik says that the classes at Columbia are highly interactive and students must orally present their ideas and thoughts in group settings—something Derik felt uncomfortable with. "At my high school we never did that. We just took in information from the teacher. All I got out of a book was the information that I read. When we read a book in my humanities class [at Columbia], we discuss it, and I almost never add to the discussion. When the other students read the book, it stirs up thoughts and they make connections. If I do speak my mind, I feel like I do it on a lower level than my classmates. I think I may always struggle with this feeling of intimidation but I've learned how to cope with it."

One way Derik copes is by improving his writing skills so that the work he turns in compensates for his lack of class participation. He has also met with his professors to explain why he doesn't fully participate in the discussions and to ask for their advice.

Derik reminds himself that even though he may not think as critically and analytically as his peers, he is rich in life experiences. "I have a few more life experiences being middle class and working. A lot of them haven't played sports and most come from wealthier families than mine. In casual talk, my friends may come up with something from a poet. A lot of what they're saying sounds academic, whereas I talk about something that has happened in my life. I think that's a kind of smart, too."

FUELING MOTIVATION

Without motivation, almost nothing would get done. Motivation is the force that propels you to complete assignments and accept new challenges. Imagine dragging yourself through every task with only a half-hearted effort. Not only would important work go undone, but life would get pretty boring.

Motivation is most often fueled by enthusiasm. Although some people may seem to be born with a sunnier disposition, you can develop the enthusiasm to make you happy and successful. Enthusiastic people typically show greater peace of mind, higher self-esteem, a stronger sense of well-being, and even better physical health. This leads to increased success in school and in the workplace.

Here are a few ways to add enthusiasm to your life:

1. **Engage in activities that you enjoy.** Make a list of the top ten things you enjoy doing and do at least one of them a week, suggests Erik Olesen in *Mastering the Winds of Change*. "Studies

have found that people who do more of what they enjoy rate their lives better within six months," he says.

2. **Associate with enthusiastic people.** "Enthusiastic people have an energy that you can't help but be affected by," says Harold Bloomfield, a leading psychological educator. "Being around them can make you feel upbeat and positive."

3. **Seek inspiration.** Look for books, movies, art, or music that has a positive effect on you. Sometimes you can find a character in a story or a few lines of a song that you identify with—feed off this energy and use it to enact positive changes in yourself.

4. **Take on a new challenge.** Make it a priority to learn something new or engage in an activity that you find challenging. Your enthusiasm for this activity will spill over into other areas of your life.

5. **Give yourself a pep talk.** "Try telling yourself to be more upbeat and enthusiastic and you may be surprised to find how well it works," Olesen says. He suggests visualizing yourself in a particularly enthusiastic moment. "Remember what it felt like, and the feeling may come back."

6. **Develop optimism in the face of setbacks.** When you experience a setback at school or work, you may automatically think, "I'm a failure." Instead of generalizing like this, think of the isolated event. Maybe you didn't get an A this time, but that doesn't mean you never will. Work toward next time instead of dwelling on past setbacks.

SOCIAL SKILLS

The ability to put people at ease is undoubtedly one of the hallmarks of emotional intelligence. You maintain mental and social poise by skillfully handling emotional reactions in others. One of the most difficult emotional reactions you will ever have to contend with in other people is anger, particularly anger vented toward you. Learning to resolve conflict constructively is key to developing your emotional intelligence. "How we work through our differences, to a large extent, determines our whole life pattern," writes David Augsburger in *Caring Enough to Confront*.

One principle to keep in mind when settling a dispute is expediency. For example, when you know that someone is upset with you, don't wait for them to come and make amends. Make an

REAL WORK

IN THE REAL WORLD

Indra Nooyi, *CEO of PepsiCo*

ndra Nooyi, PepsiCo Inc.'s Chair and CEO, follows a simple mantra, "Performance with purpose." Her initiatives at PepsiCo truly illustrate her commitment to both. Recognized as a "world-class leader," the powerful and influential Nooyi focuses on the global good, rather than serving her own interests, as reflected by her direction for PepsiCo. Nooyi has been instrumental in shifting the main profit sources from sugar and caffeine based products to healthier alternatives. It was Nooyi that prompted PepsiCo to purchase Tropicana and Quaker Oats and trailblazed the removal of trans fat from their products.

With such a powerful title and clout in the business world, Nooyi no doubt has access to the greatest business mentors around. When asked the best advice she ever received, she referred to the wisdom of her father: one should always assume positive intent when interacting with others.

"When you assume negative intent, you're angry. If you take away that anger and assume positive intent, you will be amazed. Your emotional quotient goes up because you are no longer almost random in your response. You don't get defensive. You don't scream. You are trying to understand and listen because at your basic core you are saying, 'Maybe they are saying something to me that I'm not hearing.' So "assume positive intent" has been a huge piece of advice for me."

Nooyi recognizes that misunderstandings occur in human interactions, but positivity is powerful and disarming. As Nooyi puts it, "When you assume positive intent, I think often what happens is the other person says, "Hey, wait a minute, maybe I'm wrong in reacting the way I do because this person is really making an effort." Seeing Nooyi's success, it is clear that "assuming positive intent" is a habit worth developing.

Source: Nooyi, Indra. "The Best Advice I Ever Got." Fortune 500. 30 Apr. 2008. CNN Money. http://money.cnn.com/galleries/2008/fortune/0804 /gallery.bestadvice.fortune/7.html

attempt to reconcile as soon as you know there's a problem. When you ignore the problem, your silence is often interpreted by the other party as rejection, and feelings of rejection tend to fuel anger. Most people want to resolve a conflict as much as you do, but maybe they just don't know how. Believe the best in other people, and that's what you'll usually get.

When trying to resolve a conflict, begin your message with the little word "I," as in "I feel frustrated that you didn't ask me before borrowing my computer." Avoid remarks that begin with the word "you," which can sound like an accusation, as in "You always do that." Rather than belittling the person you're at odds with, focus on reaching an agreement.

Healthy relationships are essential in life. To be an emotionally intelligent human being, you need to make people a priority. Relationships will not thrive if they are third or fourth on your "to do" list. Although this will require a commitment of your time, energy, and resources, it's important to keep relationships with other people alive. Schedule a lunch date with a friend or take your nieces and nephews for a walk. Even simple activities like that will strengthen your relationships and enhance your social skills.

your EQ in action

The coping skills you will need to live in our frenzied, competitive world will require more than just a high IQ. Learning to cope with life's complexities demands the full engagement of your emotions. It also means learning to take care of yourself. At the core of emotional intelligence is the ability to live at peace with yourself and others. Being at peace with yourself doesn't mean overlooking your deficiencies—instead, offer yourself the same forgiveness for mistakes and the courage to improve that you hope others will extend to you. From there you're off to a good start toward success and happiness.

CHAPTER THREE

I don't know what I'd like to do. That's what hurts the most. That's why I can't quit the job. I really don't know what talents I may have. And I don't know where to go to find out. I've been fostered so long by school and didn't have time to think about it.

CHICAGO PHONE RECEPTIONIST,
QUOTED IN STUDS TERKEL'S *WORKING*

There is a job, and a future, waiting for you, as long as you really want to work. There are opportunities galore, as long as you make the effort to seek them out. There are tested ways to success in the job market.

ROBERT O. SNELLING, SR., IN *THE RIGHT JOB*

C onsider a typical high school freshman's nocturnal musings on what it means to use the career planning and placement center:

The career planning and placement center is a secret building in the middle of campus, where seniors are escorted at night, blindfolded, for initiation into inescapable careers. Jobs are assigned on the basis of alphabetical synergy, a scientific technique developed in California during the mid-seventies. Alphabetical synergy pairs career and candidate by matching the first letter of the student's last name with the first letter of a career. For example:

Michael Crosby: double major in economics and physics.
Career selected by Alphabetical Synergy:
Crosby …c …CHEF …c …PLAYER …No, wait a minute—
****************CONTRACTOR****************

futures and options

MATCHING YOUR INTERESTS WITH A CAREER

Still blindfolded, Michael is given a burlap sack containing the tools of the trade: hammer, nails, hard hat, and keys to the trailer that will be his new headquarters, along with a map specifying its exact location at the construction site in Death Valley, California.

Then he wakes up, screaming.

The moral of this nightmare? Simple. Don't be afraid to investigate your career center. It won't hurt you in the light of day. Don't wait until three days before graduation and expect to nail down the perfect job. Go early—during your freshman and sophomore years—to gather information about the fields that interest you. Career centers have a wealth of materials including books, company files, videos, and names of contacts. Trained career counselors are a valuable resource: they can help you get that summer internship, help you write your resume and prepare for the interview, or lend an ear as you talk through postgraduate job possibilities. Take advantage of this service.

Most placement centers offer interest surveys. Take them. These inventories are a good place to begin figuring out what you want to do.

One such test, the Strong-Campbell Interest Inventory, compares the responses of the test taker to those of professionals in various occupations. You can get an idea of the careers people with similar interests have chosen, pointing you toward jobs you may not have considered. The inventory also helps you identify your natural learning style, which can be a good thing to know before you spend years and thousands of dollars on a program that may not fit your style. If Strong-Campbell results tell you that you are more of a practical learner, for example, you'll want a short program focused on specific skills. That way you'll be able to walk away with a degree you can use immediately to further your career. On the other hand, if you find you are more of an academic type, you may be happier in a longer course of study—even if you risk becoming an eternal student. In any case, it's important that you meet with a career counselor who can help you interpret the results of the tests you take.

"But don't rely solely on standardized tests," says Tim Dalton, a senior at Columbia University. "Many students who seek career guidance think they can just fill in the boxes, stick numbers into a computer, and then get a printout on the career they should pursue. The tests are a starting place—you must look within yourself for the answers."

Sometimes these tests can be off target. Anne, a friend of mine who is an editor, completed a survey that indicated she could be a dental hygienist—a job in which she has no interest! Like a hygienist, however, Anne does enjoy working quietly by herself or with a small group of people. The moral? Consider the broader interest profile as well as the specific job suggestions.

Cyrus Vesser, who worked for twelve years before returning to school to get his doctorate in history, says that brainstorming helped him choose his career. "The self-assessment tests and group discussions provided by my university were useful," says Cyrus. "Five years of wrong leads can be avoided by self-examination and experimentation in areas which spark your mind."

Many students fear they won't get a job after graduation. They consider only a few of the thousands of possible professions from which to choose. Students who don't know what they want to do frequently accept jobs they hate, or for which they're unsuited.

Most likely, that's not how you want to spend your career, or your life. You can do better than that. Use your imagination! There are thousands of jobs available.

Your first step? Relax. You are going to get a job in the career of your choice, even if you currently have no idea of what you want to do.

Your second step? Explore the careers available to you—by reading, interviewing people, investigating your career center. Realize how many options you have.

Your third step? Commit yourself to the process of discovering what you want to do.

Your fourth step? Chart your possible career path(s) by listing:

1. **What you have done** (your previous volunteer and work experiences, such as having a part-time salesclerk position at the Gap clothing store)

2. **Where you are now** (your current volunteer or work experiences, such as doing summer volunteer work for the Humane Society)

3. **Where you want to go** (other experiences you need to plan for now, such as preparing to interview with an honorary society on your college campus for the purpose of developing your leadership skills)

Your fifth step? Take action.

Chapter 2 dealt with those characteristics that are unique to you. It asked you to identify both your strengths and your weaknesses and encouraged you to conduct an introspective look inside yourself. Now let's focus on what you can do with your newfound understanding of yourself in the professional world. In your journal, label a section "Personal Inventory Assessment" and devote at least one page to each of the following categories: interests, talents, skills, likes and dislikes, goals, values, and ambitions. Be sure to fill everything in. Don't worry if some of it doesn't make sense. Your thoughts will develop after you have a chance to reflect on your initial responses.

personal inventory assessment

INTERESTS

1. I am curious about

2. I question

3. I'm concerned about

4. I'm fascinated by

5. I like to think/read/write about

TALENTS

1. I am good at these kinds of activities (physical, intellectual, creative, social, religious, etc.):

2. People compliment me on

3. People encourage me to

SKILLS

1. Specific skills (such as public speaking, car maintenance, word processing, etc.) that I have:

2. Skills that I want to learn:

LIKES AND DISLIKES

1. About people—their characters, habits, shortcomings, influences, etc.

   Likes   Dislikes

2. About working environment—indoors or out, with people or alone, small company or large, etc.

   Likes   Dislikes

GOALS, VALUES AND AMBITIONS

1. I like:

2. I want to accomplish:

3. When I die, I want to be remembered for:

4. In life, I value these things most:

5. Contributions I want to make to the world:

6. Things that give me peace of mind:

survey your qualities

Below are some essential characteristics every career seeker needs, regardless of what the inventory says. Take stock. Which characteristics best describe you? Which least describe you? How might you improve your weak areas before you graduate? If you analyze these things yourself, you'll be well prepared for your first salary review when your manager tells you what you've done well and where you stand to improve. You can't become better at something if you don't know what you need to improve.

Supportive

Decisive

Follow-up

Organized

Detail-oriented

Ethical

Confident (not cocky)

Fair

Honest

Keeps promises

Long-term vision

Sense of humor

Winning attitude

Ability to separate the trivial
   from the important

Sets and keeps high standards

Able to manage stress

Even-tempered

Works well with all kinds of people

Sets goals

take the next step

After you've completed your self-assessment inventory, analyze your responses. What are you learning about yourself? Is a pattern of what you'd like to do beginning to emerge? You don't have to draw any permanent conclusions now. The important thing is that you've identified your skills and interests.

What's so important about that? What's important is that you can use this knowledge to select your career options. Many people spend years in unrewarding careers before they realize that their jobs do not utilize their skills and interests. Consider the frequency of the midlife crisis as evidence. You are learning a different path—and you haven't even graduated from college yet.

ask the right questions

You have surveyed your skills and interests. Now it's time to consider what jobs you might be interested in. First, check out the list in Appendix G titled "Occupational Outlook at-a-Glance". This list contains 50 jobs expecting a ton of growth over the next ten years. Obviously, the list is a mere sample of the hundreds of thousands of jobs available to you. As you look over just a few of the possibilities, try to imagine what type of working environments each has, what training would be required and how they would mesh with your areas of interest. Also, try to consider what it is that you value in a job. Would you prefer a job predicting a lot of growth in the near future? How about money? What kind of salary do you feel you need to live comfortably? Then, try answering the following questions:

1. What do you value in a job? Is it the people? Location? Growth-potential? Salary?

2. How do these values affect what types of careers you might be interested in? Would you be willing to sacrifice any of these in the process of finding a perfect fit?

3. Do these values match your interests? For instance, if your interests tend to lean towards a career in a non-growth related field, are you comfortable with relinquishing some financial security?

4. Can you think of other pros and cons that come into play when deciding on a career that would really suit you?

The above are important questions. Finding out the answers will help you make informed decisions. Remember, you don't have to know all the answers right now. The purpose of the list is simply to jump-start your thinking about career possibilities and their potential growth. For now, all you need to do is start a running list of four or five areas you might be interested in. Over the next few years you'll explore these interests, narrow your focus, and eventually choose a career.

learn to reason

Why do we accept what we believe? Reasoning provides an answer. To reason is to understand the underlying motives and logic of our beliefs.

Vijali Brown, *real-estate business owner*

When Vijali began as a LifeBound intern, she was a senior at Johnson & Wales University, majoring in marketing. An internship was part of the requirement for her to graduate. She looked forward to working at LifeBound because the president was a former director of marketing and she wanted that exposure. She was able to compile a portfolio of brochures, statistical data, and website plans, all of which helped promote LifeBound.

At the internship, she could see LifeBound emphasized product development. The team was busy creating new books and curricula to fit course needs, and there was just one marketing brochure, one website, and no other routes to get the company's message out. She saw an opportunity to contribute her passion to sales and marketing to this startup company.

She took the initiative to create promotional brochures. One was for the company's keynote speeches and seminars, given by LifeBound president, Carol Carter, in coordination with Carol's publicist.

Another brochure promoted internship opportunities at local colleges.

When Vijali was hired to work full-time at LifeBound, she made the machine run more smoothly by keeping track of customer satisfaction, organizing tracking and invoicing systems. She kept track of Carol's innovations, as well as her busy national travel schedule of workshops and speeches.

While working for LifeBound, her father offered her an opportunity to be his business partner in real estate. She went to night school to get her real estate license and is now a small-business owner, too!

She now applies what she learned at LifeBound as a small-business owner: building customer loyalty, follow-up, looking for areas of improvement, and generating leads.

Lex Kaplan began college thinking that he wanted to be a lawyer. Originally from Englewood, New Jersey, Lex majored in journalism. As president of his college political magazine, he fell in love with reporting and writing. He enjoyed it so much that when he graduated he freelanced for the *Phoenix*, a Boston periodical. He used his writing experience there to help him land a job at the *New Yorker* doing fact checking and writing "Talk of the Town" pieces. But after a year he feared that being a journalist would make him a dilettante—a writer without a specialty. So, without reasoning, he reverted to his pre-freshman beliefs and enrolled in law school. He quickly realized his mistake. While he was a hard worker, he discovered something about himself at law school.

"I found out I wasn't a fighter," he says. Competition on campus for corporate jobs was fierce. Lex found himself disliking both the competition and the idea of corporate law, which to him, "seemed like a form of death." This time, Lex used his experiences in considering his next career move. He knew he wouldn't be happy as an attorney. So he turned down a job with a law firm in New York and decided to combine all his skills by starting up his own magazine.

Throughout your college and working careers, you will continually have to (1) come up with your own ideas and (2) convince others of their validity. Once you've reached a decision, opinion, or point of view, get used to defending it both orally and in writing. You'll feel more confident, even among your toughest critics, when you back up your claims.

You probably have ample opportunity to practice that skill now. For example, let's say your parents don't approve of the major you've chosen; they don't think you will make enough money from it to earn a living. When you have carefully thought through the decision yourself, you can more clearly articulate why you chose as you did. Even though your parents still may not agree with you, at least they will respect the reasoning behind your judgment.

Lex gave a star performance in the art of persuasion when he came up with a novel idea for a magazine that would fill a void in the market. He gave a seven-page proposal to an acquaintance he knew was interested in investing in the arts, and the man gave him $50,000. During the year that followed, Lex enthusiastically pitched his concept to writers, friends, and investors. Within the year he had (1) convinced some of his former colleagues at the *New Yorker* to work for his magazine, called *Wigwag*; (2) contracted articles from a number of known authors like Alice McDermott, Ralph Ellison, and Richard Ford; and (3) raised $3 million. All this he did from his two-bedroom apartment in New York, making the most of his "cold" phone calls and "blind" visits. Because Lex Kaplan believed in his project, so did many others.

doing the right thing for the right reasons

You came to college with a certain set of preconceptions, and you are also probably very aware of your parents' expectations. It is important to understand how these influences affect your decisions and to evaluate what is important to you—what really interests you. "Don't let somebody else persuade you to enter a career based on their idea of what's right, or practical, or that you can always fall back on," advises Nancy Wingate, a journalist and freelance writer who majored in English in college. She knew she didn't want to teach, but she wasn't sure exactly what she would do with an English degree. She did know that if she worked hard and kept pursuing her interests, she would find work that satisfied her. "Everyone kept asking me, 'but what are you going to do with a degree in English?' I would just smile and say, 'I don't know, but I know I'll find something.' Sure enough, my first job (still during college) was as a part-time editorial assistant; my first full-time job was as a television producer—both jobs I absolutely loved!"

Steve Fort, an engineering supervisor at the Lockheed Martin space facility in Florida, was motivated by money. "Quite frankly, my biggest goal in college was to get a well-paying job. I was rather single-minded in my pursuit of money because I thought money would lead to the good life. Now I wish I had spent more time considering what it was that I enjoyed rather than what would make me the most money."

"Too often, freshmen lean toward whatever will bring in the most money right after graduation," muses Mary Hopkins, a graduate student and editor of the *Daily Texan*, the student newspaper at the University of Texas. "The job market fluctuates more than it used to; top-paying jobs one year may drop out of sight the next. And at the end of a life, what does it matter how much something paid compared to how much you were able to contribute to the world?"

Mary makes an important point. People are motivated by different things. For some, money isn't nearly as important as finding fulfillment in their work. It's not that they don't want money altogether. It's just that if they must choose between a career that promises a good salary, but isn't work they care about, and a lower-paying job that they love, they'll choose the latter. In fact, there's a trend in this country called "voluntary simplicity," meaning people are scaling down their lifestyles and "getting back to the basics." Discovering what matters to you is essential because you aren't only choosing a major, you're choosing a lifestyle.

Even after you're established in a career, you will periodically need to evaluate what is motivating you and decide if your work is taking you in directions that are important to you. Cruce Stark was a professor in the English department at the University of Delaware. His career was moving along as he planned. He was doing all the right things—writing solid, scholarly articles and getting published. On a yearlong sabbatical in Latin America, he realized what he really wanted to do at that point was to write a novel.

"During that trip I started asking questions about what I really wanted," he says, "about what I'd think about my life when nobody would be there except me to think about it; or when it truly wasn't going to matter what anybody else thought. Would I be happier when I was looking back at seventy if I'd been a success in my profession, with a string of highly regarded critical works, or would I like myself better if I tried to write fiction and failed? But of course I knew I wouldn't fail. If I worked as hard as I intended to, I'd have to succeed."

Cruce worked on his fiction writing for years before he got his first novel published. While he was writing, the senior people in his department at the university kept suggesting that he return to doing what he knew how to do. When his novel, *Chasing Uncle Charley*, was published, it received rave reviews from the *New York Times* and *Publishers Weekly*. As a result, he was promoted and was assigned to teach courses and lead workshops in creative writing.

"My basic realization was that, for better or worse, I was stuck with myself—so that's what I'd better get in touch with," he says. "Trying to satisfy anything or anybody else was going to leave a very important part of me very empty. Most of us spend too many years worrying what our lives will look like from the outside, as though it were some kind of movie for somebody else to see. It may

REAL WORK

IN THE REAL WORLD

Francie Berger, *large-scale LEGO model designer*

rancie Berger's childhood dream was to build Lego models for a living. Being a practical child, she assumed that no one would pay her to play, so she decided to become an architect. When Berger entered Virginia Tech's architecture program prepared to pursue a career in architecture, she had no idea that her childhood fantasies were about to come true.

During her freshman year, a toy designer gave a guest lecture in one of her classes. After hearing him speak, she decided to approach him about interning for him. Through her internship she developed a mentoring relationship with the toy designer, who encouraged her to approach Lego about creating a model design department in the United States. At this point, Lego had a manufacturing and sales plant in the United States, but all the models and designs were made in Denmark.

For her senior project, Berger designed a model Lego farm that included fourteen buildings and vehicles—she even drew up the plans and projected the costs. She then presented her project to the director of special events at Lego. "I never doubted that I would persuade them to create this job for me," she says. "My dream was going to come true. As a kid I didn't think this kind of job existed. Once I knew the possibility, I knew I had to get this job."

It took her months of following up, calling her contact at Lego at least once every month, before she was given a job. Three months after graduating from architecture school, upon her return from an extended vacation traveling around the United States, Lego called and offered her a job designing the large Lego model displays for places like FAO Schwartz and the National Toy Fair in New York City. The Lego design department grew from three people to forty-eight in 1990. Berger manages five designers responsible for envisioning the models, and she has been featured in the *New Yorker*, on the Discovery Channel, and on a PBS children's series.

come with age, but sometimes it finally breaks through—nobody's standing in line buying tickets to watch."

Now that you've defined your interests, skills, and goals, it's time to focus on the job that will incorporate them. What would you like to do if you could do anything? Really, truly, outlandishly, anything. Imagine the sheer delight of finding the career that taps your passion and allows you the privilege of being paid for doing it!

dream on

Francie Berger's story is a great example of how it is possible to find work that really matches your interests. In order to do this, though, you sometimes have to allow yourself to dream BIG and to think beyond the immediate possibilities. Once you've found your vision, then it takes ingenuity, creativity, and perseverance to see your dreams come to fruition. Now you are going to do just that. Using the insights you gained from your personal inventory, you are going to design your possible success stories. Include everything that the perfect job entails. Where do you work? What is the work environment? Does your job include travel? What is an average day like? What is your compensation (does this include your quarterly bonus)? Describe your position in detail. The goal is to make it real. Try to taste it, hear it, feel it. Don't hold back. No holds barred. Write it down.

DREAM JOB/STELLAR ACHIEVEMENT 1

_____

_____

_____

_____

DREAM JOB/STELLAR ACHIEVEMENT 2

_____

_____

_____

_____

DREAM JOB/STELLAR ACHIEVEMENT 3

_____

_____

_____

_____

Now it's time to take your head out of the clouds and focus on planning strategies that will make these dreams a reality.

the narrowing process

Once you've analyzed the bigger picture, pick two or three areas of interest and begin developing career strategies for each. You can write them down below. (If you don't know what to choose yet, come back to this after you've had more time to think.)

using what you know

The key to choosing career options is a willingness to explore. You could convert the basics of the "dreamboat job" approach to fit any possible path: poet, advertising copywriter, stockbroker, farmer, cowboy, or corporate psychic. Remember, you're interested in these careers (all of them) because you think they would be fun. So have fun finding out about them!

And while you're out pioneering, continue to ask yourself questions that will help to refine your career goals:

1. How can I gather more information about those careers that interest me?

2. Whom do I know in this field? (If you don't know anyone, do some research.) What can they tell me about the pros and cons of the work? What is needed to succeed?

3. What else can I do each week and each month to prepare myself? How can I get more experience? (Remember: Experience leads to intelligent decisions.)

life goals

It is crucial to think about what kinds of goals you have for your life as a whole. Pam Zemper of Security Pacific advises people to think about what their goals are in four areas—social, material, professional, and personal growth. "Once you have an idea of what you want in each of these areas, it's easier to choose a career."

"Your job becomes your lifestyle," says Tony Ponturo, director of media services for the beer company, Anheuser-Busch. "So you'd better like what you're doing."

Tony is right. Know what you want, even if you don't know how to get it right now. The path to a really interesting career is often circuitous.

After college, Tony identified the three areas he loved most—business, sports, and television. He moved to New York City and got a job as a page for NBC, hoping to get a foot in the door of NBC Sports. This approach didn't work. So he took an alternate route and went into advertising, working for three successive advertising agencies as a media buyer. His work on a Coca-Cola campaign earned him a shot at his firm's Budweiser account. Anheuser-Busch was so impressed with his work that they lured him away from the agency and created a position for him in their home office in St. Louis. Since Busch promotes heavily during sports telecasts, Tony finds himself working in all three of the areas he enjoys: business, sports, and television.

Larry Maslon acquired his job through a similarly circuitous route. Larry is the dramaturge for the prestigious Arena Stage in Washington, DC. His various responsibilities include helping to choose the season's repertoire, interpreting the plays, researching their historical background, and editing the theater's publications. But when he started out, Larry knew nothing of dramaturgy—he only knew his interests. A lover of stage directing and Renaissance literature, he majored in both in college. For his thesis in theater arts he directed Shakespeare's *The Tempest*, and then he wrote a paper on the play for his Renaissance literature thesis.

"Unbeknownst to me," says Larry, "by both critically examining and producing a play, I was doing a dramaturge's work." Later, intending to become a theater director, he enrolled in a master's program in theater arts at Stanford University. He was disappointed that the program primarily focused on the academic side of theater, so he directed some plays on his own time.

"Again, unbeknownst to me, I was becoming exquisitely prepared to be a dramaturge," he says. He now possesses something that is extremely rare: a challenging, steady job in the theater. He strongly advocates that every student pursue what he or she loves. He says he has benefited from following his heart, from doing what he's done "in spite of myself."

Malcolm Forbes, the late publisher of *Forbes* magazine, was quoted in *The Achievement Factors* by B. Eugene Griessman: "I think the foremost quality—there's no success without it—is really loving what you do. If you love it, you will do it well."

"You've got to have fire in the gut," says Milton Pedraza, Colgate-Palmolive Co. recruiter and marketer. "You have to be committed to your job once you land it, but in college you must commit yourself to becoming well-educated and prepared as possible, even if you don't yet know what kind of work interests you." If you don't develop a burning passion to get things done in college, Milton says, it will be hard for you to motivate yourself on the job.

get going

Your senior year of college, though it may seem like a long way off, is just around the corner. The trick to not being caught off guard by its arrival is balance: balancing the long-term with current agendas for the month, the week, the day, the moment. For now (this moment), set some career goals. Don't worry about revising them. This will come later. Time is very forgiving to those who act, which is what you're doing right now by committing to a career direction, however tentative.

"As you begin to discover what you truly enjoy, try to picture yourself two, five, or ten years after college involved in that interest," advises Bob Kinstle, a computer consultant for a large New York bank. "Imagine what your typical day might look like; then reexamine your current activities to see if they are helping you achieve that dream," he says. "College is a time for growth and adventure. You are building the foundation and honing the skills that will determine your success and happiness in the years ahead.

Find out what your school has to offer—academically, socially, culturally, athletically—and try to sample as much as possible."

turning your dreams into reality

Someone once said, "If you aim at nothing, you'll hit it
every time." For our purposes, think of your target as
being your goals, dreams, and ambitions. Consequently,
the arrows are your plans. Stock your quiver full of them—your
plans—and you're bound to hit the bull's-eye eventually.

Former college professor Lynn Troyka suggests a planning
strategy that a friend shared with her years ago. The formula goes
like this: "Envision where you want to be, then establish steps
toward that vision." Notice that this formula has two distinct
parts: a projection phase of envisioning, and a planning phase of
establishing the steps toward that vision.

THE PROJECTION PHASE

The projection phase usually comes first. It entails thinking and
dreaming about what you want (i.e., your vision). This includes the
soon-to-be realized fantasy of your acceptance speech in Stockholm
when you humbly receive the long-deserved Nobel Prize (you are
thirty-three before the committee finally comes to its stuffed-up senses and has the decency and vision to recognize you). Envisioning the
goal is where projection comes in, and that's important. But it's not
enough. Lots of people have a dream; few turn it into reality.

THE PLANNING PHASE

The second phase, planning, involves work that is more long-term.
Once you've visualized the epic ending, you have to figure out how
to get there. You do this by establishing the steps that lead you
toward the goal. The "how" part of the formula requires creativity,
tenacity, and—most difficult of all—discipline. Living your dream
means maintaining your focus on a goal and refusing to allow distractions to divert you from the time and effort needed to accomplish
it. This may sound simple, but for many people, aligning their dream
with their life habits isn't simple at all. Turning your vision into a
reality entails weathering hard times, sometimes over long periods.
You will not magically become a CEO overnight, no matter how

potent your powers of fantasy. Achieving your dream takes 1 percent inspiration coupled with 99 percent perspiration and hard work.

Dr. Michael DeBakey, a pioneer in cardiovascular surgery, including artificial heart research, and the driving force behind the establishment of the Medical Center in Houston, Texas, believes that dedication, self-discipline, and a clear direction and purpose are the keys to human achievement. "Success is the result of focusing your energies and efforts in a specific direction and exploiting your skills and capabilities to the fullest," he says. He advises students to master whatever it is they are studying. "Apply yourself fully. Once you have devoted your efforts totally to one project, you will be able to transfer those skills and habits to every other project."

It is your task to map out the road to the corner office or mid-office cubicle or outdoor post—from college classes, internships, work experience, and appropriate role models. Remember to take it one step at a time. One hundred thousand planned steps will go by much more quickly than one hundred thousand unplanned steps.

Below is a list of broad goals a college student might realistically expect to accomplish in four years of college. Look at the list closely and see how these activities begin to build on each other. For example, a summer job will help you learn the basic skills of managing responsibility, a key qualification for securing an internship. (See Chapter 10 for a discussion of the importance of internships.) Internships are usually offered only to those students who can prove from their past job experience that they are trustworthy. That's the idea. One year's accomplishments, such as a favorable reference letter from your summer employer, increase the next year's options—like getting an internship.

If this agenda doesn't fit your projections and plans, fine. Come up with one that does. As your career adviser, this book only makes suggestions. YOU make the decisions.

COLLEGE GOALS

Freshman Year Objectives

1. Assess your study skills and habits. Improve on them if they need work.
2. Get off to a good start academically.
3. Apply for a second-semester or summer part-time job.
4. Join at least one extracurricular activity.
5. Adjust to the responsibility of your new environment.
6. Have fun.

Sophomore Year Objectives

1. Apply for a summer internship (apply for more than one).
2. Begin planning a summer, semester, or junior year abroad.
3. Make at least one career contact.
4. Join one or two clubs or special interest groups.
5. Continue to make good grades and get the most out of your classes.
6. Cultivate mentors (see Chapter 12 if you are stumped on the meaning of the word mentor).
7. Visit the career center.
8. Have fun.

Junior Year Objectives

1. Spend the summer, semester, or entire year abroad.
2. Plan an internship between your junior and senior years.
3. Join another activity or honorary society.
4. Mail out preliminary job inquiry letters.
5. Become a leader of one of the organizations you belong to.
6. Prepare your resume.
7. Take some classes that don't pertain to your major but that will make you a well-qualified job applicant and a more interesting person.
8. Have fun.

Senior Year Objectives

1. Wage a full-fledged job search in early fall.
2. Make many business contacts: gather information.
3. Send out at least twenty-five cover letters with resumes.
4. Research the companies with whom you wish to interview.
5. Hold mock interviews to prepare for the real thing.
6. Land the job, negotiate your salary, and start taking home the paycheck.
7. Have fun.

Should you aim to do all these things? Probably not. Choose the activities that suit you best, and be proud of yourself for trying new things and having the vision to see and plan for the bigger picture. Don't forget the common thread that ties each year together —having fun!

As you make projections and devise a plan on behalf of your noble destiny, keep in mind the three key areas you'll need to develop: academic, extracurricular, and work experience. Strive for balance. Keep this triangle in focus—maybe it won't be equilateral, but just make sure it's got three sides.

In the spaces below, list the specific steps you think you'll have to take in order to get from where you are to where you want to be. The rest of this book will help you take the steps...one at a time.

YOUR OBJECTIVES

Freshman Year

_____

_____

_____

_____

Sophomore Year

_____

_____

_____

_____

Junior Year

_____

_____

_____

_____

Senior Year

_____

_____

_____

_____

your first five steps

 elow are five steps designed to assure achievement wherever it is you want to go. Keep them handy for encouragement and as a gentle reminder.

1. STRIKE A BALANCE

"The most valuable experience I had in college was learning that it was a microcosm of life with opportunities to grow broadly in several areas," remembers David Glenn, who was a division manager at Chevron Corp. for thirty years. "Too often people focus on one area to the exclusion of others with the idea that they will develop after they finish college and get a job."

Kip Berry, assistant professor of veterinary medicine at North Carolina State University, spent most of his time in college doing academic work. "I believe this hurt me. In retrospect, I should have diversified my curriculum and educational experiences instead of focusing only on the hard-core academic work."

In college, you'll have to balance your academic, personal, and real-world experience. Make good grades, but realize that good grades alone are usually not enough. Even if you want to be an astrophysicist, you don't want to be a lonely astrophysicist. Therefore, you also need to make room in your life for the other essentials: extracurricular activities, sports, socializing, and work.

Denise Chamblee, a pediatric ophthalmologist, remembers her college years: "I worked hard academically, but I made a distinct pact with myself not to lose sight of social and extracurricular activities. I think that has helped me tremendously in keeping my sanity through the long road of medical training. It has been an even bigger help in relating well to patients."

2. SET GOALS

Learn to set specific goals and have a plan by which to achieve them.

José Galvez not only balanced his schoolwork with a part-time job as a copy boy for his local paper, but he also set concrete goals for himself. After eight years at his hometown paper, José is now a photojournalist for the *Los Angeles Times*.

"Identify concrete goals," José advises. "Get as much out of the smaller places as you can—then run with it from there. Shoot for the stars."

3. BE DECISIVE

A wrong decision is better than no decision at all. If you spend a year as a pre-med student, loathe it, and then switch to French, you haven't wasted a year. You've learned something valuable—what you like and what you don't, or, to put it another way, what you'd be good at and what you'd be not so good at. And you've acted accordingly. Bravo for self-assertion.

Anthea Coster, a space physicist who tracks satellites at the Massachusetts Institute of Technology (MIT), was struck by the words of one of her philosophy professors. "He said that there is probably more than one right choice. What is important is not necessarily the choice itself, but, once you make the choice, what you do with it. This has probably been one of the guiding principles of my life."

Sandra Day O'Connor, the former Supreme Court justice, learned about decision-making early in her career as a trial judge. "I put all the time and effort in at the front end, trying to decide a case correctly in the first place and do the best I can. Then I don't look back and I don't agonize over it. I may have to live with the consequences, but I'm going to live with them without regrets, because I made the best decision I could at the time."

Learn to analyze your options and then make your move quickly. Don't linger in thermodynamics if neo-impressionism is what you love. Decisiveness goes a long way toward a glorious destiny.

In the words of 19th-century author Johann Wolfgang von Goethe, "Boldness has genius, power, and magic in it. Whatever you do or dream, begin it now."

4. BELIEVE IN YOURSELF

Know that you can succeed. The only difference between You and Them is that you've got the motivation to get the job done.

Jim Cochran developed self-confidence while attending the University of California–Davis. He had a part-time job for three years as a basketball referee for the intramural sports program. During his third year, he was the head student official.

"When making a call, it's all in the manner in which you carry yourself. If you blow the whistle and hesitate, wringing your hands and gnashing your teeth, people may pick up on your indecision. The fans and players will jump all over you, grabbing you by the collar and chanting 'Blood! Blood! Blood!'"

Gordon Bock, a Columbia University graduate, was a *United Press International* reporter when he heard that a *U.S. News & World Report* editor was coming to town. In a "jobs" file, Gordon had kept a 1977 newsletter that quoted the editor as saying he would hire as many students from journalism schools as he could. Gordon sent a letter to the editor reminding him of this promise, adding, "I'm volunteering to help you in this lofty goal."

The editor hired Gordon. "I think he was impressed that I took that statement and threw it back at him, instead of begging for a job," Gordon says.

5. GO FOR IT

Lauren Ward, a brand marketing manager with PepsiCo in Purchase, New York, says getting a job as resident assistant her junior year was one of the most valuable "business lessons" she learned during college.

When Lauren applied to be a resident assistant (or RA, a dorm supervisor) at the end of her sophomore year, she was refused an application because she had never lived in a dorm before. Since Lauren had transferred from another college during her sophomore year, it had been impossible for her to gain admission to the dorms, which had waiting lists. Still, the interviewing board would make no exception: there were too many people applying for the RA positions, and rules are rules.

Lauren was determined to get a fair shot. Believing in her own competence as an applicant, Lauren went up the hierarchy to the director of housing to ask for some rule-bending so that she could be considered with other applicants. She listed all of her qualifications, showed her keen interest and enthusiasm for the dorms and the women who lived there, and diplomatically presented her case. The director of housing bent the rules and allowed her to be interviewed.

My Two Cents

HOW DO I APPLY IT?

Dylan Lewis, *University of Colorado–Denver*

My life has been a series of options, different roads leading different directions, all with separate stops and detours. By recognizing these exits and the destinations to which they lead, my life has become meaningful, interesting, and entertaining. I can see the forgone paths clearly in life's rearview mirror, and as I continue to let my abilities and experiences lead the way, I am able to peer through the fog that conceals my future. My future, of course, is uncertain, but the choices I make now will pave my life's road smooth and straight.

After high school, I had no idea what I wanted to do and definitely had no idea of who I was. I had been accepted to a mediocre four-year college as a transfer student because I had finished my freshman year at a community college during my senior year in high school. I thought I was prepared for college. My grades had been good, but I was in no way ready for real college classes. Since I had some experience with college curriculum, I registered for upper division classes, but I was less than prepared and quickly dug a hole I couldn't free myself from. The ladder out was formed of the most difficult decision I would ever have to make. My father gave me a series of options, none of which included another semester at school. I considered my options, and instead of attempting to negotiate with my father, I surprised him and chose the most difficult option, physically and mentally. I decided to join the United States Marine Corps.

I served four years, working as an air traffic controller. I helped build a house with Habitat for Humanity. I volunteered for stage security at a charity rock concert. I learned about courage and respect. I gained life experience. I did something none of my friends did. I was willing to fight and die for the people of my country. I grew and I matured. I

Out of forty-four applicants, Lauren was the only one to score a perfect ten with each of the six interviewers. She was accepted as an RA.

The business lesson? As Lauren succinctly put it, "no" doesn't necessarily mean "no." People will always resist change—in school, in business, at home. Count on it. Action takers don't take "no" for an answer; they can't, if they want to get anything done. If you believe in what you're doing, whether it be yourself, your product, your ideas, or somebody else's, be prepared to utilize creative

made great friends and forged lifelong contacts. I completed my tour honorably, was awarded and discharged, so I went back to school.

I come from an educated family. My father works as a college administrator and my mother as a teacher, both of them with post-graduate degrees. All of my uncles have earned either a Ph.D. or M.D. One grandfather is a successful businessman, and the other is an architect, so I guess you could say there is some pressure to succeed. My pressure, in this sense, is not ridden with anxiety because I trust I will make the right life decisions. However, I am neither a pre-med student, nor pre-law, engineering, or business, nor do I wish to be a college professor or a teacher of any kind. I chose something no person in my family has ever chosen to study formally. I thought about what my interests are and how I can incorporate them with a lucrative career. My choice of major will not bring the highest paying salary, but I trust it will bring me happiness and success. I will graduate with a degree in English. Critical reading and writing are my passion and hopefully, my career will be closely related.

So, here I am, twenty-six years old, a veteran, a soon-to-be college graduate with a great outlook on life. I chose to become a better person. I chose to join the Marines. I chose to return to college and graduate. In the future, I will make other choices, but none will be as important as the choices I've made since leaving high school. I have made the life I want to live, not by comparing to my relatives or friends, but by having the courage to take charge of my identity and my future. Every choice made will have rewards and consequences. I have reaped many rewards and suffered few consequences, but in order for my fortune to continue I must continue to look ahead, eyes towards the future and my mind on the goal.

strategies to combat the stonewalling you'll find yourself up against time and time again.

Lauren, like Jim, believed in herself and convinced others of her abilities. If Lauren hadn't been a hundred percent confident when she had her appointment with the director of housing, she would have been cooked. But once her foot was in the door and she had the interview, she had no problem convincing the panel of interviewers that she had potential.

Now it's your turn. Take the ball and start running.

CHAPTER FOUR

Education has really only one basic factor . . .
one must want it.

G.E. WOODBURY

The direction in which education starts a man
determines his future life.

PLATO

While writing this book, I gave a few seminars in the New York area to high school seniors preparing for success in college. At the beginning of each seminar, I distributed a questionnaire to get the students thinking about what really scared, bothered, excited, thrilled, bored, or disgusted them when they thought about college. The opener was: What do you fear most about starting college? Here are some of the responses from the students in one seminar:

"I fear failing my freshman year."

"I fear the extra work that I will actually have to do."

"I fear loneliness, being stuck at a college that I hate, and failing out."

take the plunge

MANAGING YOUR TIME AND STUDY HABITS

"I fear studying all day and night."

"I fear that college will be a letdown from what I've imagined."

"I fear not having a good time."

"I fear getting lost."

"I fear not making friends or finding my classes."

"I fear too much pressure and too much work."

"I fear not doing well academically."

"I fear not fitting in."

"I fear that I will become so socially active that I will not pay attention to my classes."

"I fear not being able to compete, work, and do well."

"I fear the responsibility."

"I fear I will not be able to work my way through school and support myself."

"I fear not finding a date."

"I fear I won't like my roommates. I'm afraid of leaving home and trying to meet new friends."

"I fear being on my own."

"I fear that I won't have a good time."

"I fear that I won't succeed."

"I fear the academic load."

"I fear not 'getting something' from my education."

"I fear that I will oversleep."

"I fear not doing well in class, having problems with roommates, and running out of money."

"I fear not being able to complete, understand, or do well on tests."

"I fear academic difficulties and no free time."

"I fear too much work and not enough discipline."

Notice any pattern? Almost everyone is nervous about starting college. They fear that they will be unable to keep up with the academic and personal challenges that college poses. That's understandable. It's a big transition from high school. But it's like the first day of school in first grade. It only seems like a big deal until the second day, after which you know what to expect.

The key is to convert your fears into positive actions that will help you conquer your academic weaknesses and master the skills needed for success in college. Once you've learned how to manage your time and develop your study skills, you will be up to the challenge.

"I never studied in high school," says Jon Jannes, a former high school basketball star who became an education major at Northern Illinois University. "It took me two years of college to learn to study effectively." Jon spent those first two years at Black Hawk Community College.

Unlike Jon, Matt Jacobson was a top student at Alleman Catholic High School. He was on the honor roll, captain of the football team, and class valedictorian.

"I didn't study much in high school—I just made sure I was ahead of everyone else," says Matt, now a pre-law freshman at Northwestern University. "But college was a lot different. I was so overwhelmed and excited about being away from home for the first time that I didn't study much my first semester. As a result, I didn't do very well. Since I'm on scholarship, I'll have to do better next semester." One of the challenges Matt faces is improving his grades while honoring his extracurricular commitments—as a fraternity pledge, a member of the pre-law association, and an assistant at the campus library.

Succeeding scholastically in college is very similar to succeeding in every other area of your life: first, make an honest self-appraisal of your strengths and weaknesses, then develop a game plan to achieve your goals.

selecting a major

Some college students know from Day One that they want to major in chemistry to become doctors, or major in business or a particular field of engineering. For these students, there is generally a set curriculum defined by the college with some latitude for elective courses.

However, if you're like many college freshmen, and you haven't decided on a major, you may want to stick to a broad, general curriculum for your first year until you can narrow down your true interests.

As a freshman, you will be required to take the general courses that are required for any four-year degree. These courses are usually referred to as the core curriculum. For most universities, it takes approximately the first four semesters to complete your core. This places you at the end of your sophomore year—the time at which your major takes a front seat. The last two years of your undergraduate studies are geared specifically to your major; therefore, it is before you begin your junior year that you absolutely have to have decided on your major course of study. Don't despair if you don't know what you want to major in as a freshman— you've got plenty of time to decide. Your best bet is to find classes that are offered within the core (there are generally choices rather than a rigid list) that appeal to your tastes. From there, you may begin to get a feel for where your interests lie.

As a peer advisor, Julie Balovich speaks with many freshmen who simply aren't sure what they want to study and what career they want to pursue. "What you learn from not picking a major in your first year, and being open to new things, is that there is a lot more out there than you originally thought. Even if you do decide what you want to do, there are ways to experience more than just English or mechanical engineering. By making a point of taking at least one really random, non-required class every semester, I found out to my surprise that I was very interested in evangelical Protestantism, the politics of developing nations, and the genre of autobiography. I also found out that I was not interested in deconstructionism or bureaucracy in government. I feel like my wide range of interests will give me more to offer law schools in the way of diversity when application time comes around. Instead of saying 'I'm undecided,' I think we should say, 'I'm discovering' or 'I'm exploring.'"

Suzanne Babinsky believes it is important to choose the more challenging courses, even when they aren't required. "The harder classes kept me on my toes. They held my interest because I had to focus harder on the material. And when I decided after teaching high school science that I wanted to go to medical school, I had no problem getting in because I had taken the rigorous prerequisites."

Employers often urge students who are undecided on a major to gain a broad liberal arts or business education. "I believe that businesses should go back to basics in recruiting, should forget about the business schools, and recruit the best young liberal arts students we can find," says Felix Rohatyn, a senior partner at one of New York's largest investment firms.

Darren Walker, an investment banker in New York City, agrees. "Resist the temptation to specialize in anything. In the long run what will benefit you most are good writing skills, good reasoning skills, and people skills. My greatest disappointment was realizing that law was an unfulfilling profession for me. However, because of the wide breadth of my academic background and extracurricular activities, I was well positioned to move into a number of different professions."

Here's a recap:

1. Take at least one elective each semester you are in school.

2. Remember to say, to others as well as to yourself, "I'm exploring" instead of "I'm undecided."

3. At least in your first two years, resist specializing. Take a broad range of courses.

When Steven Harwood began his college career, there was a demand for professors. So he decided to get a doctorate in biochemistry and a job in academics. When he graduated, however, the job market was dry. He then decided to go on to medical school and eventually specialized in nuclear medicine.

He advises students to find out what the real job situation is. "Also take a wide variety of courses and get as much enrichment experience as possible. Be flexible and be prepared to change. The job situation may be different by the time you finish four years later."

Arnold Popinsky, a potter and former art professor, remembers, "Concern over good performance and a safe curriculum were too dominant in my mind...it kept me from seeking adventure in my college experience." He advises students to take risks and to enroll in courses outside their majors.

Colleen Smith, a counselor who runs a program for women over fifty returning to school, has the following recommendation: "Study what you love. Don't think you have to have it all figured out in advance, because life takes amazing twists and turns."

Jesse Keller, a junior at Yale University, originally decided to major in computer science because he felt it would be broad enough to allow him to participate in whatever field he chose after college. But after several semesters, he realized the standard computer science curriculum was not meeting his needs.

"I arrived at the idea of an interdisciplinary major—'The Impact of Information Technology on Society.' With this trendy title, I approached the sociology department and suddenly had a new major. My course requirements are drawn from the sociology, computer science, and engineering departments. As a senior, I will write a thesis dealing with some aspect of the impact that all of our progress has had on our day-to-day lives. I am looking forward to doing the research—it's my own version of computer science."

Here are some examples of what your first two college semesters might look like:

THE FIRST-YEAR SCHEDULE: SOME IDEAS

Sample A

First Semester	Units	Second Semester	Units
Freshman Composition	3	Freshman Composition	3
Algebra (or Calculus)	3	American Government	3
Introduction to Psychology	3	Astronomy	4
French I	4	French II	4
Economics	3	Art History	3
Total	16	**Total**	17

Sample B

First Semester	Units	Second Semester	Units
Freshman Composition	3	Freshman Composition	3
Biology	4	Calculus	3
American History	3	Music Appreciation	3
Spanish I	4	Spanish II	4
Racquetball	1	Anthropology	3
Total	15	**Total**	16

Consult your school catalog or a counselor for more information on courses and majors.

General advice: Take fewer, not more, courses during your first semester. You'll have many adjustments to make, so it's best to be underextended rather than overextended. If you take fifteen or sixteen units, you'll be in good shape. Also, work as little as possible during your first semester to give yourself time to get used to school.

A good scholastic start should be your first concern. The knowledge you gain in college—and the grades you earn to show for it—doesn't assure job success but it will make you more attractive to a prospective employer. Good students are organized and responsible; top marks show you're able to learn and willing to work and apply yourself. Aside from helping you get the job, a sound education will open all kinds of other doors for you. An educated mind is your most valuable asset.

improving your ability to learn

Frank Landy, an industrial organizational psychologist at Penn State University, teaches introductory psychology on a regular basis. "My first class each semester is on study tips," says Landy. He discusses different methods of learning, taking notes, and preparing for various exams. "If students learn basic habits of discipline and time management early, they will do best over the long haul," says Landy.

"I plunge into the material at the beginning of the semester, so I expect students to know what they're doing," says Doug Finnemore, who teaches a calculus-based physics course for engineers at Iowa State University. Finnemore expects students to hit the ground running once he starts class; but if they need help, he encourages them to seek him out, or to ask any of the teaching assistants who lead discussion sections. "The people who do well in my course come to class and work throughout the semester, while the ones who do poorly show up once in a while."

If you're not a great student, don't be overwhelmed by past failure. There are certain tips that work well for all kinds of people—those who are commonsense smart, those who have high IQs, and those who may be infinitely wise. Consider the skills that all good students have, regardless of their particular learning aptitude:

1. Critical thinking
2. Active learning
3. Good study and test-taking habits
4. Time management
5. Priority setting
6. Effective note taking

LEARNING TO THINK CRITICALLY

The first step to successful studying is being a good student. College is more challenging than high school. Rote memorization of facts won't cut it—you'll need to learn to think critically. "Learning to think is the most important thing you can learn in college," says Bobbie Katz, who attended McGill University in Canada. Bobbie is now a lawyer with Milbank, Tweed, Hadley, & McCloy LLP, a Wall Street law firm. He had wanted to be a gym teacher when he first started college, but the more he found out about the profession, the less suited to it he felt. Ultimately, he opted not to pursue physical education. But because he had a broad liberal arts education, he learned to make good use of his mind, disciplining himself to think in increasingly complex ways.

BECOME AN ACTIVE LEARNER

Since one of the primary goals of college is to learn how to learn, you must become an active learner. How? Well, one way is to finish your assigned reading before you attend the lectures. That way, the professor's comments become a review for you—not an introduction.

But don't think you can do the reading and skip the class. That's what Jason Moore tried to do during his first semester at the University of Washington. Much to his dismay, he discovered that some of the material covered on exams came from lectures.

If discussion groups led by graduate teaching assistants supplement your professor's lectures, attend them. "Go to class, take notes, and reflect on what you've learned," recommends Gigi David, a curriculum coordinator for a private elementary school.

DEVELOP GOOD STUDY HABITS

Nimbleness of mind is nurtured by developing good study habits. Below are several basic learning principles endorsed by memory experts.

Resist the urge to cram. The brain operates best when you feed it information repeatedly, over a period of time, rather than all at once. Therefore, plan to study a certain amount of time every day. Before a test, reread your notes several times over the course of two weeks and you'll have better recall.

Take study breaks. Your brain can pay close attention to only one thing for so long. You begin learning with a high attention span, but after a while, it drops off. Research shows that jumping from one activity to another, however, increases your mind's ability to retain material. For instance, read for twenty minutes; then play an instrument, exercise, or call someone on the phone. Then come back to your studies. Of course, if a learning period is going well and you're at a good pace, don't make yourself stop. You may lose valuable momentum. But such instances are rare. It's much more common to have lost attention and not be aware of it.

Set up your ideal study environment. When you are studying, do you like it quiet, with few or no distractions, or does a little background music and having other people around actually help you concentrate? Discover your optimal learning environment, then create that atmosphere for yourself.

Pick your best time for learning. As a college student, you will probably be able to determine your class schedule. Use that flexibility to your advantage. "I work best late at night," says Karen McMillen. "So my best semesters were those where I had no taxing classes earlier than 9 or 10 a.m. I hit a slump right after lunch, so I found that giving myself two to three hours in the middle of the day worked well. I could focus better on my classes if they were scheduled during my 'peak brain function' times."

Jill Rudidich, a computer technical specialist, could tell in her first five minutes of studying if her time was being spent effectively or not. If it wasn't, she went running or accomplished something else on her "to do" list. "Don't sit around putting in hours if you're not absorbing," she says. "Make sure your study time is quality time."

Give your brain a regular workout. Memory experts say crossword puzzles are one of the best forms of brain work. Begin with simple ones, then progress to those that are more difficult. Here are a few other suggestions for developing your mental prowess. Pick one or two that you don't normally do; that way you'll be adding variety to your thinking processes. The goal of these exercises is to stimulate your brain to think in new ways.

1. Build something—a birdhouse, a model airplane, etc.
2. Repair something—fix a broken bicycle chain, the latch to your door, or, if you feel inclined, take a stab at your car's engine!
3. Grow a garden—herbs are especially popular right now, and window boxes are suitable for dorm rooms and other cozy living quarters.

Consider This...

HOW TO TEST BEST

Know the structure of the exam. Do the easiest questions come first? If so, do all questions count the same, no matter what their level of difficulty? Will the questions be multiple choice, essay, or a combination of both? Find out ahead of time so you can study accordingly.

1. **Be prepared.** Sharpen pencils and bring an extra pen. You might also want to bring a book or your MP3 player, so you can relax before the test.

2. **Get a good night's sleep.** If necessary, spend a week getting on a sleep schedule so you don't come in blurry-eyed.

3. **Eat a healthy snack.** An empty stomach is a distraction.

4. **Don't cram.** Instead, review relevant material several times over the course of a few days instead of just the night before.

5. **Don't panic.** If a question seems hard for you, it probably is for everyone else taking the test, too. Skip that one and move on to the other questions, then come back to it.

Source: Adapted from Kaplan & Newsweek "Tipsheet," 1999 edition.

4. Work on a cube puzzle or other kinds of "brain teasers."

5. Practice visualization. Think of a personal challenge you face. Perhaps you need to talk with your roommate about a problem in your relationship, or maybe you need to take an important test. Picture the steps that will move you closer to the desired outcome. Play around mentally by imagining several approaches you could take to meet the challenge. Also, when learning something new, visualize the information in mental pictures. Think about how what you are learning connects to something you already know. Try new methods of note taking that incorporate visual images. For example, draw a diagram of the information you are covering in a lecture or during your study time.

Engage your auditory senses as well. For example, repeat what you are reading aloud; this study technique might help ingrain the material in your mind.

MANAGE YOUR TIME

Time is money, so why not budget it? Even a billionaire's calendar has just twelve months. As a student, you have many different classes, and if you're going to pursue the extracurricular activities or part-time work that will help you become well-rounded, you're going to have to make a time budget and then stick to it. There's no other way. It doesn't have to be elaborate. Consider Benjamin Franklin's typical schedule:

5 a.m.	Wake up, wash, and dress. Plan the day; breakfast
8 a.m.	Work
12 noon	Lunch, read
2 p.m.	Work
6 p.m.	Relax; dine; review the day
10 p.m.	Sleep

It's simple enough, and yet this daily schedule served Benjamin Franklin well for over sixty years.

Part of managing time well, is knowing when to say no. Richard Branson, founder and chairman of UK business venture group Virgin Group Ltd. learned this can be a challenge. "I turn people down with extreme difficulty sometimes, because the people I'm saying no to are people I don't want to discourage. And it should be difficult. Saying 'no' shouldn't be an easy thing to do, and you have to be good at it. I often used to dodge doing it myself, and hide behind other people and delegate it. But if you're the boss, that isn't the right thing to do."

Jim Collins, a recipient of the Distinguished Teaching Award at the Stanford University Graduate School of Business, has a practical approach to managing responsibility. He writes, "When you start with an honest and diligent effort to determine the truth of your situation, the right decisions become self-evident. It is impossible to make good decisions without infusing the entire process with an honest confrontation of the brutal facts." His direct approach to decision making seems logical and simple, but its implications in your everyday life may prove challenging. But, if you have the desire to make your life easier and more productive, organization will slowly become part of your life, not an addition to it.

Why is writing down your schedule so important? For one thing, writing things down commits you to action. If you just keep your priorities in your head, you may or may not remember what you have to do. Second, writing down your schedule helps you to determine which things are most important. The do-or-die things you have to do each day take priority over things you should do if you can find time. Third, crossing things off your list at the end of each day gives you a sense of accomplishment. You realize that you are getting from one point to the next and that you are setting the agenda. Your schedule enables you to be in control. Following are some sample schedules from college freshmen.

Let's be realistic. You may not want your schedule to be this detailed. But you'll accomplish more by having a daily game plan.

SET PRIORITIES

Philosopher and creator of the scientific method, Francis Bacon, probably said it best, "To choose time is to save time." You won't waste time on things that don't matter if you identify your priorities. But before you can decide which task to tackle first each day, you have to set goals. These goals should encompass your daily life as well as the life you have planned for the future. A good way to start is to divide your life's goals into four categories: long-term (entire life), intermediate (the next 10 years), short-term (the next six months to a year), and daily. Include detailed goals that will satisfy spiritual, educational, health, social, and financial needs and desires. As your list becomes longer and more detailed, it will be necessary to prioritize your goals. The following questions will help you prioritize tasks and stay focused on your daily journey toward long-term success:

1. Which task demands my immediate attention?
2. If I cannot complete this task today, what will be the consequences?
3. Does this task help me move toward my short-term, intermediate, and long-term goals?
4. If not, is there something I can do to change the task(s) into something more oriented toward my goals?

Throughout the day, keep asking yourself: "What is the best use of my time right now?" It will only be a matter of time before you notice that your world is more ordered and purposeful. Taking charge of your time will help you with one lifelong goal—that of achieving your personal best.

Sample Schedule 1

MONDAY

6:30	Wake up, breakfast
7:15	Read history assignment
9:00	Calculus
10:00	Freshman Composition reading before class tomorrow
11:00	Astronomy
12:00	Lunch
1:00	Library time
1–2	Calculus homework
2–3	Finish rough draft of paper on Hemingway's A Farewell to Arms
3–4	Read Chap. 4 of Astronomy text; review and highlight class notes
4:00	Visit Julia Plant, composition instructor; review rough draft; make notes for revision
5:00	Golf class
6:30	Dinner
8:00	Revise composition paper; double-check calculus homework
9:30	Madeline's surprise birthday party in the dorm
10:30	Sleep

To do today:

1. Buy Madeline's birthday card
2. Invite Eric to coalition meeting
3. Finish History
4. Double-check calculus homework
5. Finish draft of paper

Sample Schedule 2

MONDAY

8:30	Wake up
9:30	Management Information Systems
10:30	Computer Center—run program
11:00	Begin reading The Odyssey
12:00	Introduction to the Humanities
1:00	Lunch
2:00	Accounting
3:00	Marketing Club meeting—bring advertising plans
4:00	Library time
4–5	Accounting homework
5–6	French lab work
6–7	Read at least to page 50 of The Odyssey
7:00	Dinner at Student Union with Cynthia and Alex
8–9	Write rough draft for composition assignment on Keats's "Ode on a Grecian Urn"
10:00	Watch the news, read the newspaper
11:00	Review French for tomorrow's test
11–12	Organize/write schedule for tomorrow

To do today:

1. Finish French assignment
2. Run program
3. Begin reading The Odyssey
4. Meet with Marketing Club
5. Double-check accounting homework

Josh Carter, financial analyst

J osh Carter hasn't even graduated from Fisher College of Business at Ohio State University yet and says he is already living his dream job.

As an investment banking analyst intern in the Global Retail Group at the Merrill Lynch & Co. Inc. in Manhattan's World Financial Center, he works full-time, and carries out the same responsibilities as a full-time professional financial analyst.

Before interning with LifeBound in 2007 as a market analyst and researcher, he assessed his personal goals. Josh was inspired to work in investment banking by Warren Buffet, the CEO named the richest person in the world by *Forbes* in 2008.

While interning with LifeBound, Josh reached out to schools, universities, and publishers world-wide. "I learned the importance of interpersonal skills while contacting different organizations," Josh said. "I realized the importance of managing relationships and representing LifeBound in a proper manner."

Josh is on his way toward career success, drawing inspiration from the people he works with. "These are very affluent, driven people who identify themselves with their success," Josh said. "I work directly with top-level management."

He admits that the work is demanding, but being part of the Wall-Street action is highly rewarding. He has worked with companies like Abercrombie & Fitch, Nordstrom, Inc., Tiffany & Co., and The Home Depot, Inc.

TAKE EFFECTIVE NOTES

Frank Landy, a professor at Penn State, once found the notebook of one of his students. "Since I had just given what I thought was a particularly clear, well-delivered lecture, I opened the book to see what kind of notes the student took. To my dismay and surprise, the student had written down only the anecdotes and stories that described the main points. The real meat of the lecture was scribbled in the margins as an afterthought."

Professors will often use stories or real-life applications to explain a concept or term. "The bones are the theory, while the flesh

Consider This...

TIPS FOR BECOMING A BETTER WRITER

1. **Keep up your journal.** You'll be able to look back over your entries to see if your thoughts are coherent. Do your sentences make sense? What style do you use?

2. **Write letters.** Instead of picking up the phone to call your friends or parents, try writing. Do your thoughts flow easily? If they don't at first, don't worry. And remember that you are going to improve with practice (as well as lower your phone bill!).

3. **Read magazines and the newspaper.** Analyze the writing of columnists and reporters. What is clear and crisp about their writing? How could you apply the same techniques?

4. **Have a friend look at and comment on your writing.** Your teacher is not the only resource for feedback. Meet with a friend or two outside of your composition class and do some peer editing. Analyze their writing and ask them to make constructive criticisms of your own work.

5. **Write your thoughts down in lists that you can refine later.** Jotting things down before you have to write—or think—them out will help you crystallize your original thoughts.

is the story," says Landy. To truly learn the subject matter, you must listen for and grasp both.

To take good notes you must go to class. Don't kid yourself. You need the material your professors give you in their lectures no matter how well you've read and retained the information in the texts.

Most professors will organize their lectures around several controlling points. Obviously, you can't write everything down, but the main ideas—which your professor may write on the board or summarize at the end of each lecture—are what you want to record on paper and commit to memory.

Some students organize their lectures in outline form. Others write in more of a prose style, which they can highlight later on. Occasionally, students who are having a hard time grasping a concept will bring mini tape recorders to class to record the professor's lecture (with permission). They can then review the taped lecture later and organize their notes in a way that helps them understand. Find a style that's comfortable for you and stick to it.

Keep your notes organized and in one place. Date each set of notes so that you can easily match the lecture up with the corresponding text chapter. If necessary, go back and rewrite your notes after the lecture. Or sit down with your professor during his or her office hours and make sure you are grasping the information.

Review your notes. In the same way that you must continually review the summaries after every chapter, you must continually review your class notes. If you keep up with the material along the way, studying for exams will be a lot easier. You can't cram for life, so start your good planning habits now. You'll be prepared for the long haul.

achieving your personal best

n the first half of this chapter, you learned about how to become a better student. Among other things, you now know how to set priorities and how to take effective notes. To achieve your personal best, however, you will also want to add a few additional skills. In the second part of this chapter, you will learn more about how to develop your potential.

GET TO KNOW YOUR PROFESSORS

When John Diaz was a reporter for the *Denver Post*, he also served as part of a weekly local TV panel that dealt with issues central to the state of Colorado. During the summer, John taught a newswriting course at Colorado State University.

"I was amazed at how few students sought me out," he said. "The ones who went the extra nine yards to ask me outside of class how they could improve, benefited the most from the course."

John was surprised that one of his students, a journalism major, said she didn't have time to read the newspaper.

"That's like an aspiring doctor who doesn't have time to be with sick people," John says. John was able to help this student organize her time so that she could read the paper every day, and he helped her brainstorm other career avenues to ensure that journalism was what she truly wanted to pursue. John was both a teacher and a mentor to her.

Few college students bother to get to know their professors. They don't take advantage of office hours unless they fail a test or miss a class. Remember that your college professors are an invaluable resource.

REAL WORK

IN THE REAL WORLD

Warren Buffet, *financial mogul*

arren Buffet, one of the wealthiest men in the world, was born on August 30, 1930. From the start, he demonstrated an aptitude for managing money and calculating numbers in his head.

At the age of eleven, Buffet purchased shares of Cities Service Preferred at $38.00 per share. He watched as the stock fell to $27.00 per share, and sold when his shares rose to $40.00. Seeing the same stock hit $200.00 after his sale, taught Buffet a first-hand lesson in investing.

Despite having no interest in pursuing higher education, his father, a stock broker, managed to persuade Buffet to attend Wharton Business School at the University of Pennsylvania. Although he transferred to University of Nebraska-Lincoln where he graduated, Buffet learned the value of education and applied to Harvard Business School for graduate studies.

When Harvard rejected Buffett, he attended Columbia University. Investors Ben Graham and David Dodd both taught at Columbia and conveyed investment principles that led to great success. Interestingly, these people, once graduate teachers in Buffet's life, later opened doors to professional opportunities.

Graham, for instance, after mentoring Buffet, later offered him a position working for his partnership. Buffet, after perusing an edition of *Who's Who*, saw Dodd listed as Chairman of GEICO, an auto insurance company. He visited the company shortly thereafter, gaining entry only after knocking on the door until a janitor answered. In an otherwise empty office, he was escorted to Lorimer Davidson, the Financial Vice President. His self-created opportunity gave Buffet the chance to learn about GEICO and its business practices. He later acquired GEICO through his investment corporation Berkshire Hathaway.

Clearly, Buffet's experience demonstrates the importance of taking the plunge and making the most of opportunities and relationships along your path.

Source: Kennon, Joshua. "Warren Buffet Biography: The Story of Berkshire Hathaway's Billionaire Chairman." *About.com.* 2009. <http://beginnersinvest.about.com/cs/warrenbuffett /a/aawarrenbio_2.htm>.

Margie Oemero, an honors student at the University of Texas, agrees. "A lot of students are intimidated by their professors. They worry that the professor will feel bothered if they seek him out. My experience is that it is worth it to build that mentoring relationship." During her sophomore year, Margie took an honors seminar on marriage taught by a prominent researcher. She enjoyed the material and took the time to get to know the professor. "Now I work for him, have taken graduate courses with him, will do my senior thesis with him, and may write an article with him. Deciding on a graduate school will be so much easier with the help of a professor who knows which departments and professors are reputable."

Colleen Smith felt extremely intimidated by one of the psychology professors in her graduate program. "I was sure he had evaluated all of my faults and decided that I was unfit for the profession," she says. "During a staff meeting, I was describing a new client that needed to be assigned to a counselor. As I spoke the professor started scowling—I felt like I would either start to cry or laugh hysterically any minute. So I made a joke about how he was scowling. Everyone laughed, including him. It turned out he was trying to figure out who would be the best counselor for the client. He was not thinking negatively about me. In fact, I soon found out he thought I was a talented counselor. That experience reminded me that teachers and employers are human—they are much easier to work with if we take them off the pedestals we put them on. This man has turned out to be of great assistance to me in my career, encouraging me and sending leads my way."

Diana Cuddeback, a hospice social worker, believes finding a mentor was one of the most important experiences of her college career. During her sophomore year at Sacramento State, she took the required abnormal psychology course. Over the course of the term she sought out her professor for questions and advice. The following year he offered her a position as teaching assistant for the course (she was still an undergraduate student). Through the experience of being a teacher assistant, she got firsthand training in leading discussion groups, grading papers, and supporting students. Her professor was also able to see how she handled the responsibility.

During Diana's senior year, this professor nominated her for the Most Outstanding Senior award, which she won. He encouraged her to attend graduate school. "He provided opportunities for me to grow and learn about myself. He also introduced me to other faculty members. His friendship and encouragement helped build my confidence and self-esteem. Under his guidance, I began to see myself as a professional, as someone who had natural abilities to develop."

Start to visit your professors' offices during the first few weeks of school. Go over your class notes with them to make sure you properly understand key concepts. Let them know that you are truly interested in learning their material. They will be impressed by your diligence and your willingness to go above and beyond what is expected. If you have a good rapport with a professor, he or she will probably give you the benefit of the doubt if your grade is on the border between an A and a B. If you are trying harder than anyone else to learn the material, chances are good that your professors will recognize and admire your tenacity.

What about the aloof professors who would rather spend time doing research than talking with undergrads? Well, you're going to meet them. So instead of giving up and assuming that all professors are like that, go to the ones who are willing to help. And remember: you are the consumer. You are paying for your education, and you deserve your professors' attention. Each semester you'll probably have at least one professor who becomes your favorite. Pursue the aloof ones, too. This will build your confidence, and it will prepare you for the aloof people you will need to build relationships with in your career.

Think of your professors as senior advisers. They can ask you questions regarding your major, start the wheels in your head turning, inspire you to superior effort, and give you insights on how to learn, think more broadly, and achieve your goals. The best professors you have in college are similar to the best managers in the working world. Learning from them will go a long way toward discovering what being the best means—as a manager or as a teacher.

It's the students who work hard to build successful relationships with their peers and professors who make the best grades, get the best recommendations, and go on to get top jobs.

Kevin Dellsperger, a cardiologist and professor of medicine at the University of Iowa, believes the mentoring relationship was one of the most valuable and enjoyable experiences of his college career. The relationship with his mentor turned into a lifelong friendship and professional relationship.

During his freshman year at Newcomb-Tulane College in Louisiana, Kevin heard a lecture given by David Wieting at a meeting of the Biomedical Engineering Society. The lecture was about prosthetic heart valves. "After his lecture, I was excited and told my friends and family about Dr. Wieting. I also thought I wanted to work with him during my time at Tulane. I actually made an appointment to talk with him about working in his lab. Unfortunately, at that time he had nothing available, but he put me in contact with another faculty member.

"During my junior year, I took Dr. Wieting's physiology course, and he rekindled my great interest in prosthetic heart valve work. This time he did have a position in his lab. Without a doubt, those last two years were the happiest of my undergraduate years. I must have seemed like a child of four or five, constantly asking him questions about heart valves and bioengineering principles.

"He may tell you otherwise, but I would not be where I am without his guidance. In our program, we were to do research as part of our curriculum. I remember during the summer of my junior year asking David for advice about prosthetic heart valves and complications. After two or three weeks I told him I wanted to design a new valve. He had a smile on his face and asked me what it should look like. I told him I didn't know. He told me to think about it and bring him a design. Well, several weeks later I had a brilliant idea. I took it in to David and the look on his face was one of shock. He went to a locked file cabinet, took out a book of his personal ideas and showed me a nearly identical thought. I believe it was at this time that our relationship changed from student–teacher to student–friend–teacher.

"The next year, working on the valve and in the lab with him was wonderful. I was having such great fun that in March or April I strongly considered delaying medical school for a year to get a master's degree. It was at this time that David was the best mentor I could have had. He told me emphatically that since I always wanted to go into medicine, I should not delay my training. He said that other research opportunities would come to my attention and that I could jump on the bandwagon.

"We kept in touch after I graduated. When he left Tulane he joined Mitral Medical International, a heart valve manufacturer, and asked me to come out during the summer to help set up the lab and do some testing. His job as my mentor was not over, as he directed the research portion of my Ph.D. work. Now I believe that I can scientifically contribute as an equal partner for the first time. While my emphasis these days is not primarily heart valve prostheses, I am still active in that area with collaborative efforts with David. He is like a big brother to me. I value his advice and care deeply about him."

MASTER YOUR COMMUNICATION SKILLS

"No higher-level job can be obtained without a good command of the language," says Steven Harwood, chief of nuclear medicine at the hospital for Veterans Affairs in Bay Pines, Florida. "Writing skills are the most important skills you can develop—especially for obtaining higher management–level jobs. You must be able to clearly communicate your ideas to others."

Mick McCormick, a Nike, Inc. sales director, believes written and oral communication skills are essential for success in the workplace. "I have seen qualified, gifted people passed over for top promotions because they could not communicate their ideas effectively. Corporations value verbal skills."

"Look for examples of great writers so that you can have the best models for your own work," says Greg McCaslin, who has taught students from kindergarten to college. "Read the newspaper, ask your teachers to let you see the work of some of the best writers in your class, and seek styles which vary from your own." Greg, who taught for fifteen years and became director of the New York Foundation for the Arts, says that the determination to improve and a non-defensive response to criticism will overcome any lack of aptitude in writing skills.

Freshman composition may be one of the most important classes you take in college. Even if it's not required, try to take a writing class your first semester. Learning to become a good writer means learning to communicate, to refine and develop your thoughts—so that what you mean to say, or what you think, is clear to others. If you learn to be a good writer as a freshman, you will be successful in your sophomore, junior, and senior-level courses, when you will be required to write research papers and do special assignments. Also, beyond the freshman level, essays become the norm.

In the business world, good writing is essential. Throughout your career, you'll likely be writing memos, business letters to clients, reports, strategic and planning proposals, persuasive or informative speeches, and more. If you can communicate effectively on paper and orally, you'll have an advantage over those who know how to manipulate numbers, but know little about expressing themselves or their work.

"I try to make it fun," says David Plane, who teaches geography at a large state university. He helps his students understand their audience by asking them to write from the point of view of someone in the field. "I ask them to write on a topic and pretend

Consider This...

TIPS FOR BECOMING A BETTER SPEAKER

1. **Contribute to class discussion as often as possible.** As you begin to share your ideas and ask questions, you will become more comfortable speaking in public and articulating your thoughts in front of groups of people.

2. **Assume a leadership position in your extracurricular organizations.** Whether you are the president or a committee leader, you will have many opportunities to practice communicating your ideas in a group.

3. **When you have a formal presentation to prepare, practice your speech in front of a friend.** Ask your friend to give you feedback. Did you enunciate your words clearly? Were your ideas interestingly presented? Did you speak too fast? Too slow? Too quietly?

4. **Enroll in a public speaking or debate class where you can hone your speaking skills.** Not only do communication classes teach you specific tips, they also give you plenty of chances to practice.

5. **Find out if your college has a student chapter of Toastmasters International,** an organization that is specifically designed to help you become comfortable and skillful in public speaking.

that they are an urban planner. What questions would that person ask? How would they best explain and communicate their ideas to a reviewing committee or to their managers?" The following week he might ask them to write a paper from the manager's point of view, presenting the urban planner's proposal.

Becoming a good writer means becoming good at revising your thoughts and observations. Writing, like thinking, is a process. Working on several drafts means distilling your ideas. So, get comfortable with rewriting, crossing things out, and throwing away some of your initial thoughts. That's part of the fun of writing.

Among the many composition books available, I think *The Simon & Schuster Handbook for Writers* by Lynn Troyka stands out. It explains how to become a good, even a great writer. It also contains everything you need to know about the rules for writing. After your freshman year, you'll use it to write research papers for your higher-level courses.

Here's an excerpt from the book that should help clarify how you (and everybody else) can master the art of writing:

> "Many people assume that a real writer can pick up a pen (or sit at a typewriter or a word processor) and magically write a finished product word by perfect word. Experienced writers know better. They know that writing is a process, a series of activities that start the moment they begin thinking about a subject and end when they complete a final draft. Experienced writers know, also, that good writing is rewriting. Their drafts are filled with additions, deletions, rearrangements, and rewordings."

So remember that good writing means practicing. And be patient with yourself. You're embarking on many new things at once.

asking for help

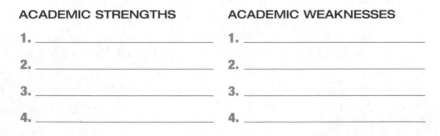f you find out early that you're having problems reading, writing, or understanding class material, get help fast. There are plenty of people available to help you in these areas. You can hire a professional, or you can go to one of the tutors your campus may provide. If you need to take a semester off to refine your study skills, do it. It will be well worth your time and energy in the long run. Better to make mediocre grades for one semester than for four years.

Christina Bernstein felt "unmotivated" during her sophomore year in college. She was especially challenged by the language requirement, which calls for four semesters of a foreign language. After taking the first semester of her junior year off and living with a family in Bogota, Colombia, Chris was able to return to school speaking Spanish fluently. She not only finished up her language classes, she also had new enthusiasm for the rest of her studies.

To get you started focusing on your study skills, fill in the academic evaluation chart below:

ACADEMIC STRENGTHS	ACADEMIC WEAKNESSES
1. _____	1. _____
2. _____	2. _____
3. _____	3. _____
4. _____	4. _____

if at first you don't succeed . . .

You may fall short of some of the goals you set for your freshman year. Maybe you won't achieve a 3.0 average or become captain of the women's soccer team. Instead of dwelling on your defeats, think about ways to improve next year. Can you sharpen your study skills? Manage time better? Better apply yourself to your studies until you improve? Whatever your problem, see what can be done the summer before your sophomore year begins. You may want to spend part of the summer taking reading and writing courses so that you'll have better study skills as a sophomore. You may want to take a year off to attend a community college where you can refine your basic study skills. Whatever your reasons for not meeting your goals may be, analyze what happened and develop a strategy for remedying the situation.

Maybe you gave it your best shot and you've come to the conclusion that you're just not cut out for college. Okay, it's not the end of the world. It does mean, however, that you'll have a somewhat different path, which may lead you to something equally as rewarding as the college-grad path.

Jack Naughton never graduated from high school. He sold Fuller cleaning tools and La-Z-Boy recliners until he brainstormed an invention. He imagined a reclining chair that dentists could use to treat their patients more effectively. He patented the idea internationally and made his life's fortune from that one idea. The original chair, by the way, is now in a world-famous museum—the Smithsonian Institution in Washington, D.C.

However, unless you have the unbridled ambition and fortitude to forgo a traditional education, you're better off staying in school. You may never be on the dean's list or make Phi Beta Kappa. That's okay. The most you can do is *try*, learning as much as you can, and going forward. Most people improve with time.

CHAPTER FIVE

A wise man should have money in his head,
but not in his heart.

JOHNATHAN SWIFT

A big part of financial freedom is having your heart and
mind free from worry about the what-ifs of life.

SUZE ORMAN

As the first decade of the millennium comes to an end, the world is facing a terrible financial crisis. Americans, once perceived as wealthy beyond words, are not immune from the downturn. In fact, many Americans are victims of a mortgage crisis causing foreclosures, bankruptcies, unemployment, and business closings across the nation. The stock market became a roller coaster depleting fortunes almost over night. A society raised on instant-gratification, is learning humility and patience. Now, as most Americans rebuild they are also reevaluating what's truly important to them.

How does this impact you as you prepare for college? You're in a place where you can create your financial future by getting off on the right foot from the start. What you do, or don't do, impacts your

finances for college students

YOUR MONEY—HOW TO GET IT AND WHAT TO DO WITH IT

future in ways you probably have not yet considered. Lenders are less forgiving than in previous years, putting a magnifying glass over any signs of financial irresponsibility.

"I was shocked when I needed a new car and couldn't get a loan," said Samantha, a twenty-four-year-old graduate from Cornell College. "I knew I made some financial mistakes in school, but who knew they'd haunt me," she said. Samantha is not alone in this experience. The freedom that comes with heading off to college is bittersweet. On one hand, you decide what you spend your money on. On the other, you pay the bills. This chapter will help you plan financially, not only for school but also for the "real-life" that follows.

the importance of planning

As the old adage goes, "Fail to plan, plan to fail." This couldn't be more true than when applied to financial planning. Whether you're in college or a professional, planning begins with assessing how much money is coming in and how much money is going out. In other words, budgeting. "I was amazed at how quickly things added up," said Luke, a sophomore at Arizona State. "Living with my parents, I had no idea what things like toilet paper, notebooks and eggs cost. It was a huge reality check when I got through the grocery line during my first shopping trip in college. I wound up putting more than a few things back."

Creating a budget may seem daunting, but it's actually quite simple if you take the following steps:

1. **Assess your income:** For college students, the following sources of income are most common: summer job money, scholarships, grants, student loans, allowances, and paid internships. Regardless of the source of your income, you need to know exactly what you can count on per month.

2. **Assess what's outgoing:** Really take a look at your needs for each month. Consider toiletries, food costs, rent, cell phone, car insurance, etc. What about big upfront expenses like books, contact lenses, deposits, etc?

3. **Assess the gap (if any):** Do you have enough to cover your expenses? If not, what makes more sense—increasing your earnings or cutting back on your spending? Can you realistically take on a job during your first semester? How much do you need to earn? As you assess your needs, use the sample monthly financial planner found at the end of this chapter. Also, on financial advisor Suze Orman's website, www.suzeorman.com, there is a comprehensive expense calculator. There are many "hidden" expenses often forgotten. Using these tools will keep you accountable.

As Mike, a junior at Penn State recalls, "By the time spring break freshman year rolled around I had a $2000.00 credit card balance and an overdrawn bank account. I was shocked when I realized the charges I had from bounced checks and late payments. I eventually had to call my parents for help." It wasn't just Mike's financial state that suffered either. "I would be sick to my stomach when the bill arrived. It ruined my first year of college," he said.

SAMPLE COLLEGE STUDENT MONTHLY BUDGET

Income:

Parental support, College fund/savings	2,575.00
Student loan ($2,500/yr.)	208.00
Part-time job (20 hrs. /wk.)	800.00
Total	$3,583.00

Expenditures:

Tuition ($15,000/yr.) (9-month payment plan)	1,600.00
Transportation (car payments, gas, insurance, repairs)	400.00
Phone	60.00
Utilities (electricity/cable, water, gas)	60.00
Groceries and necessities	200.00
Rent	500.00
Taxes	160.00
Entertainment	75.00
Total expenditures	$3,055.00
Amount left over for savings	$528.00

Source: Adapted from About.com's Monthly Budget Worksheet for College Students, 2009, at http://financialpla. about.com/cs/budgeting/l/blmocolbud.htm.

Fortunately, Mike was able to turn things around. "My parents helped me create a budget for my sophomore year. It was nice feeling in control as opposed to scared all the time."

As Mike learned, having a budget is not a restrictive thing, but an empowering one. He was able to treat himself occasionally to concerts, new clothes, and dinners out without having the experience tainted with guilt. Those moments, after all, are meant to be enjoyed.

In addition to saving your sanity and money in college, planning will serve you after graduation as well. Many companies will offer their employees 401ks. A 401k essentially helps employees build wealth and plan for their future. A company matches their employees' savings by a certain percentage. Over time, the savings really add up. For those who go on to start their own businesses, there are SEP plans to assist in saving for the future as well. For now, being aware these plans exist is the important thing. When you start looking at employment, you'll want to research them in greater detail and even meet with a financial planner. Often times a financial planner's expertise will go along way in paving the way to financial security.

not all banks are created equal

Once you have your plan in place, you'll need a reputable place to bank. Before heading off to college hop online and research the banks in your school's city. You'll want to pick the one that best serves you. Consider the following:

- Is this bank in a convenient location? Can you walk to it if you have to?
- Does this bank charge you if your account falls below a specific balance?
- Is there a charge to use the debit card machine (watch these—they can take a bite out of the budget!)?
- Is there a checking fee?
- Is the bank affiliated with the college? If so, does that provide benefits for you?

Once you've chosen a bank, vow to yourself to keep at least $200.00 in a savings account. Emergencies arise and having the cash available will ease your mind when your roommate accidentally locks you out and leaves town for the weekend or your car breaks down and needs repairs.

spend only what you have— and not all of it!

Once you have a budget, a place to bank and a savings account, it should be smooth sailing right? For the most part, that's true. There are some things to look out for though. One of them is the temptation to spend.

"Getting into Southern California University seemed so glamorous," said Tara of Des Moines, Iowa. "I couldn't wait for my life on the West Coast!" After Tara arrived on campus, however, she felt really out of place. "I was a fish out of water at that school," said Tara, who's since transferred. "I spent so much money trying to keep up with my wealthy friends. I think I just finally realized that when I spent money I didn't have, I was living a lie."

College will be a melting pot of backgrounds. Some of your friends will dine on sushi and some on Ramen Noodles. No matter what your circumstances, you must remain true to yourself in all areas, including financially. Honesty is usually met with respect, so don't hesitate to say, "Thanks for the invite, but I'll meet you after dinner" or "I'm saving for spring break, but catch me next time." Others will understand more than you think. And if they don't, who cares? There are plenty of people on campus to befriend without wasting your time on a few with elitist attitudes.

confusing wants and needs

A s mentioned earlier, Americans have been reassessing whether their daily latte is a need or a want. Have you taken a close look at your own spending? Maybe you hear yourself saying, it's only a twenty dollar manicure. I can afford it." True, but getting manicures twice a month will cost $480.00 by the end of a year. All of those channels? They can cost you an easy $1000.00 annually. Most college students find that going to school requires some sacrifices, especially financial ones.

The good news is that there are often great deals to accommodate a student's budget both in college towns and on campus. Check out the school paper for coupons and weekly specials that can help stretch a buck. Check movies out of the library instead of renting them or going to the theatre. Carpool as a way of saving gas money and making friends. As Taj, of NYU told us, "It didn't take long to realize that used books were just as good as new and a whole lot cheaper."

You'll soon find at school most of your peers are making similar adjustments. Later, you'll look back and think, "We were just scraping by, but they were the best times of our lives!"

stay out of credit card debt

W hen you walk through the student union your first week, you'll undoubtedly see kiosks with credit card vendors wooing you to sign up for a card. This advice may surprise you, but do it! A credit card is an incredible convenience and downright necessary in times of an emergency. Using one responsibly demonstrates your character and proves your sense of responsibility in the marketplace. As discussed further in the chapter, your credit score indicates how well you handle money. Keeping your score high is important later when you want a new ride or a downtown loft.

Credit cards get a bad rap, but the reality is spenders make bad choices. It doesn't take long to see four digit credit card balances, as Will from Michigan found out. "I don't know what I was thinking playing the 'big man on campus' those first three years," he told us. "I charged everything! Finally my second semester senior year, I could hardly stand to open a bill." Will got out of his situation by cutting up his cards and taking action. "After graduation, I had to move back home, while my friends got apartments. It was tough, but I've almost paid them off."

While credit cards are great resources, they can quickly become a nightmare if not paid off on a monthly basis. Follow the steps below for good credit card usage:

- Only carry one card for emergencies. Having several is more tempting and difficult to keep track of.
- Have the phone number for the card stored in your phone. If the card is lost or stolen, you'll want to cancel it immediately.
- Only charge what you can afford to pay at the end of the month.

If you have found yourself in the credit card trap, consider the following:

- Cut up the cards, with the exception of one for emergencies.
- Determine the interest rates on all of the cards.
- Pay the minimums on all cards except for that bearing the highest interest rate. This is the card you want to pay off first, since it's costing you the most money. Put as much as you possibly can down on this ABOVE the minimum to pay it off.
- Once you pay off one card, start paying down the one with the

next highest interest rate, and so on until you have paid them all off.

- Reward yourself for a job well done!

Remember that credit card interest rates can run as high as 20 percent for use of the card. That adds up quickly! Pick one with a low interest rate and no annual fee. Also keep in mind that if you miss a payment your credit rating will go down and your interest rate could go up. Once that happens, the great pair of skis you bought on sale will now have cost you a small fortune.

writing bad checks

Writing checks, even for things you need, when you don't have money in your account to cover them is a common mistake made when managing finances for the first time. Companies process checks in different ways. Some even treat paper checks like check cards, electronically debiting the money from your account upon receipt. The fees for bounced checks and overdrawn accounts add up amazingly fast and are hard to get out from under. Think of signing a check as giving someone your word that the money is already in place to cover the purchase.

forgo payday advances

It seemed so easy," English major, Michelle Diane mused. "I needed some cash to repair my car, and I stumbled upon a payday loan business down the street. They asked for a paystub and loaned me $500 that day. I didn't think about how much of my next paycheck it would take to pay the loan back with interest and fees. I actually needed to take out another advance to be able to repay the first one on time. By the time I finally paid everything back, I'd spent $300 extra dollars."

Payday advances are loans with high interest rates. Cash advances and payday loans are rarely the best solution to money woes. Resist the temptation to use them. Even negotiating with vendors you owe regarding an extension to make your payment is a better solution than a payday advance.

lease responsibly

As we mention later in this book, dorm life is an incredible experience. Some students decide to forgo life in the residence hall for their own place. If you choose to do the same, you'll likely want to find something near campus—and affordable. Since a lease is a legally binding contract, be careful before rushing in. Once you've given your signature it's too late to decide the apartment is too expensive or too close to the subway.

When you find a place that interests you, ask the landlord for a tour. Note any damage to the place as you walk around. The landlord will likely ask for a damage deposit, and you won't want to be penalized for the aftermath of the former tenant's wild parties. Provided you maintain the place well, the deposit will be returned to you in full.

If you decide to live with roommates, understand that unless otherwise stated in the lease, you are each responsible for the entire amount due for the rent. This is called Joint and Several Liability. In other words, your landlord will not care that your roommate agreed to pay 50/50, but dropped out of school. Nor will it be the landlord's responsibility to track down her half of the rent. The landlord can collect the entire lease amount from anyone that signed the document. If your roommate bails on you, you will have to pay your landlord and track down reimbursement on your own time. A word to the wise: Choose your roommates carefully. This caution holds true when co-signing a loan. Remember, as a co-signer you are assuming liability for the payment should the primary party fail to pay. Never ask a family member or friend to co-sign on a loan or sign a lease unless you can make the payment—it's a good way to damage a relationship.

Below is a lease clause illustrating the option between tenants either paying individually or joint and severally. Such a clause clarifies whether you are jointly or individually responsible for the rent and other provisions of the lease.

Obligations of co-tenants

Tenants will pay rent *(check one)*:

    ☐ Individually

    ☐ severally/jointly

and in the event of late rent:

    Tenants will be held accountable individually/jointly *(circle one)*.

It may sound obvious, but take the time to read the lease. "I was in a pinch to sign my lease," notes Mitch Johnson. "The landlord insisted another group was ready to sign, so we wanted to get our paperwork in right away. We didn't realize the terms of the lease had us paying for a $400.00 carpet cleaning service. Of course, this was something our landlord forgot to mention."

More information on lease provision can be found at http://www.cmu.edu/policies/Landlord-Tenant/leases.htm. We highly suggest reading over a full copy of the sample common lease agreement before signing a binding one. For an example go to:

web.wm.edu/sharpefellowship/Files/sampleleaseagree.doc

prepare today for tomorrow's purchases

For many college students, buying a home seems light years away. While it may be a few years off, your decisions in college will directly impact whether you have the opportunity to own a home later.

Even a few years ago, an American making a modest living could move into a palatial home with no money down using an ARM (Adjustable Rate Mortgage). Since the mortgage, or monthly payment, was adjustable, a few years after purchasing their homes, the rates went up. The owners could no longer afford the monthly mortgage. Many home owners surrendered their homes by sending house keys back to the lender. Everyone learned a valuable lesson about lending and purchasing beyond the ability to pay.

As a result, lenders are more careful then ever. This is where a good credit score comes into play.

your credit report score: what it means and how it works

Nationwide credit bureaus store information on the financial behavior of every adult in the United States. The credit bureaus derive their information from the banks, lenders, and business owners with whom the consumers do business. In addition, they have records of lawsuits, broken leases, defaulted student loans, unpaid judgments, and bankruptcy filings. After a few months, any unpaid bill is usually reported to the credit bureaus.

Based on the information received, the credit bureau determines a consumer's three digit credit score. A low credit score indicates a consumer is a business risk, while a high score indicates that the business risk is minimal. The number can change with your behavior in the marketplace. The credit bureau then profits by selling this information in the marketplace.

Having a low credit score will negatively impact your life. Lenders will charge higher interest rates on loans, require a co-signer, or refuse to lend money at all. Landlords may reject requests to lease apartments due to the perceived risk. Some employers will not hire based on low credit scores. After graduation, you may not receive loans necessary to purchase a home or car, or even attend graduate school. In short, the consequences range from inconvenient and expensive to complete limitation.

As a consumer you have rights under The Fair Credit Reporting Act. Visit the Federal Trade Commission's web site at www.ftc.gov to find out more about your protection under this act. You are entitled to one free credit report per year from each of the three main credit bureaus, Equifax, Trans Union, and Experian. It makes sense to pull yours and review your score and the entire report. Discrepancies can often be corrected with some effort on your part.

Contact information on the big three:

- Equifax—www.equifax.com
- Trans Union—www.transunion.com
- Experian—www.experian.com

Also, to better understand your credit score and report visit www.MyFico.com.

protect yourself from scams and identity theft

Unfortunately no matter how responsible you are, there are other threats to your credit score as well. Financial scams have always existed, but due to information available in cyberspace, identity theft is on the rise. Identity theft occurs when unscrupulous people prey on innocent consumers by stealing information such as social security numbers, credit card numbers, etc. The information is used to make purchases and establish lines of credit. These people will con for information, break into computer databases, and rummage through trash for paperwork with personal information. As victims can attest, the damage is devastating.

"I received a call about winning a sweepstakes while studying one night," said Connor, a student at University of Oklahoma. "I know it was gullible, but I was pretty psyched. I gave my social security number and address. It sounded so legit, I didn't question it. I had no idea they were stealing my identity. I spent a fortune getting out of the damage done."

Your grandfather's advice, "If it sounds too good to be true, it probably is," was right on. Never give personal information to anyone over the phone, and whenever possible, shred documents with personal information. If someone calls indicating they represent your bank or another financial institution, end the call immediately. Then call the financial institution yourself.

If you find an error on your credit report or think that fraud is occurring in your name, you must do the following:

- When you first spot identify theft, check all of your accounts to determine if they were affected. You may want to alert these financial organizations that you have been a victim even if those accounts aren't affected in order to keep representatives vigilant. Close the accounts that were affected.
- Change passwords, choosing those that cannot be guessed. Don't use your pet's name, birthdays, etc.
- Contact the fraud department of the three major credit bureaus to place a fraud alert. The other two will be automatically notified, but be proactive and call all three.
- File a complaint with the local police department. Make copies to supply to vendors.

- File a complaint with the Federal Trade Commission. They have a Theft Affidavit on their website.
- Notify the Social Security Administration at (800) 269-0271 or www.ssa.gov/oig/hotline.
- Keep a paper-trail. This is the difference between being a victim or a victor. You should record every email you send, keep a log of all calls and follow up on every phone call or in person meeting with a letter. Keep a copy for your file as well.

Your instincts will generally be a good guide, but con artists can be disarming. Be on the lookout if you've won "big cash" prizes when you haven't entered a contest or if you've been offered a no-interest loan with bad credit history. Also, when bargain-shopping online, be wary of any deals that seem too low—they might be stolen, fake, or even nonexistent. Advance fee scams require that you pay in advance for a credit card, scholarship, or loan—but get nothing in return. Keep your antennae up and your money in hand.

Source: "What to do if You're a Victim of Fraud." *Microsoft*. 26 July 2006. <http://www.microsoft.com/protect/ yourself/personal/fraud.mspx>.

paying for school

While this chapter explores a variety of ways to pay for school, you will want to do some investigating. Scholarships and grants, for instance, are often awarded to the student diligent enough to do their research and find applicable ones. Keep records of every step you take and get organized. Strict deadlines are the name of the game when it comes to receiving financial awards.

SCHOLARSHIPS AND GRANTS

Short of winning the lottery or having VERY generous parents, scholarships are the ideal way of paying for school. Why? Because unlike loans, scholarships do not have to be paid back. Scholarships are essentially an investment made by a person, organization or company in your education, gifted to you for meeting predetermined criteria.

Most people are familiar with academic and athletic scholarships, but there are countless other types of scholarships. Some

INSIGHTS

FROM AN INTERN

Chelsey Emmelhainz, *publishing student*

Chelsey admits that paying for college was not something she had to think about. Her grandfather was a financial whiz and had kindly set aside money for her education. That said, she still had to budget. In her words, "After all, $800 a month to pay for rent, food, school books, electric bills and internet wasn't going to be enough to keep me from pulling my hair out. And, it wasn't going to last forever."

So she got a job.

Chelsey was committed to her academic success. She knew working 40 hours a week and taking a full class load would be a major juggling act, but she was determined to make it work. "I got a day-by-day planner and budgeted out my time the same way I did with my money: three hours for homework, one at the library, five at work and one, well-earned hour, spent in front of *Grey's Anatomy*. By figuring out my peak "brain" hours, I was able to schedule my homework and my day without sacrificing too much sleep, which I found really helped. To my surprise, the plan worked. At the end of my second semester, I earned a $500 scholarship for academic success!"

In some ways, Chelsey's schedule helped her budget her time even better. As

she says, "Looking back at my planning, I realized that the tight schedule kept me from procrastinating and helped me enjoy the precious hours spent with friends. In essence, working gave my brain a break from school, and school gave it a break from work. Refocusing my attention everyday gave me energy and kept me from getting burnt out. Additionally, the time I earned with friends was  no longer quite as stressful considering that I now had a little extra cash to pay for pizza once in awhile."

Chelsey is still in school today, and is now juggling work, school, and her internship with LifeBound as a developmental editor. She realizes that time and money management is an ongoing process. "Overall, I'm still fine-tuning the crazy schedule and financial needs of my life," says Chelsey. "Sometimes I have to work a little more to pay for that new ink cartridge or sacrifice some hours at my job to ace my French exam. Either way, college and finances are a constant balancing act. And finding the right combination of the two is the only way to succeed in both and, for me, to keep my hair firmly planted in my head."

require having a particular faith, performing community service or even having a specific ambition such as news-casting. The best thing you can do is start early! Scholarships are competitive and often take time to secure. Often times they require a written essay. In your sophomore and junior years of high school, begin reaching available scholarships on line. Your guidance counselor and school librarian will also be a help in recommending scholarships. Also, do some online checking on your own: www.finaid.org/scholarships is one of many sites to kick-start a search. Beware of scholarship scams though—if you have to pay money to get money, it probably isn't on the up and up.

While there is some initial legwork, the pay-off for securing scholarships is huge. Even obtaining partial scholarships can make a big difference after school when payments start.

Similar to scholarships in that they do not need to be paid back, grants are awarded on need. Check www.finaid.org for a grant database.

STUDENT LOANS

Student loans are a common way of paying for education and a great investment in yourself. Since your college years will provide you with new insights, expand your horizons both professionally and socially, and introduce you to dreams you never knew you had, you will definitely reap rewards for borrowing the money. Just keep in mind when borrowing for college; you will need to pay back every dollar borrowed—plus interest.

There are three categories of education loans: student loans (Stafford and Perkins), parent loans (PLUS loans) and private loans. The interest rates can vary with the maximum set by the government. Some repayment plans are more flexible than others as well. Therefore, some advance research here is a good idea.

For federal loans you will want to start by filling out a FAFSA (Free Application for Federal Student Aid). This will request a detail of your financial need. If for any reason you are denied, don't hesitate to reapply. A variety of changing circumstances can affect your eligibility, for instance a sibling starting college at the same time.

You will receive a financial award letter from the college. All too often, from that time on, student loans are out of sight, out of mind, until graduation occurs. Then, repayment begins and the responsibility can seem daunting. If you've borrowed money for college, you'll be less intimidated by repayment if you remember the following:

1. Borrow only what you NEED: You may qualify for more, but assess what you can live on and limit yourself.
2. Understand the full extent of your responsibility upfront.

Start by keeping good financial records during school. You should be able to easily access amounts borrowed, copies of promissory notes, the names of your lenders and the interest accruing on each loan. Keep a binder of the loan information divided by promissory notes, receivable statements, and acknowledgements of loan money credited to your student account.

Because student loans are often provided by several lenders, both federal and private, it really helps to have a log outlining the details of each loan. This is as simple as creating an Excel spreadsheet. Below is an example of what log entries can look like. The log will help keep you on track towards paying off the loans.

The following are two examples of log entries from the Financial Counselor website:

Year	Loan Type	Loan Amount	Int. Rate %	Pay Amount	Lender's Name & Telephone No.	Lender's Address
1998	Perkins Loan	$1,500	5.0	$40.00	School Credit & Collections 888-555-8898	123 Washington, Chicago, IL 60606
1999	Federal Direct Loan	$1,000	6.32*	$50.00	Fed. Direct Loan Service Center (800) 848-0979	P.O. Box 4609 Utica, NY 13504

* 1999 Federal Direct Loans had a 6.32% variable interest rate with an 8.25% cap.

The table on the following page outlines what variations of a loan schedule can look like. Before repayment begins, arrange a meeting with your financial advisor. They will assist you in understanding your commitment and the lenders' expectations.

These figures are fixed payment amounts in which principal and interest are included.

Loans are all simple interest loans. Interest is always calculated on the unpaid balance at the time of billing.

These amounts are meant to be used as guidelines. The actual payment amount of your loan may vary.

ESTIMATED MONTHLY LOAN PAYMENT TABLE

Total Loan Balance	Number of Payments	5%	7%	8.25%	9%	10%
2,000	36	59.94	61.75	62.67	63.60	64.53
2,625	48	60.45	62.86	64.08	65.32	66.58
3,000	72	48.31	51.15	52.60	54.08	55.57
4,000	108	46.07	50.03	52.08	54.17	56.31
5,000	120	53.03	58.05	60.66	63.34	66.08
6,000	120	63.64	69.66	72.80	76.01	79.29
7,000	120	74.25	81.28	84.93	88.67	92.50
8,000	120	84.85	92.89	97.06	101.34	105.72
9,000	120	95.46	104.50	109.19	114.01	118.93
10,000	120	106.07	116.11	121.33	126.68	132.15
12,000	120	127.28	139.33	145.59	152.01	158.58
15,000	120	159.10	174.16	181.99	190.01	198.23
17,000	120	180.31	197.38	206.26	215.35	224.66
20,000	120	212.13	232.21	242.65	253.35	264.30
22,500	120	238.65	261.24	272.99	285.02	297.34
26,000	120	275.77	301.88	315.45	329.36	343.59
30,000	120	318.20	348.32	363.98	380.03	396.45
35,000	120	371.23	406.38	424.65	443.37	462.53
40,000	120	424.26	464.43	485.31	506.70	528.60
45,000	120	477.29	522.49	545.97	570.04	594.68
50,000	120	530.33	580.54	606.63	633.38	660.75
60,000	120	636.39	696.65	727.97	760.05	793.00
70,000	120	742.46	812.76	849.29	886.73	925.00
80,000	120	848.52	928.87	970.62	1013.41	1057.00
90,000	120	954.59	1044.98	1091.95	1140.08	1189.00
100,000	120	1060.66	1161.08	1213.28	1266.76	1321.00

Note: The interest rates are variable for Direct Loans and Federal Family Education Loans and are adjusted once a year, on July 1. The other Federal loans have fixed interest rates and remain the same throughout the life of the loan.

Source: Adapted from https://www.fc.campusoncall.com/cgi-bin/home.pl?campus=syracuse

what is default?

efault is the failure to pay loans back according to the terms outlined in your promissory note. The consequences for defaulting are serious as outlined below:

- Notification to national credit bureaus resulting in a lower credit score
- Declination of further loans
- Garnished wages
- Late fee charges and collection costs
- Withholding of state and federal tax refunds
- Your possessions may be repossessed
- The cost of a lawsuit

From the list above, it's easy to see that it does not pay to default. If you find yourself in bad financial straights there are alternatives to default that won't hurt your future in the long-term. Economic hardship programs extend grace to borrowers who cannot pay. These programs usually suspend the necessity of making payments for a predetermined time period. This allows a borrower to "get on their feet" without penalty. Interest still accrues on loans during deferment and forbearance period.

loan forgiveness

f you have a heart for public service, you may find your professional path qualifies you for loan forgiveness. For some nonprofit, public service jobs, and government positions, particularly in the military, there are opportunities for loan forgiveness. Ask your financial aid advisor for details during your exit interview.

Usually, there is an outline of criteria for loan forgiveness. For instance, a program may require a teacher to work in a low-income city for a specified duration of time. Sometimes only certain loans will qualify depending on the criteria. Be sure to explore this option as you prepare for graduation and plan for your career. If you can save tens of thousands of dollars and gain some public service experience in your field, you might find the option very appealing.

For more information on loan forgiveness programs, check out: http://www.finaid.org/loans/forgiveness.phtm

REAL WORK

IN THE REAL WORLD

Suze Orman, expert on personal finance

 Who would have thought that Suze Orman once considered herself as unintelligent? Yet as a child growing up that is exactly what she thought. In fact, intimidated by her college's foreign language requirement, Orman dropped out of school for three years and waited tables at the Buttercup Bakery until she was twenty-nine years old.

Her magnanimous personality earned her favor with her customers. When they learned she had an idea to open her own restaurant, they gave her a $50,000 loan interest-free. With the intention of handling the money responsibly, she invested with a Merrill Lynch broker. Rather than serve Orman's interests the broker invested the money in volatile funds. It was gone within three months.

During this time it occurred to Orman that she might make a good broker herself. She applied for a position and was accepted. Unwilling to sweep her loss under the carpet, she sued Merrill Lynch while working for them. The company eventually settled with her for the amount and interest. In the meantime, Orman became a rising star within Merrill Lynch.

Today, Orman is renowned as an expert on personal finance. She has written seven consecutive New York Times' bestsellers. She is a contributing editor for two of Oprah's magazines as well as the host of the award-winning Suze Orman Show and Financial Freedom Hour on QVC television. Her shows are aired on both television and radio.

Recently, Time magazine named Orman one of the "Time 100: The World's Most Influential People". Other honors and awards include her contributions to ensuring human rights around the world, the financial empowerment of women, and finding a cure for MS. .America's financial guru lives by the motto she shares with millions: "People First, Then Money, Then Things."

Source: "About Suze." *SuzeOrman.com.* 2009. <http://www.suzeorman.com/igsbase/igstemplate.cfm?SRC =SP&SRCN=layout_aboutsuze&GnavID=2>.

loan consolidation

After graduation, I was shocked by the number of bills arriving from lenders," Carolyn Stark, a recent college graduate, said. "It was crazy to make six separate payments on a monthly basis. Not to mention tough on the budget. By consolidating, I make one payment. It's a lot cheaper than what I paid before."

Carolyn learned the benefits of consolidation quickly. Consolidation lets a company assume all of your student loan debt and charge you in one invoice for all of them. It extends the repayment period substantially, so you often pay a lesser monthly payment over a longer period of time. For a strapped graduate, this can be a huge advantage. The trade-off can be a larger amount paid in interest depending on your credit score.

A word of caution: don't consolidate until you review your promissory notes. Some loans, like the Federal Perkins Loan, may disallow loan forgiveness for military service if you consolidate. Also, although your monthly payments may be lower after consolidation, because you are paying over a longer period of time, you will pay more over the grand scheme of things. Make sure consolidation makes sense before signing the dotted line.

For more information on all of these subjects, be sure to take a look at Appendix A in the back of this book which covers this section in greater detail. Additionally, these sources are excellent references if you have more questions:

- *Financial Counselor:* https://www.fc.campusoncall.com/cgi-bin/int_exit.pl?campus=syracuse&start_time=Sep-11-2008-14:28:47&page=exit_Provisions
- *FinAid:* The SmartStudent Guide to Financial Aid: www.finaid.com

summary

Our future is created by the things we do today. Just by reading this chapter you have taken the first important step to a good financial future: informing yourself! The choice to have success, wealth and a great life belongs to you. It is never too early to take responsibility for your future. By doing so, you will be among the many who took the current economic climate and turned it into a financial opportunity.

CHAPTER SIX

*The most exciting breakthroughs of the 21st century
will not occur because of technology but because of
an expanding concept of what it means to be human.*

JOHN NAISBITT

We're changing the world with technology.

BILL GATES

You've probably heard the expression, "To whom much is given, much is expected." This statement definitely applies when it comes to technology. Technology provides a world of information at your fingertips. By typing a few keywords and hitting the search button you can find virtually anything on the internet. On the flip side, since research can be completed with relative ease, more research may be required. In other words, convenience comes with an expectation of proficiency.

By knowing how the computer can work for you, and by being open to continuous learning, you'll be primed for success. In this chapter, you will learn how technology is used in college and how to best prepare yourself for advanced learning. You will also learn about the limits of technology and the discipline needed for using it effectively.

the technology age

GIZMOS YOU USE

If you are a completely tech savvy student, you can skip this chapter except for the section called "Socializing with Technology".

should i buy a computer?

For starters, you may be wondering, "Do I *have* to buy a computer before heading off to school?" Understandably, this may seem a large investment when other expenses such as food, housing and books are demanding your summer job money. Having a laptop, however, is a huge advantage for college students. Balancing classes, your social life and possibly a job means planning study time as wisely as possible. A laptop will allow you to jumpstart that term paper when you're hanging out in the Student Union, waiting for the bus to go to work, or sitting with a spare half hour between classes. Additionally, if you have an internal wireless card on your laptop or a broadband card, you can be ready to use all aspects of your computer anywhere you want.

If you can't afford to buy a computer yet, you'll need to do some advance scheduling. As Ann Crandall, a recent college graduate, found out the hard way, without a computer this planning is critical. "I had no idea the computer lab at my university closed at 11 p.m.," Ann said. "After my waitressing shift ended, I planned to pull an all-nighter making the final edits on a term paper. When I saw the lock on the building door, I freaked out! Luckily my boyfriend lent me his laptop or my prof would have docked me a full letter grade for turning the paper in late."

Be sure to ask the following questions:

- What are the hours of the campus computer center? Inquire about availability of computers there. Is there usually a line to use one? Is there a time limit?
- Is legal file sharing and music/video downloading allowed?
- If you have a particular area of study in mind, how dependent will you be on a computer to finish classwork?
- When you visit the campus, do you see other students relying on their laptops for note-taking?
- Will your professors require PowerPoint presentations?
- Does your college have a laptop loaner program?

If you decide to purchase a computer, allow yourself enough time to research different brands and seek advice from several people. Often, if you can tell a sales representative how you plan to use your computer, they'll help with solid recommendations. Also, find out what type of programs you will need so that you can load the computer with the right software. Ask students currently enrolled in your programs of interest what they recommend in a computer and programs. You may even be able to roll the cost of a computer into your student loan, so don't be afraid to ask about the option when meeting with your financial aid adviser.

what do i need to know about using technology in college?

FORMS OF TECHNOLOGY ON CAMPUS

Technology changes faster than we can type these words. It seems the latest and greatest breakthroughs in technology become obsolete overnight. The important thing to remember is that in college and in the real world following graduation, your ability to stay current on changes, adapt, and commit yourself to learning will separate you from the pack. The following table outlines commonly used technology, but keep your eyes open for advances:

FORM	HOW USED	PURPOSE
Text Messaging	Abbreviated messages sent using the keypad on a cell phone.	Texting is a way to send a quick note while on the run and a fun way to keep in touch with friends.
Email	A service that sends immediate messages to recipients that also have an online email account.	Email is used professionally and socially as a quick form of communication.
Twitter	A form of sending real-time short messaging across multiple networks. A "tweet" is essentially a response to the question, "What are you doing?" The response is a 140-character response sent from various devices.	Twitter keeps people connected socially. Businesses are now using Twitter as a form of marketing short, succinct messages.
Social Networking	Websites on the Internet that invite people to join as members. Members can search for other members as a form of reconnecting. Examples of these sites include: LinkedIn, Facebook and Myspace.	Social networking sites provide a way of connecting personally (with old friends for example) and building professional connections.
Digg.com	A website that compiles various forms of information from news, images, and video. The information is rated for popularity by the number of views. The most popular content makes the front page.	Digg helps people stay connected with what the general population deems relevant through popularity.
Blog	A shared online journal where people can post entries.	Blogs are used to keep a group posted on day-to-day events. Professionally, they may be used to share career highlights and demonstrate compelling writing.
Kindle Electronic Books	A portable reading device.	E-books are used to wirelessly download books, blogs, and magazines.
MP3	A handheld device used for downloading music and books.	MP3 players are a convenient way to access a variety of music and information in the palm of your hand.

COMPUTER PROGRAMS: THE BASICS

Since most high school teachers require typed term papers and essays, you are probably already familiar with basic word processing programs. Microsoft Office is a suite of products including Microsoft Word (the most commonly used word processing program), PowerPoint (a program used for designing presentation slides), Excel (a spreadsheet document program), Outlook (a time and contact management system) and Access (a database management program). These programs are considered "the basics." They are relatively straightforward and easy to learn.

Since there will be plenty of other information to digest when school begins, spend some time brushing up on your Microsoft Office skills before your college career begins. As UCLA freshman Tim Scoggins put it, "There was enough to take on getting used to a college work load. I would have felt buried if I didn't know the basics of Word."

Your high school computer lab is a great place to start. Often times an instructor can provide Microsoft Office tutorials that take you through each program step-by-step. It's easy and worth it. Familiarize yourself with desktop publishing programs Adobe InDesign and QuarkXPress as well. These programs are commonly used in business to protect others making unsolicited edits to documents.

If you don't have a computer lab at school, or the tutorials aren't available, check out classes at community centers, the library, or ask a friend for some tutoring. Also consider taking computer courses during your freshman year. Even if you don't have an IT focus, the courses can often pass for electives, and you will undoubtedly use the skills later on.

COMPUTERS IN TRADITIONAL CLASSES

Technology is used in and out of class in many ways to enhance learning. In class, the most common application used is note-taking. Many schools have lecture halls equipped to facilitate the growing use of technology. If possible, scope out the lecture halls on campus, to get a sense of how the university promotes the use of technology.

As far as other forms of technology in the classroom—anything goes. Expect to see professors presenting on PowerPoint while a podcast recording of the lecture takes place. Some professors now even use classroom response systems, also known as clickers. Similar to a TV remote, teachers can pose a question and get immediate feedback from students using clickers. Answers are tabulated and presented back to the class as a survey result.

Keep in mind that while technology brings a new dynamic to education, even the latest and greatest technology may not overcome your life-long aversion to math. Take initiative and form study groups that meet for an hour before your favorite TV show. Just incorporating a social element may make those painful subjects more fun.

ONLINE CLASSES

Technology has opened the doors of education to an online student body. As a result, students who otherwise could not attend school receive the benefit of an education. In fact, many people have even earned college and graduate degrees entirely through online programs. Kyra Banks is one of many students to earn a degree online. "With my mom battling cancer and needing full-time care, online classes were the only way I could realistically finish school. I was able to do my classwork and be available for Mom."

Typically, colleges build structure to online classes through course management software like Blackboard and WebCT. Both systems include email with the instructor and classmates, open discussion boards and a grade book allowing students to keep track of their successes throughout the semester. For the most part though, the benefit of an online class is the flexibility it offers busy students.

If you have access to a computer, the idea of taking Psychology 101 in the comfort of pajamas may have you shouting, "Sign me up!" Who can blame you? Online courses require no dress code, no note-taking (lectures are generally online chat discussions) and are usually enhanced with multimedia and resource links to keep them interesting.

Before forgoing a classroom experience, however, consider some of the drawbacks of online classes. Taking courses solely online means you miss direct interaction with professors and classmates. Independent study can pose some self-motivation challenges and be a bit isolating. Finally, although online programs are more widely accepted today than in years past, some schools will not accept transferred online credits.

However, if you've chosen online courses as the right path for you, make a point whenever possible to arrange "out of class" meetings

Amanda Larghe, *design student*

Growing up in a small town in South Dakota one might not think that my technological expertise would be even close to top-notch, but with my parents being near gurus with the PC, I was probably more technologically advanced than most that came out of advanced computer classes in high school," says Amanda.

By the time Amanda went to high school, she could tell you about everything- from the top of the line graphics cards to the biggest memory cards available. Her parents were constantly updating their machines with new cards and chips, so she was all too excited to get their old ones. As she puts it, "Where I grew up not every twelve-year-old kid had their own computer in their bedroom."

Once Amanda began school at the University of South Dakota, she realized how lucky she was to have such technically savvy parents. Almost immediately, she found she was helping everyone on the dorm floor with technical problems such as reformatting their machines. Even for a college student experienced in technology, Amanda had some surprises: "My biggest challenge and honestly eye-opening expe-

rience was when I had to use my first Mac computer. These were like the strangest things to me in the beginning. Not only did I have no idea how to use a mouse with only one button but I could not even figure out how to get a CD in and out of the thing."

By taking classes and just practicing, Amanda is now proficient with the Mac and much more. Amanda realizes that technology is ever-changing and with that in mind, she works hard to master new programs and systems. Rather than shying away from change, she embraces it. In her words, "I welcome the excitement and challenges of all the new programs and technological advances ahead."

Amanda is now a Graphic Design Intern with LifeBound and finishing school at the Art Institute of Denver. She assists in the design of publications and other materials used by the company. According to her, technology has opened doors. "I credit much of my technological knowledge to many things such as pursuing a path in graphic design and of course on receiving my internship with LifeBound. Technology has changed my life drastically from when my family got that very first computer to today, and I know that it has also greatly increased many opportunities for success in my life."

with other students. Taking time to meet for coffee and interact face-to-face will often make your learning experience that much richer. Kyra said that by sharing her unique circumstances with her online classmates, she formed a supportive network online and off. "My online classmates even came to the house for study sessions while a nurse cared for my mom. It really helped me feel a part of something."

Also, if you intend to begin your studies online and transfer to another school, research in advance the policies regarding acceptance of transferred credits. Doing so could save you substantial time and money.

HYBRID CLASSES

A hybrid course is a combination classroom and Internet course. They involve meeting in a classroom once or twice a week at a scheduled location and time, while the remainder of the coursework is completed online. Professors require participation in both aspects of the class by subscribing to an email list, discussion with an instructor, and extensive collaboration with others in class. Usually, professors assign work and make announcements via course management software like Blackboard or WebCT. Hybrid classes strike a great balance between straight traditional and online classes.

RESEARCH ON THE INTERNET

Researching on the Internet can be kind of like taking a sip of water from a fire hydrant. There are so many articles, websites, blogs, and message boards that the trick really becomes finding relevant information from credible sources.

Search engines like Google are a good place to start. Start with a broad search and become more specific based on the results you get from it. Sometimes it helps to write down the search terms used for each search to better track the results they yield. Then, separate the material not only by relevance but by credibility as well. The opinions on message boards and blogs are great to expand your views, but don't cite them as gospel truth. Turn to credible sources and journals for the meat and potatoes of your research.

Credible resources often used in college include:

LexisNexis: www.lexis-nexis.com

As one of the largest online databases of researchable information, LexisNexis archives content from newspapers, magazines, legal documents, and other printed sources.

Proquest: www.proquest.com

Another database of researchable information, Proquest has a collection of aggregated databases. Typically, colleges and universities subscribe to these databases and provide students with passwords.

Google Docs: www.google.com

This is a lifesaver for group research projects. It keeps everyone on the same page. When one student creates a document, they can invite others to chat using their emails. This allows for easy collaboration on presentations, spreadsheets and essays.

Google can also be used to send updates to your email address of relevant information. If you know you will have a research paper on Western Civilization due at the end of the semester, you can request RSS feeds for timely updates directly from Google on the topic throughout the term.

If you've been assigned research, ask the university librarian to walk you through the databases available on campus. The librarians have a wealth of knowledge and they are usually happy to point you in the right direction. "My first college paper was intimidating," Brian, a college junior at Metro State in Denver, reports. "Thankfully I started early and made friends with the librarian. After she walked me through finding material, the following papers were a breeze."

With endless resources, keeping an outline of information you discover will keep you organized. A well-researched and well-outlined paper practically writes itself.

USING TECHNOLOGY IN BUSINESS

We've referenced many devices, websites, and technological resources used both for academic and social purposes. The advances in technology are also impacting the way businesses operate. Marketing departments quickly caught onto the idea that they could promote products by creating a Facebook page and sending advertisements to their target demographic and fans. In addition, blogs have become a way to reach a consumer audience, garner feedback, and develop loyalty.

The term Web 2.0 refers to the viral nature of the Internet. Where businesses once relied on website traffic, they can now expand their reach through social networking resources. A college student keeping abreast of the advances is a huge asset to companies wanting to cast a larger consumer net. Essentially, for the tech-savvy, the sky is truly the limit.

REAL WORK

IN THE REAL WORLD

Sergey Brinn and Larry Page, Google creators

ow was a search engine like Google created? By the forging of a friendship between two students working on a research project.

Sergey Brinn and Larry Page were both students at Stanford University working on doctorates in computer science when they began working on an assignment together.

For their research project, the two determined that a search engine listing results according to popularity of pages would yield the most relevant results. Realizing they were onto something, both left their Ph.D. studies with the intention of running with their business idea.

After securing a glamorous office space—their friend's garage, they hired Eric Schmidt, an experienced technology executive to run the company. The two raised $1 million in capital from family, friends, and investors and launched to the masses. It is now the world's most popular search engine, headquartered in the heart of California's Silicon Valley. As for the two friends, they are billionaires and cultural icons due to ingenuity, determination, commitment, and of course, technology.

Sources: "Larry Page Biography". Biography.com. 2004. A&E Television Networks.
<http://www.biography.com/search/article.do?id=12103347>.

PLAGIARISM

Plagiarism is essentially using another person's writings or ideas and passing them off as your own. The consequences of plagiarism can include lawsuits, failing grades, suspension from school, and even expulsion from a program. While the practice of plagiarizing has been around long before technology, some people mistakenly believe that they can plagiarize and hide behind the abyss of cyberspace in today's world. That could not be further from the truth.

Schools are now relying on websites like turnitin.com and copyscape.com. Turnitin provides professors with an "Originality Report." The site searches billions of archived papers, journal articles, and periodicals looking for any instance of duplicity in a student's paper. It then ranks a paper with a percentage of copied material and sends the report to the instructor. Copyscape takes another approach. It uses a site's web address to find sites copying content without permission.

Whether you are researching on the web or from a journal off of a library shelf, you can avoid false accusations by citing accordingly. Since most schools now have a zero-tolerance policy with respect to plagiarism, there is no room for misunderstandings. Ted Hazik, caught plagiarizing, warns other students, "It's not worth it! All I needed to do was cite the source I used. I was pounding out the paper at the last minute. Luckily, I wasn't expelled, but I got an F on the paper and whole thing was pretty humiliating."

SOCIALIZING WITH TECHNOLOGY

Learning takes place outside the classroom as well as inside. You're entering a new community and that community will have a profound impact on your future. The old adage goes, "It's not what you know; it's who you know." In reality, it's both.

Today, technology is really boosting the "who you know" factor in people's lives. Connecting with peers through social networking sites, email, and text messages not only keeps you in touch, it also keeps your name in front of people as you look at career options.

Socializing with technology does, however, have some pitfalls. Students must be mindful of the following:

The WHOLE WORLD is watching:

Yes, spring break in Mexico was crazy and fun, but posting the pictures on MySpace can cost you that awesome internship, should the interviewer see your page. A current trend for interviewers is "background-checking" through social networking sites. Be yourself, just be discreet. Since pictures of under-aged students standing next to kegs don't impress professors or prospective employers, keep those off your page. As a private-business owner, Nancy Altman warns, "I always surf the web for background information about prospective hires. I can learn a lot about their judgment

just by searching MySpace. It never fails to amaze me what people are willing to advertise about themselves."

The same idea holds true for video. Who doesn't want to relive the best party ever by sharing the video highlights with friends? The truth is what seemed funny last weekend may be embarrassing if it resurfaces on YouTube five years from now. Once something makes it into cyberspace, it usually stays out there forever. Think twice before calling, "Lights, camera, action!"

Make friends carefully

Social networking sites provide a feeling of anonymity. We tend to be more relaxed and more open when we think we are not identified. It's very easy to get caught up in casual flirtations only to realize you shared more than you intended or that was good for your safety.

"My online chats with Don were laid back at first," said Brinn, of Hawaii University. "I guess being so far from home had taken a toll on me. It wasn't long before I thought he was the one. When he said he needed my Social Security number to book an exotic international vacation, I was ready to hand it over. Fortunately, my roommate stepped in. I later found out Don was Brad when I saw him on TV after being arrested for fraud."

Stories like Brinn's are not uncommon. Don't disclose your personal information online.

Emails can be forwarded!

It's the same old story—Beth was only venting when she expressed (vehemently) in an email her frustration regarding an unreasonable professor. Her best friend knew Beth's name-calling was just her way of blowing off steam. The problem is Beth didn't send the email to her best friend—she sent it to the professor!

People often absentmindedly send and forward emails to the wrong address, sometimes with irreversible consequences. A good rule of thumb is this: If you can't say (or write) anything nice in an email, don't send one at all.

The same warning applies to the sweet, but private, email meant only for the eyes of someone special. "We would send each other some pretty romantic messages," Tanya said. "Later, when I broke up with him, a friend told me Tom forwarded those emails to everyone in his fraternity. I was so embarrassed; I actually considered dropping out of school!" People are not always their most rational selves in romantic relationships. If a relationship sours, even your innermost thoughts can be sent to hundreds of people with just the click of a button.

Just because technology allows you to connect with friends at any time, doesn't mean you should!

Nobody wants a sermon, so we'll keep this brief. Texting in class or talking on your cell during a date can make you look self-important, ignorant, and rude. Even though it's tempting to pick up a call or respond immediately when you get a text, people will notice and respect your courtesy if you wait.

HOW TO COMMUNICATE SUCCESSFULLY ONLINE

"Netiquette" is the term that defines the guidelines of cyberspace communication. Anytime you substitute writing for face-to-face interaction keep in mind the following:

- Remember that without facial expressions, voice inflection, and body language, it is easy to misinterpret the meaning of written words. Read your emails before sending them. Looking at your message through the eyes of the receiver (as opposed to the sender) will give you some insight as to whether you should hit SEND.

- Save abbreviations (How R U) for texting good friends. Professors usually appreciate more formality. It takes more time, but write it out.

- Capital letters are great for emphasis, but they can overstate urgency even be interpreted as shouting (Example: AS SOON AS POSSIBLE!).

- Always state the subject in the subject line. This is particularly important if you are emailing during business. The subject matter helps busy professionals prioritize responses and search for the same email at a later date.

- Have a professional sounding email address (your first.lastname@emailaccount.com is usually a good rule of thumb. Keep your CutesyGirl123 and SamTheMan email accounts to your friends.)

- Don't fill in the address of the recipient until after you've written the email and have reread it. This will alleviate inadvertently sending the email to the wrong person, or sending it before you've completed writing.

TECHNOLOGY V. FACE TO FACE

Keep in mind that technology is designed as a compliment to real life interaction, not a replacement.

In a hurried world, taking the time to meet in person with someone separates the extraordinary from the ordinary. Meeting with friends and professors will bring you closer to them. Moreover, when a professor can place your face with your name, you're more likely to be top of mind for research and scholarship opportunities. In addition, the professor who knows you is the one who will be able to sing your praises in a letter of reference to grad schools or an employer.

"The most influential person in my college career was my psychology professor," says Karl, a recent grad from Michigan State University. "We'd meet for coffee and discuss my career path. He offered me work as a teacher's assistant one semester and wrote really complimentary letters to grad schools on my behalf. Forming that relationship opened a lot of doors for me."

There is no doubt Karl is right. Taking the time to get to know those around you off-line definitely makes the difference. Sometimes the best time spent happens when the cell phone and computer are turned off.

summary

The German philosopher, Arthur Schopenhaus once said, "Change alone is eternal, perpetual, immortal." As we said in the beginning of this chapter, technology is changing and advancing constantly. Whether you've already submerged yourself in it or you are now braving a whole new world, your commitment to keeping abreast of technological changes will distinguish you from your peers both at school and later on the job. The saying that "knowledge is power," proves true in life. Obtaining that knowledge only requires the desire and initiative to attain it. Take the initiative to be great.

CHAPTER SEVEN

*Freedom is not worth having
if it does not connote freedom to err.*

MAHATMA GANDHI

Responsibility educates.

WENDELL PHILLIPS

eaving home to attend college was really my first experience of being on my own," remembers Ingrid Damiani. "All of a sudden, it was completely up to me to decide when and how much I studied, how late I stayed out, and how I spent my money."

The freedom you experience as a freshman can be thrilling. The responsibilities that come with it, however, can be overwhelming. "How you face decisions in college can determine whether your college experience is filled with challenges you master or a series of crises that drain you," says Ingrid's husband, Tim Damiani, a psychiatrist who has counseled college students. "Many of the personal habits you establish during your college years will follow you through your life."

be on your own

BALANCING THE DEMANDS OF YOUR WORLD

residence-hall life versus life off campus

iving in a residence hall is one way you can make the transition from your parents' home to being on your own easier. Residence halls are usually less expensive than living on your own; most provide meal plans so that you don't have to worry about grocery shopping and meal preparation during your first year. Residence halls also come with built-in support systems. In addition to being a source for many new friends, they offer the help and support of resident advisors.

Amir Abolfolthe, a biomedical engineer and product manager, believes that living in a residence hall during his first two years of college was an important part of his adjustment to college life. "Many of the people in the residence hall are new and have the same anxieties you do. The residence hall also helps you to keep a balance between your social and academic life. When you want to play, there are always people who are ready to go out. When you need to study, you can always find someone to go to the library with. And when you are having trouble with a tricky calculus problem or are feeling blocked on your term paper, there are always other students around who are taking the same classes to brainstorm with. In my residence hall we supported each other and looked out for each other. We were like a big family."

As a foreign student, Amir found that living in the residence hall helped him to form friendships with American students. "Many of my Iranian friends lived at home and stuck to themselves on campus. I felt fortunate to be able to interact comfortably with everyone."

the dating game

College offers many opportunities to meet different kinds of people and to find out what kinds of people you enjoy being with. I'm not an expert on dating during college, since I had only one serious boyfriend in college, and that was in my senior year. Before I met him, I was frankly more interested in my studies and my friends than anything else. But I was clearly the exception. Most of my friends had boyfriends from the start of their freshman year.

Pam Zemper, an RA (resident assistant) who worked in a women's residence hall at the University of Texas, found that many freshmen are confused about how to handle relationships from high school. "These students are so excited about college. They want to meet new people and to enjoy all the new, interesting things college has to offer. But they also want to maintain the same level of closeness with their boyfriends from home. I always advised the girls on my floor to establish new ground rules with their boyfriends. If they talked every night on the phone in high school and their boyfriends want to continue this, it will hold the girls back from activities they want to try. They need to discuss their expectations about how often they will see and talk to each other. And if they are attending different schools, they probably need to talk about dating other people."

Jeanne Stark, who began dating someone seriously in the middle of her freshman year, remembers opportunities she let slip by because she was in a relationship. "He was an English major like me—he was poetic, charming, and distinctly unambitious. At the time I found him attractive and enjoyed his company. What I didn't realize was that my involvement with him was keeping me from pursuing other activities and friends I was genuinely interested in. After my sophomore year, he graduated and spent the next few months traveling around Europe. While he was gone, I became a reporter and eventually the copy editor for the school yearbook, and I began working on an honors tutorial with one of my English professors. All of a sudden, all of these doors and opportunities started to open up. What an eye-opener! I realized that I was wasting my time with someone who did not share my goals or values. A few years later I met the man I eventually married. He has shown me that the best partner is someone who shares your interests and dreams, challenges you, and cheers you on to greater successes."

This doesn't mean that it is wise to date a clone of yourself, or that college has to be the end of your high school romance. What it does mean is that it's important for you to take stock of yourself—to know what you want from your time in college and what your life goals are, and to spend time with people who support rather than distract you. Even if the person you are dating is the person of your dreams, you still need to make sure you are allowing time to get to know yourself.

Toward the end of college, many of my friends were engaged or starting to think seriously about marriage. Some of them seemed to be using marriage as an escape from the demands of academic work and graduation. Obviously, the decision to get married is personal and the right time for marriage is different for everyone. I'm a slowpoke. I just got back from my ten-year college reunion, and only five of us weren't married. I felt really out of it when people were passing around pictures of their kids. And yet, I'm not making one of the biggest decisions of my life unless it is for the right person. Why compromise?

Ingrid Damiani married her husband three years after she graduated from college. "Having time to truly be on my own, to earn my own living, and to feel like an adult in the working world has been invaluable to me in my marriage. That time on my own helped me to define my goals and to learn about myself. Looking back, I can see I grew a lot in those first few years after college. For me, that growing happened better while I was single. It was important for me to know I could succeed on my own terms before I made a commitment to someone else."

Rachelle Shaw is a pediatric dentist in Albuquerque, New Mexico, and the mother of three children. She says, "You can always get married and have children. You won't always have the opportunity to go to school. Following your dreams and achieving goals allows you to subsequently focus on your family or others, enriching all."

dating violence

Dating relationships should be fun, enriching experiences. Unfortunately, statistics reveal that sometimes they become the exact opposite. One of every five college females will experience some form of dating violence, and the Bureau of Justice Statistics report on intimate partner violence from 2000 shows that women ages 16 to 24 experience the highest per capita rates (20 per every 1000 women) of intimate violence. In addition, studies have shown that 67 percent of young women reporting rape were raped by dating partners. Even more alarming is the fact that every abusive relationship has the potential to end in murder. The same Bureau of Justice Statistics report shows that women ages 16 to 19 were killed by an intimate partner at the rate of 18 women per every 1000 murder victims, while 21 women per every 1000 murder victims ages 20 to 24 were killed by an intimate partner.

Anyone can end up in an abusive relationship, but you have to be strong to get out of it. Young men and women often become emotionally involved with their partner before they really know the person. They think they love their partner (and maybe they do), and because they are in love, they think they can and should tolerate anything their partners do, say, or prefer. Abusive relationships revolve around this kind of power and control.

Experts say the cycle of violence often begins with small things like name calling and then builds to an explosion that often results in verbal, physical, or sexual aggression. Being alert to the warning signs that trigger the cycle will make you less vulnerable to unhealthy dating patterns. Below are questions for you to think about and maybe talk over with your friends, student counselors, or parents.

Source: Rennison, Callie, and Sarah Welchans. "Intimate Partner Violence." *Bureau of Justice Statistics.* May 2000. <http://www.ojp.usdoj.gov/bjs/pub/pdf/ipv.pdf>.

WARNING SIGNS OF DATING VIOLENCE

The following is a list compiled from the National Domestic Violence Hotline and Rape Assistance and Awareness Program. If you answer yes to two or more of these questions, your partner is likely to be abusive.

- Has your relationship begun quickly and intensely, and you feel it is moving "too fast too soon"?
- Does your partner verbally put you down or call you names that hurt your feelings?
- Does he or she ridicule you for being stupid or for characteristics that he or she thinks are "typical" of women or men?
- Does your partner have a quick temper?
- When your partner gets angry, are you afraid?
- Does your partner always blame other people when things go wrong?
- Does your partner abuse alcohol or drugs?
- Did your partner grow up in a violent family?
- Does your partner always expect you to follow his or her orders or advice?
- Is your partner jealous of you when you are with your friends?
- Has your partner ever bragged about intimidating or hurting other people?
- Does your partner act self-centered and ignore your opinion?
- Do you like yourself less than usual when you're with your partner?

When you enter a new relationship, be sure to take some precautions. Below is a list of dating safety tips from the Domestic Violence Advocacy Program of Family Resource, Inc. Whenever you are unsure about the person you are dating, it is always better to be safe, so be sure to follow this advice.

- Double-date the first few dates with a trusted friend.

- Make exact plans, tell someone you trust these plans, then make sure your date knows you will be checking in with this person sometime during the date.

- Know that you will experience decreased ability under the effects of drugs and alcohol.

- If you leave a party with someone you don't know too well, make sure someone knows who you are leaving with and have that person call to see if you arrived home.

- Be assertive and straightforward.

- Trust your instincts if you feel uncomfortable and leave the situation as soon as possible.

If you are in an abusive relationship, take immediate steps to get out of it. If you think he or she might freak out and try to hurt you (a classic response of abusers when their partners try to leave them), break up in a public place and arrange for family or friends to take you home.

Also, be alert to your partner's response. If it is anything like "You're not going to leave me," be sure to tell someone (your parents or a roommate). The more people who know, the safer you are. For more information, call the National Domestic Violence Hotline at 1-800-799-7233 or reach them online at www.ndvh.org. A trained counselor is there twenty-four hours a day. The hotline provides help, not only for the victim, but for the abuser as well. If you have a hearing disability, call the hotline at 1-800-787-3224 (TDD).

HEALTHY DATING RELATIONSHIPS

Just as unhealthy dating relationships are marked by certain characteristics, so are healthy ones. Healthy intimacy is based on cooperation and equality. Here are the characteristics of a mature, nonviolent relationship:

- **Negotiation and fairness.** Seeking mutually satisfying resolutions to conflict, which includes a willingness to accept change and to compromise.

- **Respect.** Listening to each other without being judgmental, being emotionally affirming and affirmed, understanding and valuing each other's opinions.

- **Nonthreatening behavior.** Talking and acting so that you both feel safe and comfortable expressing yourselves and doing things.
- **Independence and autonomy.** Recognizing each other's interdependence, yet accepting "separateness" as non-married persons. Fostering individual identity.
- **Trust and support.** Supporting each other's life goals. Respecting each other's rights to have personal feelings, friends, activities, and opinions. Overcoming issues like envy and resentment.

Of all the demands you encounter in college, developing healthy dating relationships is one of the most critical. Every dating relationship is serious because it plays a part in defining who you are. How you relate to your dating partners, and how they to relate to you, are key to your well-being. Establishing equality in your dating relationships now will help ensure a lifetime of close, supportive relationships.

overcoming obstacles

College students face challenges of all kinds—in academic work, health, and finances, and in combating prejudice. Whatever you are facing, there is probably a resource on campus to support you. You may feel as if you are the only one who is struggling with a problem, but chances are you aren't, and there are people on campus who can help.

ACADEMIC CHALLENGES

Most colleges have a learning resource center to give students support with study habits, time management, writing, test anxiety, and other such matters. In addition, many departments offer study groups or tutoring sessions to assist students with particular subjects. Your professors will often be able to send you in the right direction to find these support systems.

EMOTIONAL/PSYCHOLOGICAL PROBLEMS

Most universities have a counseling center available specifically for students. These centers usually provide for a certain number of counseling sessions at no cost and then offer another set of sessions at affordable rates (way below the rates you would pay for a private therapist). Counselors can often provide the support or the resources you need to get through your problem.

There are also many groups in the community that can provide support for specific problems such as bulimia or anorexia, being the child of an alcoholic, or suffering from alcoholism, and programs for people who have been abused. The counseling center at your school may offer these programs or be able to send you to the right place. If not, check one of the local churches—they often host support groups in their building, and they can usually provide the name and address of a support group near you.

PHYSICAL DISABILITIES

Cyrus Sarmadi, a junior at the University of California at Santa Barbara, is hearing impaired and a foreign student. Has he let these challenges slow him down? Not on your life. So far, he has co-founded and supervised a computer club at his college, and he was a gold medalist on the Men's National Deaf Water Polo Team at the Deaf World Games in 1993. He is also in the planning stages of starting a Persian club at his school.

"My advice is to take a deep breath and plunge. If you fall, get up and jump again."

Cyrus advises other students with challenges to "take advantage of all services that are available at the university, such as note taking and tutoring services, or any other campus assistance."

Look in your school directory for an office designed to help students with special needs and take advantage of the help offered to you as a student. These offices usually have people who can solve problems quickly (such as finding you a reader, getting a ramp installed, and so on).

INSIGHTS

FROM AN INTERN

David Horn, business and marketing student

*B*eing an intern for LifeBound has taught David Horn many things about what will be expected of him after college graduation. The internship has helped him develop and understand the level of social and global intelligence that will be needed in order to be a valuable contributor to society once he has graduated from Denison University in Ohio with a business and marketing degree.

Through developing online surveys and hearing testimonials, he said he has grown a sense of pride and ownership in LifeBound that can only exist through personal involvement and responsibility. He learned what a valuable resource the Internet became when obtaining feedback from people who have used LifeBound curriculum.

"I now know that combining my love for business with my experience in education could be a possible work choice for me after college."

David created a series of online surveys in an effort to obtain feedback from teachers and students who have used LifeBound's resources. He is currently managing an intern at Denison University. David said that participating in an internship is an invaluable experience that every student should do.

"There is no better way to gain an understanding of what the 'real world' is like than through gaining work experience," David said. "An internship can also help you better understand what you are interested in and what you would enjoy doing after graduation."

After graduating in May, David is planning to initially move back to Denver, Colorado, where his parents live. After that, he is considering a job working as management for a chain of upscale dog hotels, Wag Hotels, in California.

"This may seem like an interesting life choice. But for the past four summers I have worked at a dog kennel in Denver, and would love to get a job where my passion for working with dogs and my business experience could be applied," David said.

David may also look into continuing work similar to his LifeBound internship by getting a job working within the business in order to market varying aspects of education.

Finally, he is considering graduate school, but would like to gain some work experience before making that decision.

alternative routes

Dick Christensen, a psychiatrist, remembers beginning college "in a very rigorous pre-med program which was heavy on science and light on arts and letters." Not realizing at the time that there was room for flexibility in the curriculum, he accepted the standard program and proceeded to flunk one exam after the other. Desperate and panicked, he sought out an academic advisor who allowed him to create his own curriculum. This custom arrangement was not only more manageable, but it led to a dual major in biology and philosophy. He says he learned two lessons. "Each person has unique strengths and weaknesses, and there are always alternative routes to achieving the same goal."

roadblock? detours are allowed

If you have pursued every avenue for help and you still feel overwhelmed by a problem at college, you might consider taking some time off. Carla Summers, an archivist at the University of Florida, dropped out after her sophomore year and spent several semesters waiting tables. "Taking some time off was the best decision I could have made. Before I left, I was unmotivated, under-directed, and making poor grades. When I returned to school, I had a clear sense of wanting to be there and I was very focused. My grades reflected my new sense of direction."

Jesse Keller decided to take a year off between his junior and senior years at the prestigious Ivy-League school Yale University in Connecticut. His detour was carefully planned to give him a variety of work experiences and to provide him with a refreshing break. For the first half of the year, he worked with a professor on a computer music software development project. "I found this to be a satisfying situation. I lived in New Haven and kept in touch with my Yale friends, but I worked full time (and was financially independent) in a job that was both interesting and resume-building." The second semester, Jesse worked at Microsoft as a software designer for a few months. Working at Microsoft gave him hands-on experience in his field. Finally, he spent six weeks traveling across the country before he went back to school. According to Jesse, the year off provided, "work experience from two different perspectives in the same field and a chance to see a whole bunch of possibilities as I traveled. It also gave me time to renew my academic enthusiasm."

appreciating your diverse world

Unfortunately, equality is an ideal this country has not always honored. Now more than ever we need to make a commitment to create an environment where all people have the opportunity to use their skills and to succeed regardless of race, religion, gender, sexual orientation, or disability.

"We must cooperate to compete in a global marketplace," says George Fraser, an author and founder of Success Source, LLC, a company that publishes networking guides for African Americans in various cities. "That means leveraging the collective resources of every single cultural group within our country."

A recent article in *Time* magazine devoted to diversity in the United States noted that, "Immigrants are arriving at the rate of more than one million a year, mostly from Asia and the vast Hispanic world...The impact of these immigrants is literally remaking America. Today more than 20 million Americans were born in another country."

American companies are responding to this diversity by making sure their workplaces reflect those changes in society. A recent issue of *Fortune* magazine, which featured an article on workplace diversity, noted that executives are starting to see positive results as they implement work-force diversity. "Says IBM chief Louis V. Gerstner, Jr.: 'Our marketplace is made up of all races, religions, and

REAL WORK

IN THE REAL WORLD

Maria Martinez, *corporate vice-president, Communications and Mobile Solutions Unit, Microsoft Corporation*

Maria Martinez has a great deal to be proud of. She was the first Hispanic female named a corporate vice president at Microsoft. She now runs their Communications and Mobile Solutions Unit. When Martinez speaks, chief executives in high technology and other industries listen.

Martinez paved her own road to success by first studying engineering at the University of Puerto Rico and then working at Bell Labs. As if practicing as an engineer wasn't challenging enough, Martinez realized working effectively with others posed its own set of growth opportunities. Once Martinez recognized the importance of group dynamics and team construction, she developed a keen interest in business management. She then sought out the skills and training to advance in that area. Of course, Martinez discovered it wasn't always easy.

As a Latina in technology, a traditionally male-dominated business, she told *Hispanic Business* magazine that the proverbial glass ceiling is a real issue in companies today. Her approach, however, has been staying focused despite any corporate cultural barriers. Her advice to young women interested in technology careers is to, "always set good goals for yourself and never give up." Martinez clearly realizes the importance of self-motivation. "Unfortunately, this culture has very low expectations for women and Hispanics and other minorities," Martinez said. "If you agree with that, you're never going to get anywhere."

Source: "In the High-Tech Executive Suite." *HispanicBusiness.com.* Nov 2003. Hispanic Business Magazine. <http://www.hispanicbusiness.com/news/2003/11/6/in_the_hightech_executive_ suite. htm>

sexual orientations, and therefore it is vital to our success that our work force also be diverse.'" Companies are finding that when the work force is made up of people from different backgrounds, their teams are able to come up with more creative solutions.

Ted Smith, a video producer in Washington, DC, worked as a RA in an off-campus apartment complex at Virginia Commonwealth University. One of the university's policies was to pair RAs from different backgrounds to solve problems. Usually a Caucasian RA would be paired with an African American RA. "In addition to resolving residential disputes, we also prepared presentations about resolving racial conflicts. This job helped me to see some of the challenges of living in a diverse environment and showed me creative ways of resolving problems. I use these tools every day in the work I do."

Racist or prejudiced feelings, or disrespecting others because they differ from you, can only be damaging to you as an individual as well as to those with whom you associate. These feelings can hinder you from growing. If you learn to overcome your prejudices or feelings of discomfort with those who are different, you will be an asset to your future employer. In today's world, people value those who care about the advancement of others, and who show through their actions an open mind toward people of all backgrounds.

Working with people whose backgrounds are different from yours takes practice and patience. College is an excellent opportunity for you to broaden your experience with other cultures. Through extracurricular activities, volunteering, and friendships, you can meet people who think and live differently from you. Many schools now require students to take courses that help them understand multicultural issues. The University of California at Berkeley, for example, requires students to take courses that focus on at least three ethnic groups (Asian, Latino, Native American, African American, or European).

In the words of George Fraser: "Every cultural group is like an instrument in a symphony orchestra. Each instrument brings a different tonality and character—together, the instruments make powerful music."

Sources: "America's Immigrant Challenge." *TIME.com*. 2 Dec 1993. Time Magazine. <http://www.time.com/time/magazine/article/0,9171,979725-3,00.html>

Rice, Faye. "How to Make Diversity Pay." *CNNMoney.com*. 8 Aug 1994. Fortune Magazine. <http://money.cnn.com/magazines/fortune/fortune_archive/1994/08/08/79604/index.htm>.

when there's resistance

n his book, *Out of the Madness,* award-winning journalist Jerrold Ladd tells his story about fighting to succeed
against the odds of drugs, violence, and poverty while
growing up in the projects of Dallas.

He faced many discouraging setbacks in his attempts to gain
an education and find meaningful work. At the height of his
despair, he asked, "Where was the black man's wisdom and guidance to lead us around snares and guide us through tribulation?"

Since he had no role models in his life to turn to, he found
them in the pages of history, spending hours in the library, "reading about black heroes, philosophers, and thinkers. My discovery
of dead literary role models permanently cured my doubt and made
me go back to the fundamental truth," he writes. "Knowing the
great accomplishments of my people, when they existed in their
own civilizations, started a chain reaction that would change the
foundation of my mind."

He goes on to say, "I felt that my entire life had been like that
of a man who had wings of strength and splendor. From childhood
this man had watched his brethren sweep the heavens and glide
gracefully in the sunshine. But because his wings were a different
color, he had been fooled into believing that he could not fly. He
knew his wings looked the same, were built the same, flapped the
same. But he never had proof. So he had never tried. Then he discovered in a remote cave, a cave that had been kept well-hidden,
pictures of men of his color flying in the clouds. And on this glorious day, in desperation, he jumped off a cliff, was swooped up in
the wings of truth, flapped his damnedest, and found he could fly
above them all."

Maybe you have not experienced prejudice and poverty to the
extreme that Jerrold Ladd did, but his experience of finding role
models can benefit anyone trying to overcome an obstacle. We gain
inspiration and encouragement from the stories of those who have
succeeded before us.

"There are no magic solutions," says author George Fraser.
However, he too believes that education is critical in overcoming
prejudice. His advice? "Read about people who have succeeded
despite racism. Seek out mentors and role models and learn about
yourself. Through education and knowledge of self, it is possible to
overcome the obstacle of racism. Find ways over, around, and

through it. Racism is a reality that many people have to face, but it is not a reason to fail."

Many schools have ethnic student centers (an African American student center, a Hispanic student center, a Middle Eastern student center, etc.). These offices can provide support in many ways—they can help you obtain financial aid, they can intervene in problems you may be having with the administration or professors, and they can introduce you to students who may be facing similar challenges. Some of the centers also offer mentoring programs in which they pair you with a member of the community.

Women in traditionally male-dominated fields such as engineering or science often find an effective support system when they join women's organizations in their field. Rama Moorthy, an engineer in technical sales, says that joining the Society of Women Engineers put her in touch with other women who deal with the same kinds of pressures she does.

When Anthea Coster was a graduate student in space physics at Rice University in Houston, Texas, she found that women friends in her field were a great support. "We studied together—more as a team than as a group competing against each other."

Being on your own can be scary, lonely, exciting, exhilarating, and sometimes plain uneventful. Balance the highs and lows by getting the rest, relaxation, and rejuvenation you need in order to feel inspired so that you can appreciate what is great in your surroundings and within yourself.

CHAPTER EIGHT

Is there any way of predicting the capacity to lead?
The only way I know is to look at college records.
If they were leaders during the ages of 18 to 22,
the odds are that they will emerge as leaders
in middle life.

DAVID OGILVY

Y ou've got to make it happen," says John Garcia, who says belonging to organizations is the best way to enjoy yourself and learn to relate to people, as well. John, who was a civil engineering major, was hired by Sandia National Laboratories in Albuquerque, New Mexico. Sandia sent John to Purdue University in Indiana to get a master's degree in structural engineering.

"Engineers are great theoreticians and scientists," says John, "but most of them have a hard time getting their ideas across." To balance his college experience, John worked part-time, skied, hiked, and was active in the honorary engineering society Tau Beta Pi.

Lynne Ewing buried herself in her books during her freshman year at University of Notre Dame in Indiana. "That was the worst semester I ever had," says Lynne, whose grades were far below the goals she had

stand up and be counted

EXTRACURRICULAR ACTIVITIES

set for herself. "The next semester, I joined the choir, the school newspaper, and a typically religious group. My grades went way up. So did my morale, the number of friends I could count on, and my interest level. I kept busy, managed my time, and no longer had a reason to feel sorry for myself for being from out-of-state and away from my friends and family."

Dawn Pakluda began college at the University of Texas at Austin. She wishes she had joined extracurricular activities. "I could have had a lot more fun and met many more people during college," says Dawn. "Since I only studied and worked, I feel I don't have the strong friendships and rich experiences that college should provide."

My own extracurricular college activities included joining a sorority and several honorary societies, doing volunteer work at a hospice for cancer patients, and participating in the International Students Club's English tutoring program for foreign students.

Although large group projects taught me leadership in a broad context, the one-on-one contacts I developed through my other activities helped me to, "read" people in business. I learned to listen, to question, to analyze problems, and to motivate even the most unenthused people.

Join extracurricular activities to expand your world. You'll be more interesting, and you'll learn to work with people. By better understanding others, you'll better understand yourself.

To succeed in the workplace, you must be a team player. Those who give beyond what's expected command the respect of their peers and supervisors. Chances are greater that they'll be promoted to positions where they manage and motivate others. Being valuable to an organization in college will teach you how to become valuable to a company.

Darren Walker, a New York investment banker, was president of several organizations in college. As a student board member for the University of Texas Student Union, he learned how different people competed to run the union. "When you work with successful people from diverse backgrounds, you have to learn to work toward consensus. I learned to be open to different people and different ideas. Through extracurricular activities, I learned a great deal about politics, group dynamics, and egos." Learning such skills in college will give you an advantage when you start your first job.

Companies want to hire employees who go above and beyond what is expected. If you balance work, school, and play, you'll be prepared to juggle your career and personal life. You'll learn to naturally think of new ideas and projects and you'll learn to be the first person to volunteer for additional responsibility. The busiest people are often the ones who are most likely to take on new projects because they know how to manage their time.

What exactly does the college recruiter learn about you from your extracurricular activities?

1. You are a self-starter.
2. You've got your act together enough to balance classes with activities.
3. You like people and get along with them; you can be a team player.

4. You aren't a one-dimensional grind or some gnome buried in your books. You know there's a world beyond the classroom.

5. You have sought out career-related experience.

Sometimes extracurricular activities can lead you straight into the business world. Bob Rogers, a pre-law student, says, "Working as the associate editor of the student newspaper prepares me for my long-term goals by teaching me to write, analyze political issues, and persuade readers. I have interviewed attorneys and criticized their arguments, studied how the battle for public opinion works, observed office politics within the paper, and seen the results of different management approaches."

During her freshman year in college, Jeannine DeLoche became a writer for Columbia University in the *City of New York's Curriculum Guide*, which is a student publication that reviews most of the classes at the college. After writing more articles than the rest of the staff, she was promoted to the post of executive editor. When she needed extra money that year and decided to apply for a job, she applied for an editorial assistant position, banking on her *Curriculum Guide* experiences. Her first interview was for the editorial page of the *Wall Street Journal*. Says Jeannine, "I remember the interviewer saying, 'You have real editing experience. That's unusual in someone your age.' He offered me the job right then!"

Jeannine continues to work as an assistant to the editorial features editor of the prestigious newspaper while at Columbia and is considering staying there after graduation. "In addition to joining clubs just for fun, try to find extracurricular activities which match your career interests. That way, you can develop the necessary skills and see if you enjoy the work," Jeannine advises.

participating

You may belong to the right organization, but unless you get involved, you won't have much to show for it. Joe Durrett, the chief executive officer of Broderbund Software in Novato, California, says that when he considers applicants for his company, he looks for their record of accomplishment. If the record of accomplishment is more about having been at certain places than having done something there, this tips him off that the applicant probably won't work out.

Julie Balovich, a college senior at a large university, found that she had to be responsible for seeking out ways to become involved. "The first thing I learned about student organizations is that the best way to get involved and have people recognize you is to do the grungy work. During my freshman year, I participated in several functions of the student association, and in every one I stayed after and helped clean up. Each time, without fail, upper-class persons would approach me and introduce themselves."

In addition to collegiate-affiliated organizations to join, keep your eyes and ears open for other groups that might intrigue you. Consult the campus counseling center for lists of activities. Read the school paper. Check bulletin boards. Then dive in. If you don't like your first choice, get out. Once you find a group you like, participate fully. Volunteer to chair projects. Accept responsibility. Run for office. And if you don't get accepted by Kappa Psi Whatever or get cut from the snorkeling squad, don't be discouraged. Try something else!

developing friendships

One of the greatest aspects of joining any organization is meeting interesting people, some of whom will become your close friends. Campus organizations will also introduce you to other students who are focused on their goals. Gregory Sapire, a law school graduate, recalls, "Working in student government put me in contact with a number of other ambitious students who challenged me to achieve my best. Through their experiences, they suggested opportunities—study abroad, summer enrichment programs, research positions—that I found interesting. If you hang out with people going places, you'll find yourself going places too." Another student advises, "Try to make friends

Jordan Austin, *television producer*

When Jordan Austin started surfing the Internet for internship positions as a college student, he was just looking for ideas. But then he came across the LifeBound posting for an intern candidate, and his interest was piqued. As an English major, he knew that working for a publishing company could offer the kind of real-world experience he was looking for.

Jordan got the internship at LifeBound and began helping with their various events. This included setting up for conferences where LifeBound's books were displayed, creating PowerPoint presentations for LifeBound president, Carol Carter, to use in her speeches, and assisting with set-up at parent sessions for local high schools. The LifeBound staff was so impressed by Jordan's positive attitude and quality of work, that he was offered a job at the company in his senior year of college.

Meanwhile, Jordan was also thinking about how he might use his writing abilities to break into television. Almost two years after college, he applied for a highly competitive, nonpaying broadcast internship offered at KUSA-TV in Denver, a NBC affiliate. He competed with students from across the country and, after a lengthy interview process, was hired for the position.

Jordan made the requisite sacrifices to keep both his job at LifeBound and his new internship by splitting his days between them. He would arrive at the television station at 4 a.m. and work until noon. After a quick lunch, he'd head off to LifeBound, where he would work until 5 or 6 p.m.

Jordan credits his experiences at LifeBound with helping him create every advantage for himself. "The internship helped me acquire a mindset that anything is possible, and it taught me not to let my inexperience [in television] overshadow my strong suits," he says. "It definitely helped me land the internship at KUSA.

Today, Jordan is the producer of Denver's top news show—at the same station where he got his first break! Jordan says, "I would tell high school and college students to get out there and be bold in going after what you want. After all, what have you got to lose?"

with other students who are striving for excellence. They will inspire you to achieve more." That's excellent advice. Unless you're a social recluse, developing friendships in college will be central to your happiness.

becoming a leader

A leader is one who, among other things, motivates, teaches, trains, and organizes others. Those skills will help you in almost any career—whether you want to flip Whoppers at Burger King or become president of the United States. If you develop leadership skills in college, these will keep the doors of management open for you. You may never want to manage anybody, but it's nice to be prepared enough to have the option.

Being a leader doesn't mean you have to run the country. But wherever you wind up, you will spend most of your time dealing with a small circle of people. Be a leader to them.

Bob Rogers tended to stay away from leadership positions until his black belt in Taekwondo thrust him into a leadership position. Because he had achieved so much in this widely-practiced martial art, he was automatically seen as a leader. He didn't feel comfortable immediately, but his skill allowed him to offer strong leadership to the group. He felt that the experience gave him a chance to, "see different leadership and teaching approaches and to hone leadership skills."

How do you become a leader? If you haven't done it before, just start small. Volunteer to head a committee, and then put as much energy into it as your studies allow. The most important part of your activity is gaining the goodwill of those you work with. As your confidence increases, accept more responsibility. Run for student office. If you win, great! You should accept that as a sign that your peers respect you. If you lose, don't be discouraged. As politician and Nobel laureate Winston Churchill said, "Success is the ability to go from one failure to another with no loss of enthusiasm."

WHAT MAKES A GOOD PARTICIPANT?

1. Contributes ideas
2. Organizes events
3. Volunteers to help
4. Follows through on commitments

WHAT MAKES A GOOD LEADER?

1. Has a vision of where the organization can go
2. Makes decisions
3. Motivates others
4. Sets goals
5. Plans and organizes
6. Listens carefully
7. Recognizes others' achievements and contributions
8. Inspires people
9. Delegates responsibility
10. Shares credit
11. Isn't arrogant
12. Acts diplomatically

Don't worry if you've never led before. Give it a try and see how it feels. You might hate it but you might love it. Either way, it pays to know. Student activities often have resources such as workshops or seminars to help you hone your leadership skills.

doing volunteer work

There are many good reasons to volunteer. Volunteering offers the chance to develop both leadership and teambuilding skills. Also, you'll typically interact with a diverse group of volunteers, which will enrich your life perspective.

Gretchen Van Fossan, national program manager for The Points of Light Institute, says, "Service is an incredibly valuable experience both in and out of college, particularly if you're willing to step out of your own familiar and comfortable environment in order to participate with others in community work. Helping people in situations that are different from the ones you've grown up in and working in a group with diverse perspectives are invaluable in building a real and balanced view of the world around you."

Increasingly, schools are making community service part of the core curriculum. For example, at The University of Maryland School of Law, the entire clinical law program is centered on volunteer work. In order to graduate, students must integrate two hundred hours of community service into their regular coursework. To meet that requirement, some law students have helped local high school students reclaim abandoned properties in the depressed Baltimore neighborhood of Park Heights. "One group is white and one is African American," says Daniel P. Henson III, commissioner of housing and community development, "but there's a great camaraderie between them." Next, UM is opening a law office in one of the formerly abandoned buildings to take on everything from landlord–tenant disputes to misdemeanors.

Several companies encourage community service as part of their company philosophies. For example, take IBM, which has implemented numerous community service programs to help its employees balance the demands of their jobs with their personal and family lives. One such program, Community Service Assignment, allows IBM employees to continue earning their salaries while working for nonprofit organizations.

This diversity program helps selected nonprofit, tax-exempt community service organizations in times of need, while at the same time offering IBM employees the ability to develop special talents in areas of service.

Volunteer work can also be great for relieving stress because it takes you out of yourself. Your history final will seem less catastrophic after you've worked an afternoon in a children's hospital ward, or played basketball with a fatherless child, or analyzed a famous painting with a group of high school students.

Your participation in service projects also says something very positive about you: your future employer will know that you care about people. On the job, the chances are greater that you'll treat others with sensitivity and respect. When you face unexpected snags, for instance, you'll be less likely to take out your frustrations on those around you.

If you've been a volunteer or feel that volunteering is an important part of your life philosophy, your future employer will have reason to believe that you are a good hire. After all, you have proven you're conscientious, ethical, and concerned about the well-being of others, and not just your own advancement. Employers want to hire people who will be role models for others. Good citizenship is good business.

organizations

o where do you start joining in? There are literally hundreds of clubs on and off campus. Here are several ways to find out more about campus activities:

1. Student activities office
2. School newspaper
3. Campus fliers
4. Orientation week activities
5. Friends and siblings .

Start brainstorming about what you might like to join. Then gather information and join up. Start small if you're not used to groups. Try one and then another a few months later. Below are a few suggestions, and for even more ideas, check out Appendix F, "Organizations to Enrich Your Life", in the back of this book.

CAMPUS ORGANIZATIONS

Alumni association

Amnesty International campus representative

Association for African Americans

Chess club

Crisis intervention center

Residence hall association

Greeks (fraternities and sororities)

Honorary service societies

International student club

Intramural sports and recreation

Karate club

Marketing club

Pre-law Society

Political groups

Red Cross campus representative

Religious groups

Sailing club

Ski club

Student bar association

Student government

Student media

Student newspaper

Student Union

Women's groups

Yearbook

Volunteer organizations

Campus hospital

Childhood abuse center

Drug addiction clinics

Home for the mentally retarded

March of Dimes

Mental health services

Nursing homes

Planned Parenthood

Political campaigns

Hospice program

Hospital care

Humane Society

League of Women Voters

Public Library

Red Cross

Ronald McDonald House

Sierra Club

World Wildlife Federation

Academic and professional honorary societies

Phi Beta Kappa

Tau Beta Pi

Phi Kappa Phi

Blue Key National Honor Society

Golden Key National Honor Society

Who's Who Among American College Students

Mortar Board

setting limits

To what extent should you participate? This varies according to who you are. For example, if you're a skilled opera singer or lead the nation in a competitive sport, you may benefit from focusing your energy on that skill. Take Steve Kendall, for instance. Steve's college grades were average, but Steve was captain of his college tennis team. Although his rigorous training and travel left him little spare time, his athletic and academic record prompted the college recruiter for Procter & Gamble to seek Steve out for an interview during his senior year.

"Because I was successful in a competitive sport, Procter & Gamble Co. believed I would apply the same principles of diligence, effort, teamwork, and competition to my future career," says Steve. P&G's faith was well placed: Steve worked for them for several years before accepting another position as sales and marketing director of Nabisco Brands, Inc.

So, what if your forehand is unimpressive? Does that mean that extracurricular activities are off limits? Of course not.

Leigh Talmage, for example, didn't focus on any one activity, as Steve did. She spread herself out and joined several organizations. Leigh, who is now a trader for a foreign bank, was president of her sorority and qualified to be a member of scholastic honor societies each year. She even spent two semesters in London. "Get activities under your belt," advises Leigh. "That's what counts the most at interview time." Leigh is one of five women out of 250 people in the world who trade international debt. Leigh is considering another career, too, working for a nonprofit organization. "All of the activities and leadership positions I held in college have given me solid, transferable management skills," she says. "Because of these skills, I feel comfortable moving from one industry to another."

"It's problems with people, not problems in engineering, which constitute the real power struggles," says Steven Fisher, a senior engineer for Westinghouse in San Francisco. "If you swallow your ego and learn from others in your small group, you'll pick up the commonsense aspects of the job, which the technical training you receive in college doesn't provide."

Steven, who graduated from Stanford University in California with a degree in mechanical engineering, cites extracurricular activities as the best way to learn about people and how to get things done: "That's how you prepare yourself to be successful in the long term with a company. You must realize how people work, what motivates them, and what the company can do to help them be most happy and most productive."

If you're shy and unaccustomed to being around people, it may be enough to join one organization and participate in it so that you become comfortable with the members and perhaps run for office. Stretch yourself, but take things in steps, not quantum leaps.

what if you don't get accepted into organization X?

Does that mean you've failed? Of course not. You only fail if you don't try. It sounds trite but it's true. I didn't get a lot of the things I applied for in college, but I didn't let it stop me. My freshman year, I didn't make it into the freshman honorary society. I was disappointed, but before I said, "To hell with it," I stopped to think about why I didn't make it in. Had I blown the interview? Was I not well-rounded enough? Were my grades not good enough? Most of the answers to these questions were "yes", and the other people who made it were better qualified than I was. I worked on the areas that I needed improvement in and, at the end of the year, I applied for the sophomore honorary society. I got in!

I was seriously disappointed when I applied for the Rotary Foundation Ambassadorial Scholarship (which offers opportunities to study abroad) and didn't even make the first cut. I had invested a lot of time and energy into filling out the lengthy application, getting all my professors to write me letters of recommendation, and fully researching the three countries where I wanted to study. They wanted an "ambassador of goodwill," which I thought I could be! But there were others who were more qualified, and I had to accept that.

And there were pluses that came from that disappointment. I learned how much I truly loved studying other cultures. I swore to make travel a major life priority. I also met fascinating people who were also applying for the scholarship: one of them, a unique person who spoke fluent Chinese, Spanish, and French, became my true love for the next two years (He didn't make the first cut either).

When you get a job after college, you may be initially passed over for a promotion you want. Chances are you were not as well qualified as the person who got the job. Find out specifically what you can do to ensure that you get the next opening, and take action.

How you deal with defeat says a lot about your overall character. If you learn in college how to handle defeat graciously, you'll be well prepared for the working world, where you'll need to transform tough situations into new challenges and opportunities.

So don't let defeats defeat you. Look at the situation in a broader context. Extract the positive things you learned and go on to the next challenge. Don't let the temporary setbacks take any wind out of your sails.

dealing with your supporters (and detractors)

Anytime you join a group of people, and you assert your opinion about what you think the organization should or shouldn't do, you will have some people who agree with you and others who won't. Sometimes, especially if you are leading an organization, you will have to stick your neck out for what you believe and communicate to others your vision of what the group can do.

Be cool. If people always agreed with you, you would be in dull company. The best ideas and the best teamwork come from stimulating discussions that allow all points of view to be considered. When people disagree with you—and sometimes during college and in the real world they will strongly disagree with you— keep a positive attitude and remain confident. Acknowledge their opposing viewpoints and thank them for their suggestions. Remaining mature and controlled will help you put the situation into perspective and allow you to reaffirm your position. Remember, leaders are sometimes unpopular. That's okay. It's helpful to get used to this feeling in college—to let your skin get thicker—so that

REAL WORK

IN THE REAL WORLD

Wendy Kopp, *chief executive officer
and founder of Teach for America*

egative feedback stops some people dead in their tracks, but not Wendy Kopp. While attending New Jersey's Princeton University in 1989 as an undergraduate, she submitted her senior thesis entitled: "An Argument and Plan for the Creation of Teacher Corps." Kopp's thesis outlined a plan to recruit outstanding graduates to teach in needy urban schools. She received the following feedback from her professor, "My dear Ms. Kopp, you are quite evidently deranged."

Fortunately, she was not derailed by her naysayer. Kopp sent a proposal out to prospective funders explaining the model for a nonprofit called Teach For America The response was amazing. Kopp, then only twenty-one, raised $2.5 million for her mission. She now boasts a base of 5,000 teachers reaching 440,000 kids.

Had Kopp not believed in herself and her dream, negative feedback could have derailed a program that has now helped millions of students in low-income communities across the nation. Thankfully, she had the strength to courage to keep going.

Source: "History". *TeachforAmerica.com.* <http://www.teachforamerica.org/about/our_team.htm>.

you will be more resilient when you deal with people of varying maturity levels once you start working.

Part of being both a leader and a participant is learning how to draw out the best suggestions and ideas from others. Often, discussing your thoughts with your colleagues helps you to crystallize an already good idea of your own. Recognize that sometimes it's good to change your mind, to concede someone else's points or plans. This is all part of developing your judgment.

CHAPTER NINE

*I don't like work—no one does—but I like
what is in work—the chance to find yourself.
Your own reality—not for others—
what no other person can ever know.*

JOSEPH CONRAD, *HEART OF DARKNESS*

*T*he summer after his freshman year at the University of Wisconsin, Jeff Colquhoun worked at the Kellogg Company factory near his parents' home in Michigan. Occupation? Well, what does one do at a cereal factory? Eat and run?

Guess again. Jeff frosted flakes. And when finished with his frosting duties, he stuffed coupons into boxes that the machines had missed. His was a manual counteroffensive to mechanical incompetence. It was an incredibly boring job. But for Jeff, it was by no means a waste of time. Besides earning money to help pay tuition, Jeff learned several things that helped clarify his career direction.

1. The Kellogg experience opened Jeff's eyes to people whose backgrounds differed from his. There were many people there who hadn't had Jeff's advantages, whom he might never have

the real world

WORKING PART-TIME

encountered in his "ordinary" college experience or in a more typical summer internship for the up-and-coming college student. The job helped Jeff appreciate his education. He developed real respect for people from all walks of life who worked hard for a living, regardless of job title.

2. He did not let the boring aspects of the job interfere with his work or his attitude. For the purpose of sanity, he stretched his mind and imagination. He went through the letters of the Greek alphabet forward and backward. He marveled at the mind of the engineer who designed the machine. (He thanked God for him, in fact.)

3. Jeff learned that when you're not in an ideal situation, which we seldom are, you've got to expand your mind and envision a broader context. Idle is bust.

Thirteen years later, Jeff is a doctor of ophthalmology in New York City. He went through years of studying and rigorous on-the-job training in emergency settings and operating rooms. What he learned at the Kellogg factory that summer in college—to see even the most difficult or mundane tasks in a broader context—helped him in his pursuit of a career in medicine.

Joy Wake, a marketing planner at Hallmark Cards in Kansas City, Missouri, had several part-time jobs during college. As the youngest of nine children, Joy supported herself through college. She had several work study jobs and one summer internship in Washington, DC. And she saved enough money to travel for a semester through Europe.

"Hallmark hired me because I had worked hard to put myself through college," Joy says. "They believed in me because I had a successful track record. They knew I could overcome obstacles. They also recognized that I had done different things to make myself stand out."

Instead of attending school during the day and working at night, graduate Chris Barnett did the opposite. He got an entry-level job paying $185 a week selling space in the yellow pages. He took three classes at night per semester. Although it took Chris two additional years to graduate from college after transferring from the University of Southern California to Columbia, he feels the financial and experiential trade-off was worth it.

Chris graduated college and was promoted three times within two years to a supervising position. It's true that Chris didn't have time to join extracurricular activities or participate in intramural sports, but by twenty-four, he had earned a living, put himself through school, and maintained a 3.2 grade point average at an Ivy League college. He learned about leadership through firsthand professional experience.

Gaining work experience in college is one of the best ways to prepare for your future. First, you learn to support yourself, partially or entirely, which tells your future employer that you have a sense of commitment, responsibility, and financial savvy. Second and most important, you acquire skills and techniques that will prepare you to work with others.

what work is best for you?

 lmost any job you have during college will benefit you in ways far greater than the financial. Obviously, some jobs are better than others. Before you take the first job you apply for, spend some time learning about yourself and the kinds of jobs available on and off campus.

Phoebe Finn applied to several expensive acting schools in New York and London while studying drama at the University of Maryland. To support herself and save money, she drove the campus shuttle bus at night. Not glamorous for someone aspiring to be Meryl Streep, but the job served its purpose. It allowed her to save money and attend the London School of Dramatics. Phoebe's London experience helped her land her first big job in the Folger Shakespeare Library's production of *Macbeth*.

Of course, if you've got your sights set on a highly competitive field, it may be worth it to take the extra steps necessary to get a job providing experience that will help you later on.

"Broadcasting is fiercely competitive," says Nancy Kilroy. To prepare herself during college at Yale, Nancy worked at National Public Radio, where she learned how to interview people, how to be persistent, and how to pull together information for a five-minute broadcast. "Experience is everything in broadcasting," says Nancy. "You'd better learn early on that most people have already worked at least two jobs in the profession by the time they graduate."

WHAT TO CONSIDER

There are three basic areas of work: working with people, working with information, and working with objects. You might enjoy each of these areas, but if you're like most people, one appeals to you more than the other two.

Richard Bolles, the author of *What Color Is Your Parachute?*, identifies several characteristics that can help you analyze what area best suits you. How do you answer the following questions?

PEOPLE-RELATED SKILLS

Taking Instruction

Ⓨ Ⓝ Do you like to take instruction and then carry out a plan?

Ⓨ Ⓝ Do you enjoy executing and providing support services?

Serving

Ⓨ Ⓝ Do you like helping, teaching, waiting on, or serving others?

Sensing, Feeling

Ⓨ Ⓝ Are you intuitive with respect to the needs of others?

Ⓨ Ⓝ Are you generally responsive, empathetic, warm, and able to understand the position of others?

Communicating

Ⓨ Ⓝ Are you a good listener? Do you question others?

Ⓨ Ⓝ Do you enjoy writing, giving speeches, and giving instructions to others?

Persuading

Ⓨ Ⓝ Do you like to influence, inspire, and recruit others?

Ⓨ Ⓝ Do you like publicizing and promoting causes, people, or things?

Performing, Amusing

Ⓨ Ⓝ Do you like to entertain others?

Ⓨ Ⓝ Do you like to dramatize your point of view or your own experiences as a means of teaching others?

Managing, Supervising

Ⓨ Ⓝ Do you like to plan, oversee, and develop programs with people?

Ⓨ Ⓝ Do you like to encourage and critically evaluate others, using your expertise to help them to improve?

Negotiating, Decision-Making

Ⓨ Ⓝ Do you like to discuss, confer, and resolve difficult issues?

Ⓨ Ⓝ Are you skilled in conflict management?

Ⓨ Ⓝ Do you appreciate and consider opposing points of view?

Founding, Leading

Ⓨ Ⓝ Are you able to work with little or no supervision?

Ⓨ Ⓝ Do you have maverick qualities? That is, do you like to forge your own, possibly better path?

Ⓨ Ⓝ Can you enlist the enthusiasm and support of others?

Ⓨ Ⓝ Do you delegate authority? Do you trust others to execute a job?

Advising, Consulting

Ⓨ Ⓝ Do you enjoy helping others resolve a physical, emotional, or spiritual problem?

Ⓨ Ⓝ Do you enjoy being an expert, reading, and keeping up with what is happening in one field?

Ⓨ Ⓝ Do you make effective use of contacts? Do you give others insight and perspective on their problems?

Holistic Counseling

Ⓨ Ⓝ Do you like to facilitate the growth of others by helping them to identify solutions to their problems?

Training

Ⓨ Ⓝ Do you like to teach others through lecture, demonstration, or practice?

INFORMATION-RELATED SKILLS

Observing

Ⓨ Ⓝ Do you like to study the behavior of people, information, or things?

Comparing

Ⓨ Ⓝ Do you enjoy analyzing two or more different things?

Copying, Storing, and Retrieving

Ⓨ Ⓝ Do you like keeping records, storing data, memorizing, filing, or reviewing information?

Computing

Ⓨ Ⓝ Do you enjoy working with numbers, taking inventory, solving statistical problems, using a computer, budgeting, projecting, or processing data?

Researching

Ⓨ Ⓝ Do you like uncovering hard-to-find facts and information?

Analyzing

Ⓨ Ⓝ Do you like to break things down, taking information apart and examining it?

Organizing

Ⓨ Ⓝ Does giving structure and order to things interest you? Do you always have a place for everything? Do you typically classify material?

Evaluating

Ⓨ Ⓝ Are you a diagnostician or an inspector? Do you like to assess, decide, appraise, and summarize information or situations?

Visualizing

Ⓨ Ⓝ Are you able to perceive patterns and images? Do you picture things you want to do before you do them? Do you enjoy painting, drawing, or designing?

Improving, Adapting

Ⓨ Ⓝ Do you like to take what others have developed and expand upon it? Are you good at improvising, improving, and arranging?

Creating, Synthesizing

Ⓨ Ⓝ Do you like to pull together seemingly unrelated things? Do you like to develop new concepts, approaches, and interpretations?

Designing

Ⓨ Ⓝ Do you like to create models, sculpture, or other things?

Planning, Developing

Ⓨ Ⓝ Do you like to oversee and carry out a plan? Do you prioritize and develop strategies?

Expediting

Ⓨ Ⓝ Do you naturally tend to speed up a task by organizing your objectives ahead of time? Do you have a sense of urgency or immediacy?

Achieving

Ⓨ Ⓝ Do you enjoy accomplishing tasks or specific goals? Do you like to increase productivity and create results?

OBJECT-RELATED SKILLS

Manipulating

Ⓨ Ⓝ Do you enjoy working with your hands? Do you like using your body to move objects?

Working with the Earth and Nature

Ⓨ Ⓝ Do you like nurturing, weeding, and harvesting?

Feeding, Emptying (Machines)

Ⓨ Ⓝ Do you like placing, stacking, dumping, and removing things from machines?

Monitoring (Machines)

Ⓨ Ⓝ Do you like monitoring and adjusting machines, pushing buttons, flipping switches, adjusting controls?

Using Tools

Ⓨ Ⓝ Do you enjoy using hand tools?

Operating Equipment or Machines

Ⓨ Ⓝ Do you like to have specialized knowledge about equipment or machines?

Operating Vehicles

Ⓨ Ⓝ Do you like to drive, pilot, or steer vehicles?

Precision Working

Ⓨ Ⓝ Do you like jobs such as keypunching, drilling, sandblasting, making miniatures, or performing other specialized tasks with your hands?

Setting Up

Ⓨ Ⓝ Do you like to construct or set up displays, machinery, or equipment?

Repairing

Ⓨ Ⓝ Do you like to restore, repair, or do preventive maintenance?

As a freshman, you may not be able to complete this questionnaire. But as a junior or senior, you'll have many more experiences under your belt. For now, just get a general idea of your strongest suit.

Below is a list of job possibilities.

COMMON JOBS FOR COLLEGE STUDENTS

Campus

People	Information	Objects
Resident assistant	Word processor	Library aide
Campus guide	Administrative assistant	Lab technician
Health aide	Secretarial aide	Mechanic
Study tutor	Researcher	Maintenance assistant
Lecturer	Writer (yearbook or campus newspaper)	Groundskeeper

Community

People	Information	Objects
Waiter/waitress	Legal assistant	Short-order cook
Sales clerk	Secretary	Gas-station attendant
Host/hostess	Word processor	Technician
Bartender		Gardener/yard worker

where to find work

Many colleges have job placement centers right on campus. Often campus jobs are listed there. Professors may also list job vacancies like babysitting, housework, construction, or house-sitting. You'll find a wide range of jobs and hours. Getting a job through a placement center can also put you in contact with professors who may introduce you to fields you might not be exposed to through your major.

THE CO-OP EXPERIENCE

Another way to get real-world experience is to enroll in a cooperative program. These programs are sponsored by a wide range of corporations and are designed to give students work experience while they are taking classes. You can find out more about these programs through the college placement center.

Mick McCormick, a director of sales for Nike Inc., worked in a co-op program during college. He studied electrical engineering and finance and worked for IBM as a hardware and software programmer. In addition to providing him with a stable income during college, co-op experience helped him to realize that he did not want to work with computers all day. At the same time, it gave him invaluable computer experience.

"I have the technical knowledge to do word processing, [Microsoft] PowerPoint presentations, and other computer applications I use in my present work. I also learned a lot about my working style. I needed a career where there were no barriers to getting a job done. I don't thrive when there is strong managerial control over my work."

IF WAITING ON TABLES IS NOT FOR YOU...

If you decide to forgo a traditional part-time job, such as waiting on tables, for a more educational, experience-earning job, such as working for a legal clerk, you'll have to demonstrate to your potential employer that you are worth hiring, in spite of your limited experience. If you can convince the person interviewing you that you are a quick learner who is extremely reliable, motivated above and beyond what is expected, and truly interested in pursuing a career in that area, chances are you'll get the job, regardless of your youth and inexperience. Remember that the people interviewing you were once in your place. A determined and inquisitive mind, and the capacity to work hard and achieve, enabled them to be where they are today. If a potential employer believes you have the same qualities that contributed to their success, it is in their best interest to hire you. After all, you will be graduating in a few years, and you could be an attractive employee. Ask for the chance to prove what you can do. Both you and the employer could have a lot to gain.

INSIGHTS

FROM AN INTERN

DeMarco Kelsey, *information technology student*

At an early age, DeMarco Kelsey was already reaching for the stars when he started watching the NASA channel to view space-shuttle launchings. He was also a Star Trek fan and particularly liked the problem-solving duo, Mr. Spock and Captain Kirk. DeMarco says, "It was cool to see Captain Kirk present a problem to his colleague Mr. Spock and then see Mr. Spock walk over to a computer board and punch a bunch of buttons.

DeMarco's early exposure and affinity for space travel and science fiction inspired his career choice: to pursue the innovative field of information technology. "We can use technology to improve our understanding of the world around us," DeMarco says. "For example, we can predict what's going on with the weather because of outer space satellites."

As part of his college coursework, DeMarco took web design classes at DePaul University and became a remote Web intern for LifeBound, working from his home in Chicago, Illinois, for the company located in Denver, Colorado. This was his first experience working remotely. "I quickly realized how important consistent communication would be for this position." He also said the internship gave him a strong sense of responsibility because as a remote worker, "you're entrusted to accomplish tasks without someone standing over your shoulder making sure you get the work done."

His primary responsibilities included analyzing market procedures to drive traffic to the site and customizing the user interface [appearance] and hyperlinks to create a more user-friendly environment. DeMarco also researched methods for improving the distributions of company products and services. In the process, he learned another valuable skill: meticulous documentation. "I documented every Web site I visited and every piece of information I retrieved so that LifeBound could follow up later," says DeMarco.

DeMarco also credits the internship with building his professional confidence. "Upon completing the internship, I felt more empowered to enter new technical situations based on the experience and skills I acquired," he says.

Throughout his undergraduate years at DePaul, DeMarco worked for the university's information technology services department. As an advancing professional, he will work toward his graduate degree at the University of Miami in Florida, focusing on network engineering and architecture. The position in the IT department will pay DeMarco's tuition while he gains teaching experience. DeMarco says the teaching experience is valuable for an IT professional because companies often hire trainers to instruct their employees on using software and other technical job tools.

DeMarco is considering future careers as a field technician or consultant for mega-companies such as IBM, Microsoft, and AT&T Inc. He dreams of one day building a company with his friends from college to tap a rapidly growing field that touches virtually every aspect of life.

If you don't get the experience-earning job you sought, don't despair. Follow up your interviews with a thank-you letter and reconfirm your interest in the company. If you try again six months to a year later, the company may be in a better position to take you on as an apprentice. If you know that the experience gained on the job would be more valuable than the wages you would earn and you can afford it, volunteer for the first six months. It might pay off in the long run.

The experience that such a job today will provide you with could make all the difference while competing for the job you most want later. If you have solid job experience, you will probably get hired even if the other candidate has superior grades and a more impressive background. You learned firsthand about the job and, consequently, you have much more to offer than someone without such experience.

Whichever part-time job you hold—be it gas-station attendant, hotel clerk, or real-estate apprentice—you'll learn to juggle work, school, and other activities while sustaining your motivation and sense of self-reliance. You'll have the best-rounded education upon graduation. You'll gain satisfaction from knowing that you are self-reliant, independent, and responsible for your own accomplishments; and you'll gather important data to help you make career decisions in your junior and senior years.

a final note

Jenny Harris has been out of college for three years and she is a producer for business news at CNN. She believes the key to her success (in addition to good grades) was her commitment to part-time work and internships. "I tried to get exposed to as many different industries as possible to get a firsthand look at how that industry worked. After working as a paralegal in a law firm for several summers, I realized that maybe I didn't want to be a lawyer. I had to sit back and rethink my plans."

Jenny worked on a committee at Cornell University in Ithaca, New York, that brought speakers to campus. While on the committee, she did a variety of jobs: advertising and promotion, budgeting, and setting up for the speaker. She enjoyed the work, but she didn't feel that she would enjoy doing it as a career. After

REAL WORK

IN THE REAL WORLD

Ben Cohen and Jerry Greenfield,
founders of Ben and Jerry's Ice Cream

ometimes those early-in-life jobs foretell great success later on. That was the case for childhood friends and ice cream moguls Ben Cohen and Jerry Greenfield. As the founders of Ben & Jerry's Homemade Holdings Inc., Cohen actually worked driving an ice cream truck his senior year of high school, while Greenfield worked in college as an ice cream scooper. Today, they have a claim to fame for one of the most popular ice cream brands in existence.

Each had their own false starts in life. Cohen enrolled in college, but dropped out. Greenfield graduated, but was denied admission to medical school.  After gaining some real-life experience, they reconnected and decided to enter the food business. Although the original plan was a bagel operation, the equipment proved too expensive, so ice cream became their focus.

The two set up shop in a renovated garage selling rich, homemade cones to a growing and adoring fan base. Their name soon grew and so did their reach. Ben & Jerry's expanded into a multi-state operation and their ice cream is now sold in grocery stores as well.

Perhaps what is most unique about their business is their emphasis on their social mission. The two believe not only in making a superior product, but also in promoting social value and environmental respect. Ben & Jerry's received accolades over the years for the company's commitment to the environment and the community at large. And to think it all started working as an ice cream truck driver and scooper.

Sources: Richards, Daniel. "Ben and Jerry's: The Men Behind the Ice Cream." *About.com.* 2009. <http://entrepreneurs.about.com/od/famousentrepreneurs/p/benandjerrys.htm>.

"Our Mission Statement." *Benjerry.com.* <http://www.benjerry.com/our_company /our_mission/>.

reflecting and talking with other professionals, she decided that broadcasting might be a career she would enjoy.

In order to see what broadcasting was like, she worked for the student-run radio station at Cornell. This work allowed her to experience reporting, broadcasting, writing, and news meetings—all of the facets of putting together a broadcast. She liked it, so she applied for an internship with the prestigious MacNeil/Lehrer Productions news program in Washington, DC. During her internship there, the Gulf War broke out.

"I got to be in the newsroom and experience the excitement. After this internship, I was convinced that this was the field I wanted to pursue. When I graduated, I worked for CNN as an intern for four months without pay before I was hired as a production assistant.

"All of my jobs and internships provided me with a perspective. I knew something was missing when I was working for the law firm; I wasn't happy or comfortable in the work environment. I never would have discovered what I really liked without getting the first-hand work experience that I did."

CHAPTER TEN

*What we learn to do,
we learn by doing.*

THOMAS JEFFERSON

I think the most valuable thing a college student can do while in college is to intern in his or her field of interest," says Stephanie Ward, who was the director of casework for Big Brothers Big Sisters of America in Dallas. Internships help you learn if the profession you're considering is what you really want for a career. If you do, the internship gives you credibility in the job market and a leg up on those with no experience.

"I was responsible for hiring caseworkers," explains Stephanie. "What type of internship, how they performed while at their internship, and references from their internship carried more weight in my hiring decision than grades. If a decision came down to two applicants, and one had more experience in the field than the other, *and* could verbalize what he or she had learned and discovered about him or herself, then this would be the applicant I would hire."

intern we trust

GETTING THE INTERNSHIP

Even if the only thing you discover from your internship is that you don't like the work, you're still ahead. You will have invested only your summer, not your life. Sometimes students really enjoy the coursework in a particular field, but when they actually have the opportunity to do the job, they find they don't like it. That happened to Jill Ruvidich, who had wanted to be an accountant since high school. "I really enjoyed studying accounting; however, an internship between my junior and senior years proved I found the real stuff extremely boring."

Rod Garcia, admissions recruiter for the Master of Business Administration (or MBA) program at the University of Chicago, says that internships are very useful for people who don't yet know what they want to do. "Internships give students an idea of what's out there. The experience that even an unpaid internship provides is just as valuable as, if not more valuable than, some of your key college courses."

Rama Moorthy, an engineering sales specialist, loved her engineering courses in college. She did well in her classes and received several job offers. "When it came down to it, none of the actual jobs interested me. I decided to get an MBA and apply my engineering degree in a way I would enjoy. During graduate school, I made sure to intern in several different areas so I could see what it was like doing the work I was studying. This time, when I graduated I had a much better idea of what I wanted to do."

Brigitt Berry, a quality development consultant, had several different internships in college. One of the most valuable came about through a representative she met at the college's career fair. "Different professionals had come to the college to talk about their fields of expertise. I sat down with a human resources representative and spoke with him at length about the profession; what it included and what it would take to enter the field. I was really impressed with him and what he had to say. When I look back on that conversation, I have to smile, because I asked him all sorts of questions that were of interest to me, but never really bothered to ask him what he did with the company, or if he liked his profession. I spent no time making it a two-way conversation.

"Two days later, I went to the college career center to get his address and found out he was the vice president of personnel for a Fortune 500 company. I wrote and asked if I could spend a month with his company in New York. He was impressed with my quick request and flew me to New York six months later.

"During my experience with his organization, I learned that I was not at all interested in the communications department, but that I was interested in the training and development department."

In addition to giving you a ground-level view of the profession, internships can also open the door for full-time employment when you graduate. So keep in mind that the organization you intern for will be checking you out, too. Rita Rather is a management information systems senior at the University of Illinois. An honor student with a strong personality, she so impressed management at the Cellular Telephone Company in Chicago during her internship last summer that they offered her a full-time job upon her graduation in the spring.

internships during school

Jim Cochran, an economics major from Los Alamos, New Mexico, had three internships during college. From each one he learned something different.

During his sophomore year, Jim had an unpaid internship working twelve hours a week with a commercial real estate company, Kimmel Property Management. This was Jim's first exposure to business, and it enabled him to build confidence and to establish valuable contacts. Four years later, when Jim began his first job out of college, he talked with the president of the company to ask advice on his future career. Today, Jim is still in contact with several people from his first internship.

The second internship was in a law firm where Jim worked ten hours a week during the school year. Jim learned here that he did not want to become a lawyer. He still did not know what he really wanted to do, but at least he was learning what he did *not* want to do.

During his senior year, Jim worked ten hours a week for Merrill Lynch & Co. He wanted to explore finance and investing and to continue making contacts. He enjoyed the job at Merrill Lynch, but didn't feel passionate enough about it to make it a career. He opted not to pursue a career in investing and got his first job with a real estate consulting firm.

When you know what you want to do, it can be valuable to let one internship lead to another in the same field of interest. This shows future employers that you are not only interested in them; you are very interested in them. Gordon Bock, a former reporter

INSIGHTS

FROM AN INTERN

Jeremy Hawn, public relations consultant

As one of the very first LifeBound interns in 2001, Jeremy Hawn worked with LifeBound's president, Carol Carter, to create presentations and design group activities for educational programming. As a University of Denver student, Jeremy became a sounding board with a valuable perspective. His genuine interpersonal skills and storytelling abilities made him a great candidate for leading a Peer Leadership Internship Program for high school students. He was well equipped with the traits for success.

After studying abroad for a semester, Jeremy sacrificed free-time to lead Life-Bound seminars on weekends. He shared from his own experience the things he wished he'd known in high school. "I gave them a perspective of where they could be in a few years," Jeremy said. "I was helping them bridge the gap."

Jeremy tried to help the students see him as a real person. He tried to remember who he was at their age and how he could help them now. Many group meetings with the high school students turned toward life without parental control. Although Jeremy admitted to going out a few nights a week, he also let the students know it was a balancing act. Studying needed to happen. "Sometimes there's a need to simply relax, and at other times there's a need to plan for an upcoming exam."

He was always prepared for the next move. "Find a plan and a map to get where you're going." He found his niche in a creative writing major with a minor in international studies, stayed on top of his course work, and spent his last semester job hunting.

After earning a master's degree in international education from New York University in Manhattan, Jeremy is now working in the city as a public relations consultant. The interpersonal skills that helped him connect high school students to the future at LifeBound are now helping him make a difference internationally.

with both *U.S. News & World Report* and *Time* magazine, was the youngest news director ever at Columbia University in New York's radio station during his sophomore year. One day, the nationally syndicated Campus Radio Voice called for an intern. Gordon said, "I'm interested." He was hired, and over the next two years he was heard over the air at 460 colleges nationwide, interviewing celebrities and newsmakers. That internship led to the most prestigious one of all: becoming the first undergraduate in the history of the school to teach communications at Columbia Journalism School.

The result: when Gordon graduated, he moved immediately to a reporting job with The Associated Press and Dow Jones in New York City, writing radio copy. Three months later, he was hired by United Press International at a third-year pay scale (based largely on his college jobs), and four years after that, he was hired by *U.S. News & World Report*. At twenty-six, when many reporters are moving from one-town to three-town beats, (reporter slang for a coverage area) Gordon was given a job covering eight states—and half of Pennsylvania!

Landing good internships, Gordon says, can be very important. And once you have them, he says, make the most of them. "Be gung-ho about whatever you do."

SUMMER INTERNSHIPS

"Summer activity is a great indicator of future job success," says Dee Milligan, first vice president and director of insurance marketing for Kemper Financial Companies, Inc. in Chicago. She interviews and hires many graduates straight from college. "I want to see that the applicant has taken initiative. I'm not interested in someone who has just messed around and not thought about using his or her summers wisely."

Dee says that working during the summer in a standard corporate environment gives students the opportunity to learn about the workplace—by diving in and experiencing it for themselves. It's the kind of education you can't get in the classroom.

Brenda White is from Ainsworth, Iowa, a town of with a population of 524. She attended Augustana College, a small Lutheran school in Illinois. During her junior year, Brenda applied for a nonpaying summer internship with the U.N. She was selected as one of twenty college students in the country to come to New York City.

Although the internship was nonpaying, Brenda talked to several people at the financial aid office at Augustana to see if she could get funding. And she did.

The most valuable part of Brenda's experience? She became street smart, learning to survive and thrive in a big city. After that summer in NYC, Brenda felt herself a match for any environment.

Jeff Cantany is an economics major who hopes to work for a nonprofit agency in international development. To qualify, he needs to go into the Peace Corps, and they require construction skills. So what did he do the summer after his freshman year? He worked for a builder in New Mexico. He earned a good salary, learned a trade, and was introduced to a culture very different from that of his native New York.

WINTER INTERNSHIPS

Many companies and firms have programs for students during the winter semester break. During his senior year at Columbia, Tim Dalton had a full-time, four-week internship in January with the Lawyers Committee for Human Rights in New York City. Tim worked with other volunteers on LCHR reports about human rights violations and refugee issues.

"I learned about issues not covered in the newspapers," says Tim. "Although I wasn't paid, the internship was invaluable because I gained insight into the nonprofit organizations which rely heavily on volunteers. I provided them with much-needed labor, but most of all, I enjoyed the work."

internships after graduation

Think about internships after college, too. Kim Caldwell already had a bachelor's degree in art history when she began her six-month internship at The Metropolitan Museum of Art, in New York. She got the job through the American Association of Museums, which posts job openings online. Kim was able to work in several administrative areas and visit other museums in the city.

"Becoming involved in a professional organization kept me abreast of openings in the museum field as well as informing me of the latest trends in museum policies," Kim said.

no pay? okay

Internship work seldom provides a paycheck. Particularly in some industries, unpaid internships are the norm. Your reward is the experience. This means, quite obviously, that you may have to work a part-time job to help pay for your living expenses.

I was a summer intern in Washington, D.C., between my sophomore and junior years. I worked without pay for Common Cause, a grassroots lobbying organization. I attended Senate and House hearings there. I also reported on the Clean Air Act and the daily debate on the constitutional amendment to balance the budget.

On the less glamorous side, this internship didn't pay the bills. Therefore, I worked as a waitress at an Italian restaurant atop an apartment building with a view of the Washington Monument. Because the menu there was expensive, I made good money in tips. So I only had to work three nights a week.

I remember working on the Fourth of July and feeling glum because all my friends were down on the Mall watching the fireworks and listening to the Beach Boys' concert. However, I was lucky to be in Washington. I was also lucky to have a part-time job that enabled me to have my nonpaying, though thoroughly rewarding summer internship.

meeting mentors

Lisa Heinlein, a special-education teacher, learned a great deal about how to be an excellent teacher from watching other great teachers. "Allow yourself to be taught," Lisa says. "Don't be afraid to try things and make mistakes—that's how you learn."

Lenny Feder, now a senior at Columbia, had his first internship during his sophomore year. He worked for three weeks at American Marketing. Though he had held a lot of different jobs, this was his first experience in the corporate world. His boss, who happened to have belonged to the same fraternity as Lenny when he attended college, served as a mentor. He let Lenny sit in on meetings, allowed him to help plan projects from day one, and even gave him advice on what type of suit to wear. "My mentor gave me a sense of what skills I'd need in the business world. But I couldn't just copy him. I learned those skills by myself—with my mentor serving as a guide."

Through your internships, you'll meet people who can be your teachers. Choose two or three people whom you respect to be your mentors. Pick their brains to find answers to the following questions:

1. How could I do my job better?
2. What could I do at school to prepare myself for the industry?
3. How did you become interested in this industry?
4. What are your toughest challenges?
5. What part of the job do you like the most?
6. What will be the toughest challenge facing the industry over the next five years?
7. Where is the growth potential?
8. If you were interviewing me today, would I get the job? If not, why?
9. What qualities do you look for in a qualified applicant?

Getting answers to these questions will help you learn about the profession—and about yourself. You'll gain insight, but your employers will also gain respect for your initiative.

developing a professional self-image

One of the transitions you will have to make after college is the change from seeing yourself as a student to seeing yourself as a legitimate professional. Internships can give you the opportunity to develop your professional self-image.

Carla Schnurr spent a summer on a science and technology public policy fellowship. It was sponsored by the American Association for the Advancement of Science and placed fifteen students in reporting positions in radio, newspapers, television, and magazines around the country.

Carla joined the science desk at the *Atlanta Journal-Constitution,* where she was assigned stories with other science reporters. She learned by doing. The editor would give her a story, and it was her job to research it, conduct the pertinent interviews, and write it. The editor and the other reporters coached her as she worked through each phase of the job.

"I gained confidence by being thrown into new situations where I was expected to perform as a professional rather than as a student. The internship helped me to develop my 'reporter's persona'—to be comfortable talking with all kinds of people as an adult. I remember

REAL WORK

IN THE REAL WORLD

Rachael Ray, *chef, author, entrepreneur*

While most people know that Rachael Ray is a famous celebrity cook and TV personality, many don't know that she began her career as a food buyer, eventually becoming a chef for Cowan & Lobel, Limited, Inc., a gourmet boutique In Albany, New York. During the holiday season, Ray promoted grocery sales by teaching a cooking class called 30-minute Mediterranean Meals. It was a hit that caught the attention of a local TV station. When they invited her to host a *30-Minute Meals* segment, Ray accepted.

"I did *30-Minute Meals* for five years on local television and I earned nothing the first two years. Then, I earned $50 a segment. I spent more than that on gas and groceries, but I really enjoyed making the show and loved going to a viewer's house each week. I knew I enjoyed it, so I stuck with it even though it cost me."

Today, Ray's television work includes hosting *Tasty Travels, $40 a Day, Inside Dish,* and *30-Minute Meals.* She recently won a Daytime Emmy Award for Outstanding Talk-Show Entertainment and now has a multi-media empire that includes her own magazine, *Everyday with Rachael Ray,* as well as a growing list of cookbooks.

Not only does Ray's experience demonstrate the importance of doing what you love, but it also shows the importance of being willing to accept experience in lieu of pay.

Source: "Rachael Ray Bio." *RachaelRayMag.com.* 2009. The Reader's Digest Association, Inc. <http://www.rachaelraymag.com/about-rachael/rachael-ray-biography/article.html>.

being very nervous on my first interview with the new director of the American Cancer Society. As we began talking, however, I became interested in the person and the work he did. From then on I lost my feelings of shyness around people in prominent positions. My interviewing skills really grew with that newfound confidence."

The people Carla worked with became mentors and role models. "They have become real friends in the workplace. Through their experience, I got to see alternative routes to my goals which I might not have thought of on my own."

how to get the internship

Let's hope that I've convinced you that an internship is worth pursuing. Now what? First, know that you will get a job as an intern. Banish all doubts—they aren't going to help you. Believe you are going to succeed.

Second, realize that securing an internship is very much like interviewing for your "real" job at the end of your senior year. In fact, the whole process of writing your resume, interviewing, and landing the internship is exactly the preparation you'll need for your full-fledged job search upon graduation. Now for the practical steps.

WHAT TO DO

1. Get a copy of one of the current summer internship directories for college students, or make an appointment at your school's career office. Also, be sure to check out Appendix B for a small sample of internship opportunities.

2. From the college directory and/or other resources, make a list of the internship positions that interest you. Select at least twenty.

3. Review your list carefully, thinking about which skills a potential employer might look for in an applicant.

4. Take stock of your qualifications. Look at the skills listed below and ask yourself two questions: (1) Which of these skills can I offer my potential employer? and (2) What other skills not listed here can I contribute to the internship positions? In the column on the right, add your own words to describe your strengths and give examples of something you've done that illustrates your know-how. For instance, if you've served as the head of a school club, describe how this experience helped you develop leadership abilities. The more specific you are, the better prepared you'll be for your job search.

SKILL	My strengths in this area and an example of what I've done that demonstrates this ability
Organizing	
Working with others	
Developing ideas	
Writing/researching	
Prioritizing time	
Observing	
Repairing things	
Founding/leading	
Paying attention to detail	
Following instructions	
Speaking in public	
Other	

WHERE TO GO

Geography may play a part in which internship you choose. For instance, if you're interested in banking, New York, Chicago, Los Angeles, and San Francisco would be great cities to work in for a summer. If you're interested in computers, you could work in almost any large metropolitan area, although California's Silicon Valley might be the best. Maybe you don't know which career interests you yet. No problem. Half your classmates don't know either, but they're probably not taking steps to find out. Pat yourself on the back. Okay, that's enough. Now back to work . . .

If you can afford it, seek contrast. If you're from a small town, apply for a spot in a big city. The more diversity you experience, the more versatile you'll be. Working in a new city conveys maturity, confidence, and determination to your future employers. I waited tables on the weekends so I could afford to intern for a summer in New York. I'm from Arizona, so living in Manhattan for three months was an educational experience in itself!

WHEN TO APPLY

Begin early. If you want to get an internship between your sophomore and junior years, ideally you should have your resume, cover letter, and target companies ready during the summer after your freshman year. Also, since you may not get a response from any of your top five picks, plan to send letters to at least fifteen other companies. From the twenty letters you send, expect to receive at least two offers.

WHOM TO CONTACT

Once you have considered internship possibilities based on your skills and your career interests, it's time to narrow your scope by choosing the five internships you'd like to contact first.

1. Desired career: _____

Name of organization: _____

Address: _____

_____

Contact: _____ Phone: _____

2. Desired career: _____

Name of organization: _____

Address: _____

_____

Contact: _____ Phone: _____

3. Desired career: _____

Name of organization: _____

Address: _____

_____

Contact: _____ Phone: _____

4. Desired career: _____

Name of organization: _____

Address: _____

_____

Contact: _____ Phone: _____

5. Desired career: _____

Name of organization: _____

Address: _____

_____

Contact: _____ Phone: _____

HOW TO APPLY

Now that you know which organizations you want to contact, here's what to send:

1. A resume briefly stating your objectives as an intern, your education, your work experience, and your extracurricular activities. Be prepared to provide three references, and notify these people that they may be contacted by your prospective employers. (See the sample resume on later in this chapter.)

2. A one-page cover letter explaining your interests, abilities, and reasons for choosing this organization. This letter, like your resume, should be flawlessly written and typed; see the example later in this chapter. Have a couple of your friends or your composition professor read it for clarity and accuracy. Make sure you're sending the letter to the right person. Don't rely on the information in your internship directory. It's a changing world, so call the company to verify the address and the contact person.

3. A letter of recommendation from a professor or employer (not one of your three references). The right recommendation can make a big difference because it can help separate you from the pack. When you approach someone to write a letter, let him or her know why you are asking for a letter. For example, it is helpful for a teacher to know that you have chosen her because you are proud of the research project you did in her class, and not simply because she gave you a good grade. (See the sample letter of recommendation later in this chapter.) Be sure to thank the professor or employer for the letter.

4. Consider whether it is appropriate to include a writing sample. If you have a well organized essay or term paper that received superior marks, include it. A good writing sample demonstrates the way you think, organize your thoughts and communicate.

About two weeks after you've mailed your cover letter, resume, and letter of recommendation, call the person to whom you wrote. Make sure he or she received your letter, and ask when a decision will be made. Reiterate your interest in the company, but also let the person know that you have other summer job options.

Is an interview required? If so, check out the interview evaluation form in Chapter 14.

don't give up

n Appendix B, you'll find a directory of many business-es in the United States currently offering internships for college students. Although this is an excellent reference list, don't depend on it completely. If no organization in your field of interest is listed, find one on your own! Some of the most rewarding internships will be those you research and find yourself. Use this list to land your first summer internship, but for the fol-lowing summer, go for the challenge of landing the job no one else could find. Sell yourself to the organization that may not have an established internship program.

Rama Moorthy suggests that one way to learn about a company, and to get your foot in the door for an internship, is to try to meet some of the recruiters who come to campus to interview grad-uating seniors. "Ask them if you can meet with them briefly in between their interviews," he says, "then use the opportunity to find out what kinds of internships they offer or if they would be open to creating an internship position."

If you can convince an employer to *make* a position for you, you'll be successful at selling your ideas and getting support after you graduate. The more you develop these maverick qualities, the more fearless you'll become. To be effective, you must believe in yourself. If you learn early to convince others to believe in you, you'll be several steps ahead of the game.

once you begin your internship

Some internships are better organized than others. Jonathan Bober, a curator and art professor at the University of Texas, says that internships are valuable only if they are extremely well-organized. Otherwise, you may spend your time run-ning errands rather than learning about the field. Keep in mind that you will often need to be the initiator to make your internship as valuable as possible. It's up to you to formulate some goals—what you want to learn about this career.

Pam Zemper knew she was good at understanding how an organization ticks by seeing the broad patterns. When she began her internship at an ad agency in Austin, Texas, her goal was to learn every department of advertising. She chose this particular agency because she would gain experience in television, radio, print, and public relations. "The agency I interned for had agreed to give me a chance to work in each division. But when I got there, I realized it was up to me to seek out extra projects in those areas."

Pam formed a mentoring relationship with an account executive who gave her background reading in many areas of the business. "This material was written by an advertising agency and gave me a working knowledge of the process and the vocabulary. I was able to apply this information during my internship and talk comfortably with the other executives." After graduation, the agency offered her a job.

WHEN THINGS GO WRONG

What happens when you make your first mistakes on the job? Well, if you're not making mistakes, you're probably not trying hard enough. Mistakes are the processes by which we learn. One of the main purposes of an internship is to learn some lessons that will make you better prepared once you start your "real" job after college.

Jim Burke, the CEO at Johnson & Johnson, the personal care product company, has a favorite story about his former boss. General Robert Wood Johnson discovered that Burke had failed miserably at one of his really innovative ideas—a children's chest rub. Johnson asked him, "Are you the person who cost us all that money?" Burke nodded. "I'd like to congratulate you," the general said. "If you are making mistakes, that means you are making decisions and taking risks. And we won't grow unless you take risks."

If you mess up on the job, admit it, correct the mistake, discuss it, and above all, learn from it. The greatest fool is one who will not admit his or her own mistakes and get help from others when necessary.

When things aren't going as you expected, it's time to figure out why. Were your expectations realistic? Internships will involve some drudgery; it's not going to be exciting every minute you're there. However, if you're not learning and experiencing what you had hoped for at least part of the time, there are steps you can take to remedy the situation.

1. First, set up a time to meet with your supervisor. Tell them what you see as the problem and what you think the possible solutions are.

2. Second, discuss what you believe the goals and objectives should be. Then ask your supervisor for feedback.

3. Third, clarify with your supervisor what they want you to accomplish, and together establish some specific goals for the remainder of your internship.

EVALUATING YOUR PERFORMANCE

Some organizations have formal evaluations. If yours doesn't, be forthright in asking for an honest appraisal of your work at the conclusion of your internship. Remember, you'll be able to improve only if you can take constructive criticism from those with more experience.

The following is a list of categories in which an employee is typically evaluated. Use the chart to grade yourself in each of these categories. If you believe you're doing an excellent job, put an E next to that item; if a satisfactory job, put an S; if a poor job, write a P.

PERFORMANCE REVIEW

_____ Quality of work		_____ Delegating
_____ Quantity of work		_____ Self-control
_____ Problem solving		_____ Communication
_____ Decision-making		_____ Working with others
_____ Planning and organizing		_____ Business savvy

OTHER CHARACTERISTICS

_____ Creativity		_____ Leadership
_____ Initiative		_____ Self-confidence
_____ Teamwork		_____ Attitude
_____ Judgment		_____ Maturity
_____ Adaptability		_____ Foresight
_____ Persuasiveness		

Then, go over the list with your manager. Ask for specific tips on how you can improve on your weak areas.

OVERALL EVALUATION

■ Your strengths:

_____

_____

_____

_____

■ Areas that need improvement:

_____

_____

_____

_____

■ Supervisor's comments:

_____

_____

_____

_____

---

where do you go from here?

I f you love your internship and decide that another summer at the same company would be valuable for your professional development, set things up for the following year. Many companies have an interest in cultivating students for two summers in a row so they can make them a job offer upon graduation. Just make sure to secure greater responsibilities for the next summer. This way you'll continue to develop your skills as well as make new contacts.

Then again, you may wish to keep your options open and work for another organization the following summer—in the same industry or a completely different one.

SAMPLE RESUME

Mary Ann Van Camp

6680 North Anywhere Avenue, Duluth, MN 55806   mvancamp@aol.com

EDUCATION	College sophomore English Major, Business Minor University of Georgia, Athens, GA
OBJECTIVE	Summer Internship in Marketing or Sales
EMPLOYMENT *April 2004 to present*	*Administrative assistant,* Adler & Adler Public Relations Agency. Responsibilities include working with clients and partners, answering mail, and routine paperwork.
March 2003 to April 2004	*Hostess,* Spaghetti Company Restaurant
ACTIVITIES	*Resident Assistant,* Coronado Dorm, University of Georgia. Responsibilities include organizing dorm functions, helping students adjust to college, and providing support during difficult times. Member, International Students Club; Spurs; Sophomore Student Honorary Society. Participated in philanthropy program.
HIGH SCHOOL **HIGHLIGHTS**	President, Thespian Society. Organized actors' league, performed for charities, worked with professional actors in the community. Graduated with a 3.2 GPA. Mainstream High junior-year representative to Girls' State.

References available upon request.

SAMPLE COVER LETTER

Mary Ann Van Camp

6680 North Anywhere Avenue, Duluth, MN 55806   mvancamp@aol.com

Mr. Ryan Rinaldi   September 30, XXXX
Pillsbury Company
Pillsbury Center
Minneapolis, MN 55402

Dear Mr. Rinaldi:

I am a sophomore majoring in English and minoring in business at the University of Georgia. My goal is to work for Pillsbury this summer as an intern in either sales or marketing.

Attached is a copy of my resume and a letter of recommendation from one of my professors. As you can see from my resume, I am committed to achievement, both in and out of the classroom. An internship with Pillsbury would provide me with an unparalleled "real-world" experience. Because I am a dedicated, energetic, and inquisitive worker, I would be a benefit to Pillsbury as an intern.

I will be calling before October 15 to inquire further about internship opportunities. In the meantime, if you have any questions, don't hesitate to call me at 313-888-1017.

I look forward to speaking with you soon. Thank you for your consideration.

Sincerely,

Mary Ann Van Camp

mvancamp@aol.com

SAMPLE LETTER OF RECOMMENDATION

September 25, XXXX

To Whom It May Concern:

I met Mary Ann Van Camp the first semester of her freshman year. Mary Ann was enrolled in my Western Civilization course, and she immediately impressed me as a top-notch student. She came to see me during office hours, asked questions about class lectures and writing assignments, and followed up after tests to ensure that she had learned all the pertinent information. Seldom do college students today take the extra time—especially in a survey course—to get to know their professors and to seek their help outside of class.

Although Mary Ann received a B for the course, her efforts deserved an A for the amount of time she devoted to a class normally taken by sophomores. The first semester of college is a tough adjustment period for any student, but those who persevere and learn the materials, not just to get a good grade but for the sake of learning, are truly distinguished. I know Mary Ann will get more than most out of college because she tries harder.

I highly recommend Mary Ann for a summer internship at your company. Her delightful personality, coupled with her intellect and desire to learn, will be an asset to any company or organization.

Please feel free to contact me.

Sincerely,

Robert Timmons

Dr. Robert Timmons
Department of History
University of Georgia
Athens, GA 00010

My Two Cents

HOW DO I APPLY IT?

Jordan Austin, University of Colorado, Boulder

I'm sure you've heard the saying, "It's not what you know, it's who you know." Well, it's true and not for the reasons you might think. One year after graduation, I began to look for an internship. I knew if I wanted a chance at a well-paying job, I needed experience. But to justify taking an unpaid position when my wife was still student teaching for free, I would have to look at my unpaid internship time as an investment for my future. So I made the decision to follow my dreams and make the very best of my experience.

I applied for an internship at one of the best TV stations in the country. I got it. I arranged with my employer to work part-time and I threw myself into learning. I decided to give it everything I had. No good job for a good company is ever going to be given on recommendation alone. You have to earn it.

It was a bit intimidating at first, but I quickly adjusted. If you take initiative, it's amazing what kind of respect you get. If those around you know you'll work hard, they'll help you succeed. Ask questions and ask some more questions. Make yourself a valuable member of the company's team. Volunteer to work extra hours. Above all,

Adam Edwards, a senior at the University of Michigan, is completing his third internship at Microsoft. He feels his interning experience has benefited him in many ways. "The most tangible benefit of the internships is that by doing well at them, I give Microsoft the incentive to hire me when I graduate—these days it's comforting to have a job lined up after graduation." Adam has also gained valuable knowledge about his field. "I learned a computer language at Microsoft that is taught at my school—I learned it before I took the class, so I had an advantage over people who were learning it for the first time. I've gained enough knowledge about how software is developed that I could potentially develop commercial software using methodologies and technical skills I learned on the job at Microsoft."

take some chances, and don't be afraid to make some mistakes. They'll forgive you. After all, you're an intern.

At the end of my internship, I was serving, more or less, as an associate producer. I had real jobs and had even been hired (and paid) to do some work for the station as a freelancer. I had the experience to move forward. More than that, I had the people around me who had seen me work, who liked my work and could vouch for the quality of my work.

After I had finished my internship, I applied for almost twenty TV jobs. When I was granted an interview, the people I had worked with called on my behalf. They called of their own free will to express their satisfaction with my work. The people I knew got me the job. They proved to my new employer that my resume wasn't just something that looked nice. They proved what a resume couldn't prove: that I'm a good worker and will give my all to the task at hand.

So today, I'm doing something that seemed so crazy and far-fetched a year ago. I'm a TV news reporter. There are not many industries where who you know can be as important as it is in this business. But the power of personal recommendation goes a long way in every business. So maybe it's fair to say, "It's not just what you know, it's who you know that can prove it."

MAJORING IN THE

CHAPTER ELEVEN

The world is a book and those who stay
at home read only one page.

ST. AUGUSTINE

The use of traveling is to regulate the imagination
by reality and, instead of thinking how
things may be, to see them as they are.

SAMUEL JOHNSON

P eople travel for a variety of reasons: to study, work, volunteer, or for leisure, just to name a few. Regardless of the motivation, experiencing the world offers immense personal and professional rewards. For one thing, travel can be a deeply enriching experience. By venturing out of your safe, familiar environment, you gain insights about humanity and also about yourself. Your understanding of other cultures expands, and so does your self-awareness—important elements in developing a healthy view of the world.

Even if you're not planning a career internationally, job recruiters look favorably on students who have traveled outside the United States. A summer or a semester abroad tells a potential employer that you possess attractive character traits such as the desire to learn and the courage to explore, which are key attributes for the kind of innovative

windows on the world

TRAVELING AT HOME AND ABROAD

thinking today's industries long for. Immersing yourself in another culture also develops the universally prized skill of adaptability. Your ability to adjust quickly to any situation, group of people, or environment will serve you in any occupation, particularly in today's multinational work environment.

Marty D'Luzansky taught English in France as part of a Fulbright Teaching Assistant program after he graduated from college with a major in French. He ended up working as a trade consultant with the New Zealand Trade Development Board. "I can't stress enough how important it is to take a year between undergraduate school and whatever it is you think you want to do," he said. "My overseas experience has provided me with the cross-cultural skills essential to help me effectively advise New Zealanders on the best way to succeed with their products or services in the U.S. market. The ability to see the United States from a foreign perspective is critical to my work."

the world as your classroom

Hong Kong. Buenos Aires. Cairo. London. Paris. Milan. Faraway cities like these can be your first exposure to other people, cultures, and languages. World travel can even jump-start a career that you'll love. Diane Roberts is a case in point. As she traveled through Europe, Diane became enamored with historic churches. Diane's curiosity led her on a search for studios where stained-glass restoration was done; the artists there told her that the churches and buildings in the United States were just then becoming old enough to need restoration, and they recommended that she pursue a career in restoration at home. Today, Diane Roberts is an artisan at Cummings Stained Glass Studios in North Adams, Massachusetts. "I wouldn't be working on American windows today if I hadn't spent that time in Europe," she says.

Spending time in another country can also help you clarify your career goals. Susan Finnemore studied for one semester at the University of York in England. On weekends she traveled with friends around Great Britain. In the youth hostels where she stayed, she noticed advertisements for work camps. (Important tip: There are many jobs abroad. Some can be found on the bulletin boards of youth hostels, train stations, and schools.) One camp where she worked was on a Welsh estate, where she received wages and lodgings. The camp paid for food, and Susan cooked the meals.

Susan's parents are both professors, and Susan had always planned to go straight from undergraduate school to a master's program in history. Travel gave her the perspective to reconsider her options. "If I can travel through Europe," Susan thought to herself, "I can do anything." Instead of going to graduate school, Susan decided to pursue a career in publishing. She found job satisfaction as the psychology editor of college textbooks at Prentice Hall.

Your travel experience, however, doesn't have to be as structured as the examples cited to be worthwhile. Bill and Jonathan Aikens spent three months bicycling through Europe with little on their minds except taking in the scenery. Yet they learned valuable lessons along the way. Between the two of them, they spoke five languages. Besides English, Bill spoke Spanish and French; Jonathan spoke German; both learned Italian en route! Travel can, therefore, provide another very specific, very tangible skill: speaking a foreign language.

In some fields, the more exotic the language, the more marketable employers find the skill. UPI Beijing correspondent Mark Delvecchio skipped several rungs on the journalism ladder in this way. Reporters can work ten years to win coveted overseas positions—and some can wait an entire lifetime for such jobs, to no avail. Mark, however, rose out of a reporting job at a small Connecticut paper to a job in China in just a little over four years.

An energetic reporter, Mark made rapid progress on the basis of hard work, becoming city editor of a daily after only three years in the business. However, when a job opened up on UPI's foreign desk in Washington, DC, Mark says it was his college year abroad in China and his University of Connecticut master's degree in Chinese history that made the difference. "Few American reporters speak Chinese," he says. A few months after arriving in Washington, Mark was sent to Beijing. He was twenty-eight.

learning about yourself

Travel teaches you about other places and other people, but most important, it teaches you about yourself. For example, I spent the fall semester of my junior year in Segovia, Spain, a village near Madrid. I lived with a delightful Spanish family and attended a local Spanish college, where I received university credit. I partied—in Spanish—with friends from the town while the other Americans partied in English with each other.

On weekends I took the train into Madrid and explored other nearby towns. Once, my Spanish friend Ma Paz took me outside Segovia to visit her family's village: population, twenty-five. It was out of a storybook. The only public building was a small church where a friar came to perform mass each Sunday.

Ma Paz's father, a farmer, lived with her mother in a small house next to the barn overflowing with cows. Her grandparents' house was only a ten-minute walk away, along a path bordered by gorgeous, rolling Spanish hills. Her grandparents showed us where they made wine from grapes that they pressed themselves. They were intensely curious about my life back in the United States, asking many questions about my family, my hometown, and my university. We talked long into the night.

I felt lucky to meet these generous people. When I reminisce about my semester abroad, it's not the Prado, the Alahambra, or the 800-year-old castles that leap to mind first, but my experiences with people such as Ma and her family, who taught me much more than just how to be fluent in Spanish.

The lives of other travelers have also been enriched in similar ways. Sue Flynn, for instance, traveled and worked extensively in Europe and South America prior to earning a law degree in public service. Sue's reflections on her experiences abroad prompted her to say the following: "If you can understand and relate to the conditions in different countries whose people have backgrounds so different from your own, you can come back to the United States and relate to almost any situation."

Linda Montag grew up in Pittsburgh and attended Grove City College in Pennsylvania. Although her school offered study abroad programs, Linda knew she could distinguish herself by getting work experience in a foreign country. So, with the encouragement of one of her German professors, she secured a work–study program in Germany for one summer and one semester in the field of insurance.

"My time abroad helped me develop self-confidence more than anything else I did in college," says Linda, who is now an assistant vice president of a German commercial bank headquartered in Frankfurt. "It was the first opportunity I had to truly assert myself and depend on myself completely to do everything—from finding my way around to learning my job to becoming proficient in a foreign language."

where do you want to go?

Maybe you'd like to visit France because you studied French in school. Maybe you'd like to visit Ireland because your ancestors were Irish. You've also thought about Canada or Mexico because they're closer and more convenient to visit. Below, make a list of five countries that interest you and, more importantly, tell why they interest you.

1. _____ *because:* _____

_____

2. _____ *because:* _____

_____

3. _____ *because:* _____

_____

4. _____ *because:* _____

_____

5. _____ *because:* _____

_____

If no particular country stands out in your mind as the place you really want to go, take your travel wish list and do some information gathering:

- Talk to professors.
- Talk to friends who've traveled.
- Read whatever you can about the countries that interest you.

By now you should be passionate about visiting at least a couple of those countries on your wish list. Choose the one that best fits your interest in language, culture, and education. Remember, you've got a lifetime to visit the other cultures on your list. Your first extended visit to a foreign country will forever change the way you see yourself and the world. *Vive l'experience!*

HOW TO GET THERE

Foreign travel is costly. Unless you win a scholarship such as the Rotary, Fulbright, or Rhodes, you'll have to come up with the money for your trip yourself.

Here are some low-cost options:

You can take a year off from college to work, then travel. Work hard to save money for the entire first semester and then travel for six months—or as long as your money lasts. You can travel by train with a backpack and stay in inexpensive youth hostels. It's safer, but not essential, to travel with a companion.

Advantages. You can plan for and take your trip without any outside interruptions. You can fully immerse yourself in travel: six months is a good chunk of time in which to see several different countries or to concentrate on only one.

Disadvantages. You'll be one year behind your classmates in school. However, this is actually an advantage, because you'll graduate with one more full year of experience over other applicants. Don't let peer pressure stop you.

Work in London or Paris as an au pair or nanny, taking care of children in the homes of affluent families. In exchange for your services, which also may involve light housework, you receive free room and board and sometimes a small salary.

Advantages. This is a cheap way to learn about other cultures. It affords far more experience than, say, living in a college dorm. Usually you have weekends free to explore the city and surrounding countryside.

Disadvantages. Frequently you do not have the time to venture beyond your central city unless you are traveling with the family. The job itself can be quite demanding.

After you graduate from college, you can become a Peace Corps volunteer. This requires a two-year commitment in one of sixty developing nations, working in such areas as nutrition, agriculture, education, or hygiene. Contact your local Peace Corps office for more information or call 1-800-424-8580. If two years abroad is too long for you, shorter assignments are also available. The Young Men's Christian Association (YMCA) and Amigo de las Americas offer summer volunteer programs that might better meet your objectives.

Advantages: If you don't know a foreign language, the Peace Corps will teach you. You would work with a team of other volunteers in small towns and villages. You would learn a great deal about developing countries and the people who live there. This is probably one of the most eye-opening experiences you can have abroad. Its rewards are not in dollars, but in experience. Also, being a Peace Corps volunteer tells potential employers that you are both tenacious and hard-working.

Disadvantages. Peace Corps assignments are typically rigorous, and a two-year commitment is a significant amount of time. So consider the costs before you make the commitment.

You can contact the Council on International Educational Exchange (CIEE).
The Council on International Educational Exchange is a nonprofit
member organization of nearly two hundred universities, colleges, and
youth service agencies. It runs service projects in Denmark, Poland,
Portugal, Canada, Turkey, Spain, and other countries. These two-to-
four-week programs involve voluntary community service—such as
renovation of historical sites, forestry, or social work—in exchange for
room and board. There are also long-term service projects, including
semester-long programs on Israeli kibbutzim—a collective farm.

Advantages. There's no better way to learn about yourself
than through helping others—the personal satisfaction and confidence gained through volunteer work is more than worth your
time and effort.

Disadvantages. Again, unless you choose to volunteer during
the summer, you'll lose out on time in school. Your time will probably be very structured on these trips, too. Also, conditions can often
be quite rustic.

You can study abroad—for a summer, a semester, or a full year. Nearly all
colleges sponsor programs abroad for credit, and most of these programs are open to students from other schools. In addition to joining
a program sponsored by an American university, you can enroll
directly in a foreign university in a program designed for foreign students. There are programs in virtually every country—if you really
want to study in Finland or Bora Bora, or both, you probably can.

Almost every college campus features summer- and semester-
abroad programs for credit. Check with your foreign language, art
history, or humanities departments for details, or perhaps your
school has a separate study abroad office.

Advantages. This is a great way to learn the language and the
culture while earning college credit. Living with a family abroad
can be one of the most delightful ways to experience a country in
depth. Also, you can usually apply for financial aid.

Disadvantages. Cost. Often these programs are very expensive,
including airfare and spending money as well as tuition, room and
board. Fortunately, most colleges encourage students to apply their
financial aid packages toward study abroad. Another disadvantage
is that the host family the placement service thought was just right
for you may turn out to be less than all you'd hoped for. This is rare,
however; most programs thoroughly screen the families to ensure
that they provide a nice home, good food, and a pleasant atmosphere
for their guests.

You can contact Semester at Sea. This program offers students college credit while they travel by ship to several designated countries. Check your study-abroad office for details.

Advantages. Students are able to see many different countries by ship, a thrilling means of travel by anybody's standard. You can also earn up to sixteen units of college credit.

Disadvantages. This is an extremely costly program. Since you are on a ship most of your time, you won't put down roots in a particular country. Also, instead of traveling by yourself, you are intended to stay in a group.

You can enlist in the armed services. You're trained in a marketable skill, and you get to travel around the world. Other armed services besides the Army have ROTC programs; consult your local recruiter or on-campus ROTC office.

Advantages. When you get out, you'll be able to continue your education with a healthy subsidy from Uncle Sam, or enter the job market, whichever you prefer. You might also want to consider ROTC. With this program, your undergraduate tuition at a host institution is partially paid for (usually the program pays 80 percent), and you have the advantage of not worrying about what you're going to be doing once you graduate.

Disadvantages. You have little choice in where you want to be stationed, and the time commitment is relatively lengthy—usually three to four years.

You can apply for a travel scholarship. You just might qualify for a grant or scholarship to study abroad. It is relatively easy to get scholarship money for study in non-Western countries. For example, Max Ward, a senior in Asian studies, spent a semester studying in China. His trip to China was funded by the University of Texas and the Institute of Asian Studies in Chicago.

Advantages. According to Max Ward, his experience "provided a chance for me to see a completely different way of life from my own." It moved him so much that he planned to go back to China after graduation to work. He is now working part-time for a legal aid service, where he has had the opportunity to work with Chinese businesspeople.

Disadvantages. Depending on your school, competition for travel scholarships can be fierce. Your knowledge of a foreign language, however, narrows the competition for scholarships. In the spring of her first year at Columbia's School of International Affairs,

Elizabeth Thompson decided she wanted to go to Egypt to brush up on her Arabic. (She had learned some Arabic while abroad in the past.) Elizabeth, a native of Detroit, who attended both Harvard as an undergraduate and Columbia's graduate school on full scholarship, could not afford to go on her own. When she asked an academic adviser if there were any scholarships that would send her to Egypt, he pulled an application for a grant out of the drawer. "In Middle Eastern Affairs departments," he explained, "there are sometimes more grants than students." Elizabeth spent that summer in Egypt. Since then she has taught in Syria for a year and has been admitted to Ph.D. programs in Middle Eastern studies, both at Columbia and Berkeley.

Additional Search Strategies

Here are some other sources of information about traveling abroad:

1. **The Internet and the World Wide Web.** Get online and click on a search engine; then type in the words "study abroad" or "foreign travel" and see what you can find. If you know which country you want to visit, type in that country's name; many countries have websites. Also check out chat rooms and bulletin boards where you can get tips from other travelers.

2. **Travel agencies.** Look in the yellow pages under "Travel Agencies," then call and ask about student programs. Travel agencies also have information on which U.S. cities sponsor international events. They often offer package deals that can make travel a bargain. Your on-campus travel agency is a great place to shop for bargains. Students are often eligible for travel discounts for airlines and hotels. Agencies may also offer reduced rates on airfares, tours, and other travel items. You can also get an International Student Card, which allows you to visit museums and other attractions worldwide at reduced rates.

3. **International education offices.** Many campuses also have an international education office set up to help you. They have information on programs in places as diverse as the Orient, South America, and Russia. Vince Perez, for instance, had always been interested in international relations. As a sophomore, he applied for a job with AIESEC, an international student-run foundation for students interested in economics and management, through the international education office

on his campus. Although Vince was from the Philippines, he got a paid job—$1,000 a month—in New Jersey with an American firm. Through an exchange program with Rider College, AIESEC arranged for Vince to live with an American family. Vince enjoyed the program so much that he became president of the AIESEC for the Philippines. He attended seminars in Australia, Singapore, Belgium, and Washington, DC. Vince's sister joined the same organization and landed a job in Denmark, where she now lives and works. "AIESEC was my big breakthrough," says Vince, who is now director of an international trading firm, Lazard Freres and Company in London.

travel essentials

Check with your doctor to determine whether you will need to be immunized before leaving the United States. Some immunizations must be completed weeks before you leave, so plan ahead.

For any type of foreign travel, you'll need a passport. These are available from courts and post offices throughout the country, as well as from designated passport agencies in most major cities. You'll also need a visa for travel to some countries. For visa information, you can contact the country's embassy or write to the Office of Passport Services in Washington, DC, for visa requirements.

it's never too late

If you can't afford the time or cost of travel during college, don't worry. Cathy Stanley and Kim Corley waited until they graduated before they went abroad. For two months they traveled carrying backpacks and Eurail passes. They explored England, Spain, Germany, Switzerland, Italy, and Greece. When they returned, Cathy began her job as a sales representative in the sales division of Procter & Gamble and Kim began her career with IBM.

Howard Sklar graduated from University of California, Los Angeles with a degree in French history, but he didn't think his education was complete. "I had spent four years cramming my head full of names, dates, literature, and facts—but to tell you the truth, I hadn't the slightest idea of what French culture is in real life. I'd never seen it. I'd never lived it." Howard decided to experience French culture firsthand from the seat of his bicycle. For three

Stephen Hosea, *business finance student*

Many things influenced who Stephen Hosea is today, namely his grandparent's legacy. Both of Stephen's grandparents were Colorado natives. His grandmother was one of the first African-American women to attend University of Denver, and his grandfather was a member of the first African-American military air personnel, the Tuskegee Airmen. After President Harry S. Truman racially integrated the armed forces and formed the U.S. Air Force, his grandfather continued a thirty-year career as a pioneer Black Aviator. He received numerous commendations and was a member of the elite Tactical Air Command and the Strategic Air Command. After retiring from the Air Force as a Lt. Colonel, Stephen's grandfather became the first African-American pilot for the Department of Treasury Customs Department. His grandmother also experienced many life-long accomplishments, including achieving a bachelor's degree from The University of Redlands in California. Currently, she is an amazing jazz pianist and continues to entertain family and friends.

Having such accomplished grandparents contributed to Stephen's determination and perseverance. His grandfather died when Stephen was a teen. On March 29, 2007 the Tuskegee Airmen and their widows were collectively awarded the Congressional Gold Medal. Stephen's grandmother bought one for each of the grandchildren, and Stephen's medal sits on his desk at school. It is an inspiration. "I look at it and think about my grandfather's incredible contribution to society," Stephen says.

Another life-shaping experience was Stephen's involvement with LifeBound. "I was a sophomore in high school. I was in accelerated classes, but was not performing well and was very frustrated," he said. "Through peer meetings, and group discussions with other high school students enrolled in LifeBound, I was able to sort out many of the challenges that seemed to be stalling my academic progress. I had goals I wanted to achieve, but somehow I knew I was not on the right path."

At LifeBound, Stephen decided to transfer high schools. "I became more organized and focused and started to truly enjoy my total high school experience—the academics, high school social life, and community involvement. When I was accepted at the private Marymount College in Rancho Palos Verdes, California, I knew all the hard work had paid off—and I was living up to my potential and aspirations," Stephen said.

"The internship prepared me for my next job as an admissions worker at Marymount College," Stephen said. "I graduated and obtained my associate's degree and was accepted into Loyola Marymount University in Los Angeles where I am currently enrolled as a business-finance major." He also studied abroad in England. As Stephen looked toward law school, he said he appreciates the experiences and people who helped him build his work ethic and succeed.

weeks he took in the French countryside as he pedaled his way from Paris to Pouilly. Near the end of his trip, he finally realized what fascinated him about France. It wasn't the language, the history, or the great works of art and literature. Instead, to his surprise, Howard found the heart and soul of France in its wine. Today Howard works as a wine importer in California.

Rich Matteson didn't travel during college either. Instead, he worked for one year as a restaurant manager after graduation before joining Up With People, a performance organization dedicated to promoting international understanding. After traveling to Belgium, Denmark, and Finland, Rich decided to become a full-time staff member with Up With People. He travels all over the world and stays with host families while organizing tours and performing with the cast. So don't be discouraged if you can't see the world right now. An opportunity to travel may open sometime in the near future. If it does, be sure to go for it.

travel opportunities in the United States

Although our focus up to this point has been on foreign travel, travel doesn't have to be international to be valuable. After her sophomore year at Brown University in Rhode Island, Melissa Halverstadt spent twelve months hiking, kayaking, and mountain climbing in a wilderness education program offered through Prescott College in Arizona. She learned the survival skills of leadership, cooperation, conservation, and planning.

So if you can't venture outside of the United States, yet you want to experience the world, never fear. There are ample activities and programs you can join right on your own campus and in your community that will "bring the world to you."

WHERE TO GET THE FACTS

On Campus

1. **Contact the International Students' Organization.** Almost every campus has an ISO group where students from around the world join Americans in an exchange of culture, ideas, and good times (often centered upon delectable cuisine). If there is no such organization on your campus, begin one yourself. Each week, someone from a different country gives a speech or

slide presentation, followed by refreshments and the opportunity to meet everyone. Also, there are dinners or banquets where a group of people will provide the regional cuisine, and perhaps demonstrate a traditional art or form of dress.

2. **Visit the campus residence for international students.** You could apply for a job as a clerk at the desk or as a food server. Or drop by sometime when you can introduce yourself to several students. Give them your phone number and tell them you would like to get together for lunch or dinner. Remember, they want to learn just as much about America as you want to learn about their culture.

3. **Volunteer to be an English tutor.** This is a great way to learn intimately about the culture of a foreign country through fellow students who will become your friends. Also, you can derive a lot of personal satisfaction from knowing that you are helping to open your culture and country up to someone else.

In the Community

1. **Work in an ethnic restaurant or in a business run entirely by people from another country.** Expose yourself to a different set of customs and values. Ask questions about their home country. How is it different from the United States? How do they perceive Americans? What have they learned from Americans? What has been the biggest cultural barrier?

2. **Read the newspapers to find out about cultural events.** Frequently there are specific cultural festivals that feature music, dance, and foods from foreign lands. If you have time, get involved in a steering committee to plan such an event. Chances are you'll meet fascinating people from the community who will keep you posted on similar events.

3. **Contact AmeriCorps.** AmeriCorps is like the Peace Corps, except that the assignments take place here in the United States. You work for little or no pay in places like American Indian reservations, inner cities, or remote rural communities. Like the Peace Corps, AmeriCorps involves hard work and commitment.

REAL WORK

IN THE REAL WORLD

Dr. Seyi Oyesola, *physician, inventor, entrepreneur*

We are all too familiar with the ravaging death toll of diseases deemed incurable today, like AIDS. What is equally tragic are the number of fatalities from common, survivable illnesses and injuries such as burns, trauma and heart attacks.

Dr. Seyi Oyesola is a Nigerian physician, inventor and advocate for bringing healthcare to remote places of the world. Oyesola went to high school in Cleveland, Ohio, and then returned to the Delta state of Nigeria with his family. Although he earned his medical degree while working in Nigeria, he realized as an intern that his pay would not afford him much.

Consequently, he left Nigeria. He realized that he was not alone. Others receiving their medical training in Nigeria left to pursue greener pastures. This was not Oyesola's vision for his homeland, so he began focusing on a solution.

The result was his invention, CompactOR, otherwise known as "Hospital in a Box." The system is light enough to be dropped from a helicopter, and can be powered by solar panels. It includes anesthetic, surgical equipment and hope for those who otherwise would not have access to medical care. Oyesola realizes that sufficient facilities and pay will encourage medical professionals to remain in Nigeria, but for now, his CompactOR will be a lifesaver to many.

Sources: Zuckerman, Ethan. "Focusing on the Solutions, Not the Problems: Medical Tech off the Grid in Africa." My Heart's in Accra. 6 June 2007. <http://ethanzuckerman.com/blog/2007/ 06/06/focusingon-the-solutions-not-the-problemsmedical-tech-off-the-grid-in-africa/>.

other horizons

There are many ways to appreciate and enrich your travel experience before, during, and after your trip. Brushing up on the language, reading about the history of the country, and learning about the people before you go can make you feel more at home right from the start.

Let's say you've chosen to visit France. Before your trip, you may want to listen to some French-language lessons on your MP3 player and practice the most commonly used phrases. (It helps if you've studied the language in school, but it's not essential.) What are other considerations?

1. **Art.** Every region of the world has its own unique art forms. You may want to research the region you intend to visit.

2. **Literature.** Read works by native authors as an entertaining way to learn about the country you are visiting.

3. **History.** Invest in a paperback on the country's history so that the sights you see will have greater significance for you.

4. **Music.** Listen to local radio stations during your trip. This will help you understand the language and expose you to the country's music.

5. **Philosophy.** Who were the philosophers that influenced cultural development? How has their thinking affected everyday life?

6. **Politics and Economics.** Think about the way the country is governed. How does it differ from the United States? What are the pluses and minuses? What is the economic system?

7. **Business.** What is the local commerce? What are the major industries? Is the country rich in natural resources, human resources, agriculture, or technological advances? What American companies thrive in the country?

No matter where you plan to go, from Peru to Japan, getting a sense of the country beforehand will help you feel better upon arrival. You can learn and adapt on the road by carrying a guidebook as a useful reference and road map.

This is only a partial list. Don't stop here! For more ideas, references, and sources, check out Appendix I in the back of this book. Make foreign or domestic travel a goal. Your travel adventure may just be the most important experience of your college years.

CHAPTER TWELVE

The need to be opportunistic, to think on your feet, again underscores the importance of tuning in to people— of hearing not only what they say, but the larger and underlying meaning as well.

MARK MCCORMACK, IN
*WHAT THEY DON'T TEACH YOU
AT HARVARD BUSINESS SCHOOL*

D on't wait for the business connections to come to you," says Chris Salgado, an operations manager at the Morgan Guaranty Trust Co. "You have to talk to as many people as possible, and don't be afraid of asking questions. The more aggressive you are at asking questions, the more information you'll have on which to make a decision." By visiting his school's career services office when he was a sophomore, Chris had the competitive advantage over his classmates who waited till the last minute to investigate career contacts.

Networking involves all the activities that result in contacts. Therefore, at the core of networking is a commitment to develop good relationships. Meeting people; making your career needs known to friends and relatives; keeping in touch and on good terms with

networking

MAPPING OUT YOUR CAREER STRATEGY

past and present classmates, professors, employers, co-workers, relatives, friends, and virtually everyone you know—all are important elements of mapping out an effective career strategy. Learning to network effectively can mean the difference between landing the job and receiving a form letter that reads, "Thank you for your time, but. . . ."

Your career network represents the connections you already have with the people you know, as well as those you want to establish. Therefore, Nancy Forsyth, a business graduate from the University of New Hampshire, advises, "Be gutsy. You can't expect people to help you out if you don't do something for yourself."

Nancy built strong relationships with her professors and the counselors at the career services office. "Your mentors in college have the best connections, and they care about helping you assess what you should do," says Nancy, who became an editor for Boston textbook publisher Allyn & Bacon. "But students must make the initial effort to seek these people out."

Although he had been a highly qualified student, the editor of his college magazine, and voted "Most Likely to Succeed in Journalism," David Herndon found that getting his first good job was not just a matter of talent and hard work. It also involved what he describes as "circumstance and opportunity."

"You've got to be around to get around," says David, a *Newsday* newspaper features editor. After graduating from Columbia Journalism School, David had to spend three years doing odd jobs (including compiling sections for an encyclopedia, which was "like writing high school book reports") before he finally got his break. Ironically, it came from a former fellow student who had landed a job with *SPORT* magazine and asked David to write a few articles. David did, and was then recommended for a job as sports editor at the *Village Voice*. He got the job, and over the next five years, he made up for lost time. At age twenty-nine, he moved from sports editor, to managing editor, to features editor for *Newsday*.

In his award-winning book *The Achievement Factors*, Gene Griessman writes, "Opportunities are usually for the moment, and as they pass by, there is often only a brief moment to grab them." Therefore, keep in mind that contacts are everywhere, in the classroom and out, in the office and out.

the career search

hy not use your career search as a launching pad for networking skills? Basically, for career search purposes, networking means making contact with people who can:

- Tell you about a specific job.
- Put you in touch with someone important at a company that interests you.
- Keep you in mind for a job that will open up in the future.
- Coach you in your career pursuit.
- Provide you with inside information.

- Introduce you to someone who can give you valuable information.
- Hire you.

Why is networking—or making career or business contacts—so important? For one thing, you always need people contacts, whether you're looking for a job or not. Your GPA will not be your best friend. Second, you need people to tell you firsthand how best to make the transition from super college student to super job applicant. Meeting people who can help you in this transition will be more helpful than reading ten books on how to get the job of your dreams.

In fields like finance, connections can be everything. John Carrigan, age thirty, has his own seat on the Chicago Board of Trade. He says his first contact in the field was made through a friend from high school. His three summer internships, and the contacts he made, were a foot in the door for his first post-college job trading futures for Paine Webber and Company.

WHERE TO BEGIN

Networking has, thankfully, never been easier with the social and professional networking sites available online. The easiest way to get connected is to jump online and build some accounts with these social and professional sites. You may have been using Facebook and MySpace as a way to stay connected with friends, but now they can work for you in a whole new way. Once you have your account set up (as easy as establishing a user name and password), you can start searching for connections. You may be surprised to learn that your best friend from kindergarten has been trying to find you all these years. You may also be surprised to find that his mother is director of human resources in your dream company. Make it a priority today to have accounts at MySpace, Facebook, and LinkedIn.

Although this is explored a bit more in Chapter 6, it bears repeating. Always be professional and always be safe. Keep a professional headshot as your photo or one showing you engaging in a hobby. You never get a second chance at a first impression. In addition, never give your Social Security number to anyone asking through these sites. It is fair to say, "With all of the identity theft taking place, I prefer not to take risks." Social Security numbers are only needed by employers for background checks at final decision-making time.

To begin finding possible contacts, first take inventory of your summer internships and part-time jobs. Did the work interest you?

What do you most value from your college classes and activities? What was most enjoyable?

Use these answers as clues to finding the jobs that interest you most. Then talk to people who have those jobs now. This advice should sound familiar, since you've already been "networking" with your professors, friends, and employers since your freshman year.

If possible, ask your networking contacts if you can observe them on the job. You want to get an accurate picture of a typical workday. Would you like to be alone or with people? Would you be closely supervised or independent? What environment would you work in? Would you travel?

George Fraser, author of the networking book *Success Runs in Our Race,* remembers one of his first jobs working in a department store stockroom. "I worked hard and looked constantly for opportunities to be promoted, and in doing so, I learned a basic principle of networking: Start wherever the door of opportunity opens, be it in the mail room or the back room. I see so many young people who want to start in the front office, if not higher. It doesn't work that way. Everything good that happened to me during this period was a result of people telling other people good things about my attitude. I learned the importance of developing good relationships with my co-workers. If you work hard and well with other people, you don't always need to job-hunt. Often, the jobs come hunting for you."

CULTIVATING CONTACTS NOW AND IN THE FUTURE

Much of your success in work will depend on the relationships you have with other people. If you learn early to pick people's brains, to perceive what makes them successful and to incorporate their qualities of success, you will be far ahead of your contemporaries. Know that you have much to learn from your mentors and your role models in business but you have equally as much to learn from all your other work associates.

Networking doesn't mean just making yourself visible to those in the position to give you a promotion, though that is important. It also means cultivating relationships with all the people behind the scenes. These are the people who actually get things done—the receptionist, mail clerk, messenger, office manager, janitor—and whose jobs mostly go unrecognized by the corporate hierarchy. It involves a willingness to learn anything from anyone who works with you, in any capacity.

"You never know where you will run into someone again," says Nancy Wingate. "You may not think much of the reception-ist or the intern or classmate next to you, but they may be sitting across a desk interviewing you down the line. It pays to treat every-one you work with respect and consideration."

Robert Girardot, a chemical engineer at CSX Corporation, agrees. "You never know who's going to be your boss one day," he says. He remembers when an unpopular guy became the boss. "I'm not saying you should be phony...but do not participate in office gos-sip. Be a booster. If you don't have something good to say about a co-worker, boss, or company, don't say anything." Do you remember the Golden Rule you learned way back in kindergarten? Well, it still applies, even in your professional life. Not only is following the Gold-en Rule the right thing to do, your career will also function better in the long run. Therefore, maintain high ethical standards, consistently.

Business Week columnist Paul Nadler says he always sends postcards to the office's photocopying personnel. He depends heav-ily on quick and efficient photocopies, especially at deadline time.

Building relationships with all different kinds of people will help you if you ever want to be in management. As a manager, you are a leader, organizing and inspiring and working with others to achieve professional and personal goals. How do you learn the principles of good management?

"Not by reading about great leaders whose experience is so foreign it makes it impossible to identify with them," observes Andrew S. Grove, former CEO of Intel Corpo-ration, in a *Fortune* magazine article. Grove does not endorse wilderness excursions, climbing down poles, or whitewater rafting as the secret to management suc-cess. According to Grove, good leadership and good management are learned, "the same way each of us has learned the important, unteachable roles in our lives, be they that of husband or wife, father or mother: by studying the behavior of people who have made a success of it and modeling ourselves after them."

Networking means learning from others. It also means being a teacher to others when you have the knowledge, experience, and expertise to give someone else guidance.

To illustrate this point further, let's take theoretical job-seekers "John" and "Elizabeth". John and Elizabeth were hired right out of journalism school by a major weekly periodical with an emphasis on financial news. Each held entry-level editorial positions. John was eager to learn, inquisitive, and helpful to co-workers in his training seminar. When Ann, a new co-worker, was having a hard time figuring out the computer system, John took the time to sit down and help her figure it out. He wasn't much more experienced with it than she was but he figured he'd learn by helping. When they couldn't resolve a glitch, John was the one who went to the seminar instructor and asked for help. Not only was the instructor happy to help John and Ann figure out the problem, he also became interested in the sample article they were working on. And he was impressed with John's editorial eye. This gave John the opportunity to get to know a senior editor in an informal situation, sincerely and without any grandstanding.

Elizabeth used a different approach. During the instructor's seminar, she constantly interrupted the other trainees, interjecting her opinion based on her vast experience working at her father's newspaper in a midsized, Midwestern city. Once, when Ann asked Elizabeth to share her experience about working for her father's newspaper, Elizabeth refused. Instead, she looked briefly at Ann with a bored expression and said that she'd love to if she had the time, but right now she was "consumed" with a special feature proposal for the magazine.

At promotion time, Elizabeth was still laboring on her uncommissioned special feature while John was promoted to assistant managing editor, with responsibility for developing a financial news column for college graduates. The senior editors believed John would be a better long-term choice because he was a superior teacher, listener, communicator, and motivator. In short, John was a role model. Elizabeth's poor attitude closed the doors of opportunity.

HOW HAVE YOU NETWORKED?

Have you networked during your summer internship or part-time job? Even if you have only waited on tables, think of how your success depended on your co-workers. Seriously.

An excellent waiter who is liked and respected by his co-workers is far more effective—and therefore more profitable—than the average waiter. Why? Because if the host or hostess likes him, he'll get his tables turned (cleared off and set) faster than the others. If the cook likes him, he'll get occasional special orders for his "preferred" customers. If the manager realizes how valuable his work and his good disposition are, he or she will make special arrangements (to accommodate his school schedule, for instance) just to keep him. Finally, the customer stands a greater chance of being pleased with the service. Therefore, this waiter will probably get a better tip—one of his goals in the first place.

Good human relations will help you in any job. Although some people have a natural knack for dealing with people, others have a hard time. If you are in the latter category, take heart. There are resources that can help you understand how you can better relate to people and how you can help other people feel comfortable relating to you. The classic self-help book on this subject is *How to Win Friends and Influence People* by Dale Carnegie. In it he outlines six basic principles for successful interaction. (There's so much common sense here it's easy to take this formula for granted. Don't.)

1. Become genuinely interested in other people.
2. Smile.
3. Remember that a person's name is to that person the sweetest and most important sound in any language.
4. Be a good listener. Encourage others to talk about themselves.
5. Talk in terms of other people's interests, not your own.
6. Make the other person feel important, and do it sincerely.

Networking is a relatively new word for, among other things, effective human relations. Wholesome, old-fashioned characteristics like good manners, sincerity, a positive attitude, and a generous spirit never go out of style. Together they formulate the essence of a winning career strategy.

finding a mentor

I f you haven't already, find yourself a mentor. In short, a mentor is a teacher, a coach, a guide, a guru—somebody you have a rapport with and a respect for in your chosen career field. A mentor is less a model and more of a teacher.

So how will you meet your mentor? Will he or she appear to you magically? Probably not. You must take the initiative. Seeking out a mentor will help you to define yourself and your chosen career path, so choose carefully. Asking yourself two smart questions will help you get started on your quest:

1. Which professors most inspire you? Talk to them after class. Ask them for special assignments.

2. Whom do you know that works in your field of interest? Perhaps your mentor will be a manager at an office where you get a part-time job or a summer internship. Set up an appointment to talk with that person about your career goals, and ask him or her for input or suggestions.

To be effective at networking—that is, cultivating good professional relations—you must first examine your own character and personality. Think about those people you most admire (professors, movie stars, politicians, characters from literature, and so on). Think about the people who've had the greatest and most positive influence on you. What distinguishes them from the rest of the herd? Why do they appeal to you? Why do they stand out? Learn how to ask questions of the people you work with who have more experience and more knowledge than you do. Take notes. Watch them in action. Analyze what they do. Study the people who are excelling in their fields; obviously they are doing something right.

One other thing: It's important that your mentor be someone you can get to know. If you want to be a playwright, Shakespeare might be an ideal, but he's dead. Why not cultivate a relationship with the drama professor at your local college?

Thomas Easton, New York bureau chief of the *Baltimore Sun*, found his career shaped dramatically by a mentor. In college he was reluctant to specialize in any one area. He was interested in everything from film to history to political science. When he graduated, he had a vague idea that his broad range of interests might make him suitable for journalism, but he wasn't sure.

Then, during a job interview for a chain of weekly newspapers in Connecticut, he met editor John Peterson, who had won awards as an investigative reporter. The two hit it off right away. Peterson's great curiosity and energy matched Easton's. "I asked him once if he wanted me to go out for coffee," Easton says, laughing. "And he said, 'No, I didn't hire you to get coffee. I hired you to get stories. Get out there.'"

Because of his mentor, Easton made an extraordinary career jump. After two years on the weekly, he worked for a daily for six months, went to business school, and ended up on one of the best papers in the country. Easton says the *Sun* weighed two things heavily: his business degree and a stellar recommendation from Peterson.

THE MENTOR DYNAMIC

Within your career-strategy network, there will be people whom you admire more than others because of the quality of their work. Mentoring relationships naturally tend to form around your shared interest or passion within a particular field. Therefore, your boss might be a potential mentor, but it could just as easily be someone in a different department with whom you've worked on a specific project. Many fields and industries even require a mentoring relationship. In these situations, senior members are matched with newcomers for the purpose of advancing the work.

If someone takes a special interest in you because you have been an apprentice—taking on extra assignments, staying late to help on a special project, and so on—he or she is more likely to give you advice that is not commonly available to others at your level. For instance, you may learn how to best prepare yourself for a promotion. Or you may receive detailed advice on how to do your present job more efficiently. Therefore, seek out ways you can work with or for the people you want to model your professional life after. Then learn as much as you can from them.

I also recommend that you look to a number of different people for guidance, not just one person. The world has become so specialized that a single individual cannot possibly keep up with all there is to know in a given field. For example, at last count, there were at least three different types of eye surgeons, who operate on three different areas of the human eye. Therefore, plan to draw information and support from several people, according to their area of expertise.

Athena Dodd, *clinical research associate*

After earning a Bachelor of Arts degree in biology from Reed College in Portland, Oregon, Athena Dodd thought she was on the path to earning a doctorate and becoming a biologist. As a start on this career, she worked in a biology lab at the University of Colorado at Boulder. After three years, Athena realized that she needed something more fast-paced and with real-world application. She decided to look around for an alternative to graduate school.

While attending a women's networking group in Colorado, she met LifeBound president, Carol Carter, who offered her an internship. Athena began spending one day a week helping to revise an edition of this very book. She researched and interviewed people with learning disabilities, wrote chapter sidebars, suggested graphics, and summarized reviewer comments.

This was a major change from her science background, but the experience affirmed her interest in editorial work and design, persuading her to value practical experience. It also gave her the chance to create a portfolio of work that showcased her skills and helped her land a position in a market research firm editing and designing reports.

Athena continued to reevaluate her interests and evolve in her career, but she still applies many of the skills she first learned during her internship at LifeBound in her work as a clinical research associate at a Colorado biotech company. She became part of a team that managed clinical trials for a new blood pressure drug, and her work involved constant communication with team members and vendors, as well as tracking and summarizing new information to meet strict deadlines..

She developed a strong sense of the importance of ongoing learning, applied flexibility, and the ability to multi-task. Working in the fast-paced, team-oriented environment of her internship—while reading the book she was helping to update—prepared her to effectively communicate and to meet deadlines. The experience gave her a set of universally applicable skills and confidence.

In order to actually learn from other people, you must demonstrate an inquiring mind. Ask questions, and be willing to disclose what you do not know. Be open to feedback. Ditch any attitude of arrogance; it won't get you anywhere. I'm not saying that you shouldn't be confident—you have to believe in yourself—but have the wisdom to know what you can learn from others.

What does a successful mentor–protégé relationship look like in the working world? The answer: a two-way street. Harvard Business School graduate Linda Hill, the author of *Becoming a Manager: Mastery of a New Identity*, writes that good mentoring relationships are always mutually beneficial. "The mentor offers advice and opportunity; the protégé delivers results," explains Hill. In other words, the mentor's input yields fruit. You are improving, or you are growing in your understanding of a concept, as a direct result of the mentor's influence in your professional life. This tangible evidence of personal growth and development is gratifying not only to you, but to your mentor as well.

who are my contact people?

hroughout college, you've pushed yourself to branch out, experience things, meet people, and ask questions. Beginning with your junior year, narrow your focus to the career you think you want to pursue.

Here are some good people to contact:

1. Company representatives who have registered with your career services office
2. Company recruiters listed in the publication *Job Choices* (this is revised and updated yearly)
3. Members of your school's alumni association who are in fields you want to pursue
4. Professionals in your hometown
5. Professors at your university
6. Your parents' friends; your siblings or their friends
7. Authors of books you've read in your field of interest
8. People who have given speeches in your career area

Of course, this is only a partial listing, but it should at least get you started. Keep a checklist of important people you want to meet in order to gather information. Try to meet and speak with one key person a week during your junior and senior years. Keep notes on your conversations so that you can analyze the advice you're given.

GETTING CONNECTED

Networking, for the purpose of mapping out a career strategy, entails six simple yet critical steps. First, you will need to make contact with people who already work in your field of interest. So make a list of anyone and everyone who is even remotely related to your selected career or job. If you can't think of at least five people to contact, you're not thinking hard enough.

Second, create a list of questions to ask the contact person. The goal of the questioning process is to determine whether the career path you are on is truly the right one for you. Here are a few questions to get you started:

1. What are the pros and cons of working in the industry?
2. Of working in that company?
3. Of the company's philosophy?
4. What does and doesn't appeal to the company?
5. What has he or she enjoyed the most? disliked the most?

Remember, finding the answers to these questions will help you assess whether the field and the job are right for you.

Third, with each contact you make, take notes on the responses you get to your questions. Some contacts may even offer to call potential employers on your behalf. Be sure to ask each contact person with whom else you can speak in order to gather more information.

Fourth, while you have the contact on the phone, make the most of the opportunity. For instance, if the conversation went well, you could plan to ask permission to use the contact as a future reference. Be prepared to hear "no," and try not to take it personally. The individual may not feel familiar enough with you to give an honest reference.

The previous step leads to the fifth one: prepare yourself for unexpected outcomes. For example, your contact person may invite you for an interview, so have a calendar nearby so that you can set a date. You may also catch the contact person at a bad time. If this happens, ask if there is a better time to call.

Finally, regardless of what happens, always thank the contact person for his or her time. Then follow up with a brief note of appreciation.

REAL WORK

IN THE REAL WORLD

Carol Carter, *LifeBound president and founder*

arol Carter is the woman behind the LifeBound enterprise and says her natural love of socializing has been vital to the growth of her professional story. "When I was a little kid and my parents would take me to restaurants, I would talk to the people at the tables near us and ask what they were ordering," said Carter.

Talking to strangers, even asking for directions on the street, can turn into a networking connection. Carter began extending her network of contact simply by asking friends of her brother if they knew anyone who might be able to get her a job. Many of the people featured in the profiles and biographies in these pages are real stories from Carter's own contacts and the leads they gave her to new contacts.

This book is not the only proof of the fruits of networking. Carter's impressive career has been built on a foundation of strong networking skills. Throughout her professional life, Carter has been committed to helping all kinds of students turn on their brains, discover their motivations, and tap into their abilities. Her first book, *Majoring in the Rest of your Life,* launched her writing career and gave her the foundation for the *Keys to Success* series, which has been read by more than a million students. Carter was the vice president of a major corporation, as well as the founder of a non-profit career mentoring program, of which she is still an active board member. Additionally, she is president of her own company, LifeBound, which helps students become competitive and confident enough to take on today's global world. She also trains and certifies educators in academic coaching skills.

Her passion for working with at-risk students is evidenced by her volunteer teaching at federal prison facilities and her LifeBound work teaching in the Denver housing projects. Aided by speaking Spanish fluently, Carter has visited more than forty countries worldwide and feels her brain is stretched by meeting people from different cultures and networking with people around the world. "The greatest business opportunities have come to me from asking questions of people and being curious," said Carter. "I look for excuses to talk to people."

For more information about Carter, please visit www.lifebound.com, email Carter at Caroljcarter@lifebound.com, or call her LifeBound office toll free at 877.737.8510.

ACCESSING KEY PEOPLE

Within every company or industry, there are key people. These key people are given job titles such as chief executive officer, executive director, president, or dean. Although the titles may vary, the power usually doesn't. These are the decision-makers of that institution, so they are the ones you must gain access to.

Making contact with them, however, can be tricky. To contact the key person, you must first make a good impression on the person in the other power seat: the administrative assistant. Treat the assistant with as much respect—or more—as the other people you intend to contact. Tell him or her why you would like to see the key person. Explain why you are interested in the company, and talk about your experiences and abilities. Also, ask for information on the company so that you can study it before your meeting with the key person.

The administrative assistant is the eyes and ears for the person you need to speak with. He or she is skilled at knowing exactly what his or her boss values and looks for, so this individual is the first in the chain of people to win over.

If the administrative assistant does not grant you an appointment with the executive director, be gracious. Thank the person for taking the time to talk with you. Later, send follow-up letters to the administrative assistant as well as to the key person, restating your interest. Often the initial "no" is a smokescreen. Your diplomatic, consistent follow-up may secure the appointment, so don't give up.

FACE-TO-FACE WITH KEY PEOPLE

Mapping out a career strategy eventually translates into meeting the administrative assistant and other key people for the first time. Although one of your objectives for this initial encounter is to research the company or industry, your primary goal is to make a favorable impression on the people you meet. Doing so may lead to future employment at that establishment, or at the very least open the door to some great contacts. That's why some people refer to this stage of career strategy as "getting your foot in the door."

When meeting someone for the first time, you will want to present a professional, courteous, and direct demeanor. Right at the start, you should clearly state your interests and your reasons for wanting to interview this person. This is especially crucial with a professional you've never met. Be poised and well-dressed, and don't smoke before the meeting. You'll probably have only two to three minutes to set up the appointment, so be prepared for the opportunity. Consider the sample dialogues below.

FIRST INTERVIEW

You: Hello, Ms. Marshall. Thank you for taking time to see me today.

Key Person: My pleasure. What can I do for you?

You: As your assistant probably told you, I'm one year away from graduating from State A&M with a degree in architectural design. Since your firm has designed some of the most outstanding buildings in this state, I wanted to express my interest in working with you someday. I wondered, specifically, if I might be able to set up a luncheon appointment with you or one of your junior associates so that I could learn firsthand about the qualities you seek in graduates you hire as first-year associates.

KP: I admire your foresight. Unfortunately, I'm swamped right now and would not be able to take two hours to meet with you. However, there is one exemplary employee who has worked with us for two years and who graduated from your school. His name is Jordan Simon, and he may be available to give you some advice.

You: I would appreciate speaking with him. Thank you very much for your time. I hope we are able to see each other in the next year.

KP: You're welcome. My assistant will be happy to give you Jordan's phone number. He manages our other office. Tell him I sent you. Good luck.

PHONE CONTACT WITH JORDAN SIMON

You: Mr. Simon, I am a junior at State A&M and will graduate next year with a degree in architectural design. Cynthia Marshall recommended that I speak with you about how I might best prepare to work for your firm someday. May I take you to lunch sometime next week so we can talk further?

JS: I exercise at lunch every day, but I'd be happy to meet you for breakfast if you tell me why it would be worth my time.

You: Gladly. I have a 3.6 GPA and two summers of experience working for your competitors. I am a hard worker and a team player, and I have a very creative mind. I'd like to speak with you in person and pick your brains and find out how you think, plan, and organize your time.

JS: (Interrupting) That's a good start. Where and when would you like to get together?

Before the actual appointment, make a list of good questions to ask. You shouldn't be doing all the talking. Instead, you should be listening and asking what else you can do to prepare for success. Be confident, not cocky. You may end up with an apprenticeship that could get you in the door come graduation.

narrowing your choices

Once you've completed several phone contacts and meetings, you'll have entered the narrowing phase of your career pursuit. On the basis of all the information you've gathered over the years, narrow your choices down to a few career domains. For example, if you have strong people skills and want to be in management, sales may be the place to start. If you're strength lies in information skills, you may want to begin in an entry-level position in market research. If you're strong in the area of objects, you may want to begin as an apprentice with a craftsperson or a professional in your technical area of interest.

Once you've narrowed down your career search to a few companies in your chosen industry, make a list of employees you'd like to meet with. You may not be able to talk to all of them, but consider those whose advice may have the greatest impact. Make every effort to contact these names first.

To maximize the utility of this list, consider these questions:

- Who do you think is the happiest in his or her job?
- Why?
- Is it the company, or is it that person's approach to the job— or maybe a combination of both?

Questioning as many people as possible, in a very diplomatic way, will give you volumes of information with which to make a good decision.

There you have it! Networking involves far more than just meeting people and gathering information for yourself—it's a two-way street. Sure, you will gain a lot from others, but not unless you're prepared to give something back. If you can't help someone directly, at least thank them sincerely. And when you're in the position to, you'll help others less experienced, too. Take pleasure in knowing that you're being a mentor or role model to them, just as others have been to you.

network map: chart it out!

Sylvia Robinson	Charles Dean
Alumna; VP, Interstate	Bank President, Hometown Bank
Mary Rolatta	Al Ruben
Ex-employee	VP, Finance
John Sloan	Mark Cortez
Now has own business	Financial Planner, Merrill Lynch
Anne Gibb	
Teller	

CAREER NETWORK MAP

Field:

Job:

Contact people:

1. Entry-level   3. Former employees

  a.   a.

  b.   b.

  c.   c.

2. Upper-level   4. Alumni who are now in the field

  a.   a

  b.   b.

  c.   c.

Impressions of the industry:

Pros   Cons

CHAPTER THIRTEEN

*Your biggest opportunity probably lies
under your own feet, in your current job,
industry, education, experience, or interests.*

BRIAN TRACY

*Every job is a self-portrait of the person who does it.
Autograph your work with excellence.*

UNKNOWN

S ome students are excited about resume writing. They look forward to the challenge of condensing several years of their life onto one sheet of paper. On the other end of the spectrum are those who approach the task as if they were waiting in the dentist's office for a root canal.

How about you? Are you ready to promote yourself on paper? Whatever your degree of anticipation, writing a resume is an absolutely essential component of a successful job search. In this chapter, we will help you craft an effective one as painlessly as possible. We will also assist you with two other aspects of paperwork, namely, the cover letter and the job application.

paperwork that lands the job

RESUMES, COVER LETTERS, AND THE JOB APPLICATION

the job search

A ccording to William Potter, vice president of A Better Resume Service in Chicago, the key to a successful job search is:

1. To know yourself
2. To know your market
3. To know how to market yourself effectively

By now you're well on your way to developing knowledge in two of these areas. From Chapter 2, "Discover Who You Are," you learned more about Potter's first recommendation, to know your-self. In Chapter 3, you tackled Potter's second recommendation, to know your market, by investigating the majors and jobs that inter-est you. Congratulations—you have covered a lot of ground!

Now you're ready to pick up Potter's third job search recom-mendation: marketing yourself, which is where writing the resume comes in. A good resume opens doors to interviews, so to market yourself effectively, you'll need to craft one that emphasizes your unique skills and qualities.

planning your dream resume

Your career direction will be molded in increments. In other words, everything you study and explore now will contribute to the resume you send out during your senior year. Your resume will include the whole shebang—academ-ic achievements, extracurricular activities, and work experience.

When those pieces come together, you'll compile your real, working resume. In the meantime, however, use what you've already studied and achieved to think about your dream resume. This resume will help you organize your thoughts and achieve-ments thus far into an early version of your working resume.

What do you want your resume to look like? Thinking about the answer to this question now will help you achieve the resume of your dreams. Consequently, the resume of your dreams will help you land the job of your dreams. So start planning!

Many students resist writing their resumes for as long as pos-sible. While procrastination is understandable, it won't help you in finding a job. Wait until the second semester of your senior year and you may find yourself distributing political tracts at the local mall for minimum wage. So why tempt fate when it is so easily out-foxed? Start thinking now about how you'd like your resume to look. Can't picture it? I have a suggestion: write it out.

Okay, now you know what you want to accomplish for your future. The first step toward getting there is to focus on the here and now. What does your current resume look like? Do you have a current resume? If not, now is definitely the time to begin thinking about it. Why? Because you want to land that internship, don't you? What about the part-time job? Regardless of the type of position you seek, a resume will always reflect favorably on you. It allows your prospective employer to see what you have accomplished thus far—your experience, skills and abilities, and any special training are there at a glance.

So, how do you compile your current resume? You can begin by taking a look at what you possess that might be attractive to a prospective employer. Don't be afraid to toot your own horn—as long as it's all true and not exaggerated, of course! Completing the sentences below will help you begin to craft the resume of your dreams.

my dream resume

(By the second semester of my senior year)

My grade point average is _____

My major and minor are _____

My career goal is _____

My academic honors include _____

_____

_____

My extracurricular activities include _____

_____

_____

I had a summer internship doing _____

at _____

I traveled to _____

I worked part-time as _____

My references are: _____

1. _____

2. _____

3. _____

my dream resume

My objective is _____

_____

I am currently studying _____

_____

I graduated from high school in _____

_____

Academic recognitions that I received in high school included _____

_____

My past work experience includes _____

_____

I have special training in _____

_____

I am especially good at _____

_____

My other abilities include _____

_____

Classes I have had that are relevant to the position I seek are _____

_____

_____

People who can speak highly of me are: _____

_____

And what they might say is: _____

1. _____

2. _____

3. _____

first impressions

Experts emphasize that your resume gives potential employers their first impression of you. Your resume may be the most important element of your job search because it secures the interview. In addition to making a good first impression, your resume also serves as a springboard for a prospective employer's questions. And later, it's a reminder on file of who you are.

A survey involving the top 100 U.S. companies by Robert Half, author of *How to Get a Better Job in This Crazy World,* revealed the four leading reasons that resumes are disregarded: 36 percent of all resumes contain distortions or lies; 19 percent have spelling errors; 12 percent fail to provide sufficient detail; and 10 percent give irrelevant information. Your career planning and placement center probably offers assistance in eliminating mistakes like these, so be sure to make an appointment with them. For now, here are the basic ingredients of an effective resume, in the order that they should appear:

1. **The heading.** A resume should begin with your name, address, telephone number, and email address (if you have one) so an employer will know how to reach you, should they be interested.

2. **The job objective.** Next on your resume comes the job objective, which should be stated in one sentence. Including a job objective on your resume, however, isn't always necessary, nor is it always the best approach. "By stating a job objective," writes Robert Half, "you potentially rule yourself out of being considered for other jobs in that same company, jobs that do not match precisely with the objective you've stated."

One solution to the job-objective dilemma is to drop the job objective altogether. Another option, however, is to write separate, "specialized" resumes, each prepared with basic honesty but beefing up those qualities you want to accentuate. For example, let's say your education and background has made you suitable for positions in marketing, selling, and advertising. Obviously, any of those areas might provide permanent employment for you, but one resume that attempts to cover all those bases may lack the necessary focus. Therefore, three specialized resumes should be created. One will emphasize the marketing aspect of your experience. The second will focus on your sales background and your accomplishments in selling. The third will have your advertising experience at

INSIGHTS
FROM AN INTERN

Kati Pope, *social work student*

Kati Pope began working as a LifeBound intern during her senior year at the University of Denver. Kati was inspired to work with youth after studying psychology and sociology. "I wanted an internship that allowed me to work closely within the community and help others achieve their goals. LifeBound was the ideal place for me to gain this kind of experience!"

As part of her internship with LifeBound, Kati helped at-risk youth prepare to take the GED. She also conducted LifeBound seminars for students preparing for college. Kati's ability to communicate effectively with diverse populations allowed her to motivate adolescents in a profound way.

Kati's experience as a LifeBound intern motivated her to pursue a career promoting the academic, social and emotional success of others. Kati is currently pursuing a mas-

ter's degree in social work at The George Warren Brown School of Social Work at Washington University in St. Louis. She is studying clinical social work with children, youth and families. She is also specializing in school social work, another pursuit inspired by her internship.

Kati continues to work with youth in the community as she attends graduate school. Specifically, she works for the Child Abuse Prevention Program at Jewish Family and Children's Service in St. Louis. Kati is committed to educating the community about child abuse prevention. Her experience working with diverse populations at LifeBound enabled her to educate children from all over the St. Louis area.

Kati is well on her way to accomplishing her dream of becoming a licensed clinical social worker. She hopes to one day counsel youth and families in a private practice setting.

the forefront. When you're invited for a marketing job interview, you will give the interviewer the version of the resume that highlights that aspect of your education and experience.

Since you can't, however, be all things to all people all of the time, Half recommends that you prepare a general resume so that "the disparate major focuses of your experience are given equal weight."

3. **The body.** The body, which is the largest portion of your resume, consists of four parts: (1) education; (2) job history; (3) activities; and (4) achievements. List these items in reverse chronological order, beginning with the most recent. Include any skills relevant to the type of employment sought, such as the ability to speak a foreign language, or secretarial or computer skills.

the cover letter

To get your resume noticed, you'll need an ace cover letter that accompanies your resume. You might think the best cover letter would contain a curling arrow and a boldface message reading "Resume Below," followed by a full line of exclamation points.

That might not be such a bad idea, but unfortunately this is not the kind of cover letter most employers have come to expect. The cover letter is not the domain of the abstract-expressionist avant-garde existentialist career hunter. Not as of this writing, anyway.

Basically, a cover letter lets you do two things: herald your resume and lock down the interview. By taking your highlights and personalizing them, a good cover letter convinces the reader to pay attention to your resume. Therefore, take just as much care in preparing it as you do your resume. To make your cover letter visually appealing, print it on personalized stationery or at least good quality paper. Then briefly state your most compelling qualifications and request an interview. Also, be sure to mention the reason why you'd like to work for the company.

In short, the goals of your cover letter are:

1. To express interest in the company and a specific position.
2. To engage the reader's interest so he or she is compelled to read your resume.
3. To mention a specific date when you will contact the employer, if he or she doesn't contact you.

Of equal importance, the cover letter provides you with the opportunity to discuss the company to which you're applying. Mention something specifically appealing to you about the prospective employer. This lets the "personal approach" work in two directions—yours and theirs. And it makes things much more interesting.

In respect to cover letters, *Newsday* features editor David Herndon gives another important job search tip: Give the cover letter some zing. Don't dwell on the reasons why it would be a good experience for you to work for the prospective employer; rather, always stay focused on how you can help the company. "Tell [the prospective employer] why it would be a good experience for him to work with you." Then follow up with a phone call two weeks later.

Thank-you notes following interviews are neither necessary nor expected, which is all the more reason why it's so important to send them. They need not be elaborate. Just say thanks.

the job application

Like your other work papers, the job application should be neat and well thought out. If you can, fill out the application at home. But before writing on the actual application, write your responses first on scratch paper. That way you can refine your thoughts before committing them to paper.

On the pages that follow is a fairly comprehensive sample job application. Fill it out for practice. Then look at your responses later and see what you think. Are you crisp and to the point? Are your examples convincing? Would you be interested in interviewing you based on your application?

JOB APPLICATION

Please print in ink. Attach separate sheets if necessary.

Name (*first, middle, last*): _____

Social security no.: _____

Home address *(street, city, state, zip)*: _____

_____ Home phone: _____

How long at present address? _____ Are you in the U.S. on a temporary visa? _____

In emergency, notify *(name/address/phone)*: _____

_____

List any friends or relatives working with the company, by name and relationship.

_____

_____

Have you ever worked for us or one of our subsidiaries?

Have you ever applied for work here before? If so, when?

Do you own or have access to a car?

Has your license ever been suspended or revoked? If so, why?

EDUCATION

Circle the highest grade completed:

High school   1 2 3 4   *Graduate school*   1 2 3 4   *College*   1 2 3 4

Degrees:

Name of high school:

Date entered, location:

Graduation date and grade point average:

Name of college/university:

Date entered, location:

Graduation date and grade point average:

List major and minor fields:

Name of graduate school:

Date entered, location:

Graduation date and grade point average:

List major and minor fields:

Scholastic honors:

Any academic or disciplinary probation? If yes, explain.

List extracurricular or athletic activities:

List part-time jobs:

How did you spend your summer vacations?

Are you proud of your college record? Explain.

WORK EXPERIENCE

MOST RECENT EMPLOYER:

From/through: _____ May we contact? _____

Address: _____

_____ Phone: _____

Current or final supervisor: _____

Starting position and salary: _____

How did you get the job? _____

Why did you leave? _____

What did you like the best about the job? _____

_____

What did you like the least about the job? _____

_____

PREVIOUS EMPLOYER: _____

From/through: _____ May we contact? _____

Address: _____

_____ Phone: _____

Current or final supervisor: _____

Starting position and salary: _____

How did you get the job? _____

Why did you leave? _____

What did you like the best about the job? _____

_____

What did you like the least about the job? _____

_____

PREVIOUS EMPLOYER: _____

From/through: _____ May we contact? _____

Address: _____

_____ Phone: _____

Current or final supervisor: _____

Starting position and salary: _____

How did you get the job? _____

Why did you leave? _____

What did you like the best about the job?

_____

What did you like the least about the job?

_____

Please summarize any relevant experience that uniquely qualifies you for this job.

_____

_____

_____

REFERENCES

List three persons, not relatives or former employers, who have known you for the last five years whom we may contact.

Name _____ Years known _____

Address _____

Name _____ Years known _____

Address _____

Name _____ Years known _____

Address _____

State your own personal definition of this position.

_____

Why do you want this job and why do you think you will be successful?

_____

_____

ACTIVITIES

Excluding religious or political groups, with what organizations do you now work?

_____

What are your principal hobbies?

_____

What magazines do you regularly read?

_____

How many hours do you watch TV per week?

What types of books do you read most often?

_____

Below are some of the reasons why some people want to join our company. Check four that are the most important to you and four that are the least important to you.

Most   Least

Most	Least	
○	○	The chance to be with a growing company.
○	○	The company's liberal pension policies.
○	○	The opportunity to be promoted.
○	○	The opportunity to sell.
○	○	The company's reputation.
○	○	The profit-sharing program.
○	○	Freedom from routine.
○	○	Job security.
○	○	The opportunity to travel.

What do you consider your most important accomplishment? _____

_____

What has been your most serious disappointment? _____

_____

Describe your most competitive situation and the steps you took to achieve success. ____

_____

_____

What do you consider to be your three most important assets? _____

_____

In what three areas would you most like to improve? _____

_____

Are you willing to travel? To relocate? _____

When can you start to work? _____

cover letters and resumes

O n the next few pages are some sample resumes and cover letters. These are designed to give you some ideas about how to format and compile your information. Look closely at the wording and order of ideas presented. Watch how they work together introduce and essentially "sell" the person in question. Effective cover letters and resumes do both of these things covertly while maintaining a crisp, professional surface.

SAMPLE COVER LETTER 1

Melanie McFadden

19 Circle Street (614) 555-1234   •   Columbus, Ohio 43216   •   mmcfadden@earthlink.net

Mr. James Ward   April 10, XXXX
Director of Operations
Database International
5510 Mainway Drive
Los Angeles, CA 90086

Dear Mr. Ward:

I am a senior majoring in computer science and information processing at the University of Florida.

I have followed the success of Database International. You are recognized nationally as a leader in the industry and have a reputation for providing exceptional ongoing training programs for your junior programmers.

Enclosed is my resume outlining my academic, extracurricular, and work experience of the past four years.

If you would like to call me to set up a personal interview, I can be reached at (614) 555-1234. If I don't hear from you by April 29, I'll call you.

Thank you for your consideration. I look forward to hearing from you soon.

Sincerely,

Melanie McFadden

Melanie McFadden

SAMPLE COVER LETTER 2

Sandra Magioco

9 College Road, Baltimore, Maryland 21203   (410) 555-1776

February 5, XXXX
Ms. Margaret Jimenez
XYZ Department Store
9 Financial Street
New York, NY 11351

Dear Ms. Jimenez:

I was recently speaking with Joanne Stewart, a manager with your store. Because she is familiar with my work, she strongly advised me to send a copy of my resume to your office regarding the opening as an assistant buyer in your sportswear department.

I feel confident that after reviewing my resume, you will see that I am a worthy candidate. Besides having a strong background in sales, I have worked closely with buyers for many years. Not only do I have skill in fashion display, customer service, and managing employees, I understand the demands of the retail fashion industry as a whole.

The opportunity to work with you is appealing. I look forward to your response and hope we can meet soon to discuss my resume and work history further. Thank you for your time and consideration.

Sincerely,

Sandra Magioco

Sandra Magioco
s_magioco@yahoo.com

SAMPLE RESUME 1

Jennifer Anderson

4332 Rookwood Street   (216) 555-3452
Cleveland, Ohio 44101   jennanderson@cox.net

JOB OBJECTIVE

Position as programmer with supervisory responsibilities.

EDUCATION

- B.A., University of Florida, XXXX Computer science/information processing major; liberal arts minor. GPA: 3.4.
- Junior semester abroad in Florence, Italy. Studied history, art, music, Renaissance literature, and Italian.
- Rotary scholarship finalist: May XXXX. Alternate for one year of study in Fyfe, Scotland.

WORK EXPERIENCE

- *Anderson, Inc., XXXX to present.*
  Created computer programs using Java for privately owned company in Cleveland.
- *Computer Science Center, University of Florida tutor, XXXX-XXXX.*
  Tutored freshman and sophomore students in math and computer science.
- *Borrans Corporation, Columbus, Ohio summer intern, XXXX-XXXX*
  Programmer and operations trainee, responsible for training new employees and experienced employees in need of additional instruction.

ACTIVITIES/HONORS

- *Vice President, College Democrats: XXXX-XXXX*
  Recruited students to participate in city, state, and local campaigns.
- *Treasurer, Campus Achievers: XXXX–XXXX*
  Honorary student service society.
- *President, Student Union Activities Board, XXXX-XXXX.*
  Coordinated activities from Parents' Day to spring break vacations.

References available upon request.

SAMPLE RESUME 2

George Rappaport

154 West 78th Street, New York, New York 10019 ▪ george_rapp@netstar.com ▪ (212) 555-0030

JOB OBJECTIVE   Entry-level accounting position with medium- to large-sized public accounting firm.

EDUCATION   Bachelor of Science in Accounting with English minor, University of Maryland, XXXX. GPA: 3.6.
- Dean's List, six semesters
- Junior semester in Mexico City, Mexico. Studied Spanish and Mexican heritage while living with a Mexican family.

WORK EXPERIENCE
- *Internal Auditor,* XXXX-XXXX
  HealthCare Insurance Agency, Baltimore, MD.
  Managed nine corporate accounts. Responsible for training and supervising staff of twelve.

- *Summer Intern,* XXXX
  Kenase Accountants.
  Experienced work in a small accounting firm first hand. Managed four of the company's ten largest accounts as well as eighteen long-term clients.

- *Summer Intern,* XXXX
  Business Management Legal Associates.
  Performed legal accounting and tax preparation for partners and associates.

ACTIVITIES
- Volunteer, Big Brother program, XXXX-XXXX
  Coached and served as "big brother" to two under-privileged teenagers.

- President, Blue Key (national senior honorary society), XXXX

- Scholarship Chairperson, Phi Kappa Psi Fraternity.

References available upon request.

SAMPLE RESUME 3

Gretl Pahane
gretlp@theriver.org

11 North Oracle Circle, Santa Barbara, CA 93103   (805) 555-9000

EDUCATION

- University of California, Santa Barbara—Bachelor of Arts in Oral History, May XXXX

MAJOR COURSEWORK

- Rhetoric, Religious Theory, PASCAL Programming, Political Science in the Modern Age, Squash.

EXPERIENCE

Tutor

- Dual Discovery Center, 800 Sproul Plaza, UCSB, Santa Barbara.

  Tutored socially disadvantaged high school students in various academic disciplines, with an emphasis in algebra and geometry.

Sales Associate

- The May Company, 1000 Maypole Lane, Primavera, CA.

  Marketed state-of-the-art organic disinfectants. Involved in all aspects of business, including cash and credit transactions, daily book- and record-keeping, and inventory.

Political Assistant

- Assistant to Representative Boris Bear, 8 Beach Front Bonanza Blvd., Bora Bora, CA.

  Performed administrative tasks including word processing, maintaining headquarter files, and telephoning constituents. Assisted door-to-door survey in reelection campaign; coordinated neighborhood voter registration drive.

Volunteer Work

- *Adviser,* Big Sister Program, Santa Barbara. Planned recreational activities for three inner-city teens.
- *Pollster,* Campaign to Re-elect Jerry Brown. Worked at midtown Los Angeles headquarters on voter survey phone bank. Solicited voter preferences through assertive phone skills.

PERSONAL

- Captain, UCSB Varsity Squash Team; UCSB Humanitarian Award (XXXX).

References available upon request.

REAL WORK

IN THE REAL WORLD

John Grisham, attorney, philanthropist, author

ohn Grisham, best known for his best-selling legal suspense novels, didn't start off with that dream in mind. However, anyone who has picked up his books knows how difficult they are to put back down. Each novel is filled with captivating twists and fascinating characters. Surprisingly, Grisham's own biography is equally exciting. Like his books, Grisham "wrote" for himself a life that incorporated all of his passions: family, baseball, law, and writing.

Grisham was born in Jonesboro, Arkansas on February 8, 1995. Although he had dreams of playing professional baseball in his youth, his stronger gifts won out. Grisham's confidence with numbers and logic led to studying accounting before attending law school at Mississippi State University. He then began his career as a trial attorney "going to bat" for clients in the sectors of criminal defense and personal injury. It was while working in the courtroom that Grisham heard the testimony of a young rape victim. Her testimony inspired Grisham to write *A Time to Kill*, the novel that launched his writing career.

Rather than waiting for the right time to get started, Grisham made time for his dreams. He woke up early to begin writing before his work day began. Although it took three years of writing and many rejections, Wynwood Press finally took notice with a modest offer. Grisham kept writing, this time producing *The Firm*. Not only did Grisham's second novel, purchased by Double Day, spend forty-seven weeks on the best-seller list, Paramount Pictures also bought the movie rights.

Currently, Grisham lives with his wife and two kids in Mississippi and Virginia. Since publishing *A Time to Kill,* Grisham has written one book per year. Of those written, all have become international best-sellers and nine have been made into films. In keeping with his childhood dream, Grisham also serves as the local Little League Commissioner hosting games on six ball fields he built on his property.

John Grisham is an example of a person who achieves their dream by applying talent, passion, and discipline. He is an inspiration to anyone wondering if they can have it all.

Source: "Bio." JGrisham.com. 2009. Random House, Inc. <http://www.jgrisham.com/bio/>.

some final thoughts

emember, resumes and other paperwork are simply marketing tools. On average, job recruiters will spend only about thirty seconds looking at your resume; therefore, you want to give the very best impression.

The ways you dress, speak, and follow up are also tools of self-promotion. Again, you may see a key person only briefly but you want to make a lasting, winning impression. If you follow the advice in this chapter, you will.

For more help with resumes and cover letters, check out the awesome books in Appendix C.

CHAPTER FOURTEEN

The worst thing you can possibly do in a deal is seem
desperate to make it. That makes the other guy smell blood
and then you're dead. The best thing you can do is deal
from strength, and leverage is the best strength you have.
Leverage is having what the other guy wants.
Or better yet, needs. Or best of all,
simply can't do without.

DONALD TRUMP, *THE ART OF THE DEAL*

Y ou've marketed yourself with your resume and cover letter. Now comes the big sell. You'll need to describe your experience so your interviewer knows you're prepared for the job. Rehearse for confidence. And, by all means, follow up after the interview. Here are some tips:

1. **Before the interview, do some research.** Check out the organization and the position. The better prepared you are for the interview, the more confidence you will project. Talk to people who work at the company or who hold similar positions for rival firms. Go to the library and research the company. Look in the *Standard and Poor's Register of Corporations* or the *Moody's Manual.* Check *Forbes, Fortune, Hoovers,* or other business magazines. Look for the organization's web page on the Internet. Learn the organization's history and the current climate.

you're hired!

INTERVIEWING AND LANDING THE JOB

This is the type of knowledge that helps people at both ends of the interviewing seesaw. Not only will your readiness impress your interviewer, it will also help you decide if the organization interests you. So develop questions about the company and the job ahead of time, then find the answers from your research.

2. **Rehearse.** Before your interview, rehearse answers to questions likely to be asked. Ask friends to play interviewer and give them a list of questions to ask you. When you communicate effectively, your interviewer will be convinced of your abilities beyond your "paper" credentials. If you do not have someone to help you role-play, set up mock interviews at your career services center. You

may even want to record a practice interview of yourself on a video camera and then play it back to see how you did. Without sounding arrogant, become comfortable and confident about your accomplishments. You want the interviewer to know that you are ambitious and self-assured.

Even after you've asked a friend to help you simulate an actual interview, continue to think and brainstorm about the really tough questions you're likely to be asked. For practice, go to all the interviews you're offered, even at companies you're not seriously considering. All the while, keep an open mind. The company you may be least interested in initially could be the very one that impresses you most.

3. **Dress for success.** Your appearance says a lot about you, so invest in one good interviewing shirt, suit, and shoes. Have your hair cut and styled. Look neat, alert, and enthusiastic. Again, you're promoting yourself, so you want to present the best "you" possible. Don't take any shortcuts.

4. **Relax.** If you've followed the first three steps, you have every reason to be confident as you walk into the interviewer's office. So relax, be yourself, and enjoy the experience.

SOME INTERVIEW TIPS

Now for a few tips from a veteran. Steve Kendall, a recruiter for Nabisco, appreciates interviewees who are animated, sincere, and forthright. "I want to see the applicant use examples to convince me of his or her qualifications and potential for success," says Steve.

"Let the interviewer set the pace," he continues. "The biggest turn-offs in job interviews are pat answers riddled with anxiety and interviewees who control the interview too abrasively in the first part of the conversation. Use the time in the last quarter of the interview to ask questions and gather information about the company."

COMMON INTERVIEW QUESTIONS

When Steve Kendall conducts an interview, two of his favorite questions are "Why are you interested in working for my company?" and "What are some examples of how you persuaded others to your way of thinking?" (How would you respond right now to those two questions?)

In addition, here are some of the most common questions interviewers ask college graduates. Use the sample answers as a starting point for figuring out answers of your own.

"Why should we hire you?" (Worst possible response: "Because.") This is a springboard from which to list the qualities that will make you a great employee. Be brief in giving your response and use specific examples to illustrate your points:

> I'm conscientious, tireless, and committed to going above and beyond what is expected of me. Last summer, as an intern with the New York Stock Exchange, I was always the first in to work and the last to leave at night. I made several excellent acquaintances, including the president of Merrill Lynch, who offered me a part-time job during the school year.

"Tell me about your education." (Worst possible response: "It's over.") This question is meant to find out how much emphasis you've put on your academic education. If you've made good or great grades, terrific. If you haven't, explain why: you worked twenty-five hours a week, supported yourself and your foster family of five completely, took eighteen credits each semester, got your pilot's license, and so on. If you've learned a lot from taking demanding teachers, say so, but only if it's true. Never fudge in an interview. In addition to being unethical, padding your own story in an interview is painfully obvious to people who recruit for a living.

> Although my GPA is 3.2, I've made 4.0 for the last two academic years. I took serious classes, looked to my professors as mentors, and truly challenged myself. I'm proud of what I've learned during college.

"Tell me something about yourself." (Worst possible answer: "Taurus, Cancer rising, Moon in Sagittarius.") Like the first question, this is an open-ended query. Your interviewer is interested in seeing what you choose to include in your answers. Open-ended questions reveal a lot about who you are: Are you an achiever? Are you detail-oriented? Are you reliable? Are you a fast learner? Are you good at balancing several things at once? Would you have a cool head in a hot situation? What about the personal side of you? How are you perceived by others? Are you frequently available to help? Are you patient?

Your response to one open-ended query helps answer many questions at once. Notice how the applicant below manages to answer the question skillfully while letting her personality shine through.

> I'm an enthusiastic, determined, and highly self-motivated person. I take a great deal of pride in being successful in work and play. I've tried hard to develop my outside interests—some of which my friends and family consider crazy. I like to skydive, spelunk [crawl around in caves], and read science fiction. I also love organizing big groups of people—for outdoor park concerts, the annual summer Renaissance Festival, canoeing trips, and so on. My greatest weakness is that I have so many interests; I tend to take on too much at times.

By analyzing the responses to some of these questions, you can see how much you must "think on your feet" to answer questions in positive, concrete, and self-affirming ways. But the more responses to questions you've thought through and rehearsed, the better you'll be able to "close" your interview.

Here's an additional list of frequently asked questions for you to think about and rehearse. (You'll notice that some of these questions are similar to those in Chapter 2, on defining who you are.) Compare the answers from your freshman year to the answers to your interview questions. How have you changed?

- Tell me about a specific goal you have set and achieved, at school or at work.
- How much energy do you have? Describe a typical day and week.
- Describe any experience you have had that is relevant to this job.
- Where do you see yourself five years from now?
- Where do you see yourself ten years from now?
- What was your greatest defeat, and how did you overcome it? What is your greatest accomplishment?
- What do you do in your spare time? What is the last book you read?
- What book has had the greatest impact on you?
- What interests you most about this job?
- How would a previous employer or professor describe you?
- How would your friends describe you?
- What interests you most about this job and this organization?

how you will be evaluated

here are a number of different ways in which your interviewer will evaluate you. On a scale of 1 to 5, with 1 being
the lowest and 5 being the highest, rate yourself in the following areas. Then think of one or more specific examples to support
your rating and write the examples down in the spaces provided
below:

- **Solving problems and setting priorities:** Able to understand
  and take action to solve even the most complex problems.
  Number rating: _____
  Example: _____
  _____
  _____

- **Achieving goals:** Consistently sets and achieves goals; results-
  oriented.
  Number rating: _____
  Example: _____
  _____
  _____

- **Motivating others:** Effective at communicating a personal
  point of view to others.
  Number rating: _____
  Example: _____
  _____
  _____

- **Working well with others:** Works well with and gains the
  respect of co-workers.
  Number rating: _____
  Example: _____
  _____
  _____

- **Responsibility:** Follows through on commitments made to co-workers and clients.

  Number rating: _____

  Example: _____

  _____

  _____

- **Tenacity:** Determined to work well through even the most mundane parts of the job.

  Number rating: _____

  Example: _____

  _____

  _____

- **Detail-oriented:** Pays attention to even the smallest details while keeping the larger goals in focus.

  Number rating: _____

  Example: _____

  _____

  _____

- **Vision:** Envisions a mission beyond the immediate game plan; can see all the way to the championship.

  Number rating: _____

  Example: _____

  _____

  _____

- **Resilience:** Bounces back from defeat. Treats setbacks as stepping-stones. Explores other avenues despite the difficult nature of the situation. Consistently tests new ideas.

  Number rating: _____

  Example: _____

  _____

  _____

OTHER CRITERIA

Basically, most companies will evaluate you as Excellent, Good, Fair, or Weak on four points. They are:

1. **Personal qualities:** How do you come across? Are you strongly motivated or sluggish? Are you energetic or lazy? Do you have long-term goals or are you aimless? Are you articulate or shy? Friendly or boorish?

2. **Professional qualities:** Are you reliable? Are you honest? Can you inspire others? Are you able to juggle a number of projects at once? Are you decisive? Do you follow through?

3. **Accomplishments:** Can you describe your proudest achievements? What have they taught you? How have you grown from the challenges you've faced?

4. **Potential:** Do you consider the long term? Do you place high value on continuing your education and building new skills? Will you be a good investment for the company? Do you show signs of long-term interest in the industry, or will you be off to business school in one year?

These are the kinds of questions interviewers have in mind when they sit down with you. You will find favor in their eyes if you can answer their questions with clarity.

SAMPLE INTERVIEW FORM

On the facing page is an example of a form that an employer might use while interviewing you. Take a close look at these categories and think about how you stack up right now. Try filling it out as it applies to you today. Which categories do you excel in? Which need work? If you were an employer looking over your scores, would you hire you? Why or why not?

a match made in heaven

he interview process is designed to make sure that the applicant and the organization are a good match. Therefore, as you diligently rehearse answers to an interviewer's questions; don't forget to prepare questions of your own. The answers you receive will help confirm whether or not the organiza-

INTERVIEW EVALUATION FORM

Graduate _____   College _____

CRITERIA	WEAK 1	AVERAGE 2	GOOD 3	EXCELLENT 4	SCORE
Leadership Potential ■ Personal attributes, values, and behavior ■ Ability to encourage and motivate others ■ Leadership Activities					
Strength of Character ■ Persistence when facing difficulty ■ Commitment to ideas larger than the individual ■ Motivation and discipline					
Maturity ■ Understanding of personal strengths and weaknesses ■ Commitment to learn, grow, accept responsibility, and challenge oneself ■ Passion and purpose					
Well-Rounded Personality ■ Intellectual, physical, and spiritual interests and endeavors ■ Commitment to broad-based life experiences					
Potential to Contribute to One's Community and the World ■ Past and present service and contributions to the community ■ Interest and activity toward solving world problems					
Interview Questions ■ Content clear, concise, and well presented ■ Interestingly poised					
Discretionary Comments					
TOTAL RATING SCORE (on a scale from 1 to 5)					

tion you're considering is the right one for you. To help you determine this, here is a list of questions you'll probably want to ask:

- **Job training:** What will be the job training procedure for my position?

- **Learning opportunities:** Does your organization provide an employee development program or other kind of learning opportunities?

- **Advancement:** What is the opportunity for advancement for someone who not only does his or her job, but goes beyond that?

- **Reporting structure:** What is the reporting structure for this position?

- **Facilities:** May I have a tour of your facility, especially the area this position occupies?

If you have other concerns or questions you want answered, by all means voice them during the interview. One word of caution, however. Inquiries about the number of vacation days, salary, medical benefits, pension plans, and other nitty-gritty items should be saved until later. These issues are typically discussed when you are close to being offered the job, which rarely happens in your first interview. Although you have every right to know this information before you make a final decision to accept or reject the job, there's no reason to bring them up prematurely. Doing so will make it seem as if your primary concerns are about money and benefits, rather than making sure that your qualifications fit their needs. (The chapter that follows will discuss how to initiate a conversation about your employee package and how to negotiate a salary.)

Your career center is likely to have several books and videos on how to research companies and how to interview effectively. The career services office will also have information on companies that come to interview on campus. For example, most companies give the career services office large notebooks describing the history of the company and various positions available. Again, make sure that the company will be a good match for you and vice versa. Many career offices also link company home pages to their websites. You can make sure that a company will be a good match for you only if you have sufficient information. Get it. It will allow you to be savvy and well informed in your interviews.

handling rejection

At some point during the interview process, you'll have to deal with rejection. One way to handle it constructively is to call the employer and discuss the reasons you didn't get the job. What you learn from this discussion may help you in future interviews.

Another constructive means of handling rejection is to keep a positive attitude. Keep reminding yourself: "I will find a job." Commit yourself to that end. Believe in your capabilities and overcome all objections.

It was hard for Chris Nelson, who majored in economics. After graduate school, he searched for three years for a good banking job. He kept his head up, realizing that the perfect job was just around the corner. Finally he landed a job with First Boston. If you are talented and work hard, he says, the only other quality you'll need is perseverance.

some final points

No matter how the interview goes, be sure to send a thank-you note. Thank-you notes following interviews are neither necessary nor expected, which is all the more reason why it's so important to send them. They need not be elaborate. Just say thanks.

When writing a thank-you note consider including the following: 1) Thank the person for meeting with you; 2) Mention a specific aspect of the job that you are looking forward to or are interested in pursuing; 3) Refer to a part of the interview that wasn't addressed that might help sway their opinion (This is a tricky addition. Check out sample thank-you note number two for an example); and 4) Give a time and date when you will call to follow up.

You never know what's going on behind the scenes. The company's first choice may turn down the offer, or the person who was hired may not work out a month down the road. In that case, your last piece of correspondence may tip the scales your way. Always be ready for the unexpected. Remember, "Luck favors the prepared mind."

Following, are two examples of gracious thank-you notes. Notice the placement of these elements within the letter. Then, try writing one yourself.

SAMPLE THANK-YOU NOTE 1

John Rhies

2001 Northshore Drive, Detroit, MI 48231

February 25, XXXX

Mr. Mark Nordbrach
Manager, Personnel Department
Wesley Manufacturing, Inc.
500 Sylvan Avenue
Redwood City, CA 94063

Dear Mr. Nordbrach:

I appreciate your taking the time to talk with me about entry-level management positions at Wesley.

I am especially interested in spending a day in the field with one of your division managers. I am eager to see the workings of the job you discussed—in progress.

If I don't hear from you by the end of the week, I'll call you on Monday morning, March 8.

Again, thanks for your time and consideration.

Sincerely,

John Rhies

John Rhies
john–rhies@interset.com
313-495-2501

SAMPLE THANK-YOU NOTE 2

KEVIN SULLIVAN

3000 Sutro Boulevard, San Francisco, CA 94143 • 415-224-8966

Ms. Alison McCormack   April 8, XXXX
National Recruiter
ABC Paper Products
9 Ellwood Avenue
San Francisco, CA 94142

Dear Ms. McCormack:

Thank you for taking the time to discuss with me the position of product manager with ABC Paper Products.

Though we didn't have a chance to discuss my part-time job, I believe it qualifies me for the position even more than my summer internships. Working ten hours a week over three years for the Reynolds Advertising Agency as a clerk gave me firsthand experience with designers and production artists. I was able to learn over an extended period the long-term ramifications of the wrong—and the right—paper decisions. This long-term view provided me with more insight than my three-month summer internship.

If I don't hear from you within the next week, I'll call you on Monday, April 19. I'm keenly interested in the position and the company. Again, thanks for your time.

Sincerely,

Kevin Sullivan

Kevin Sullivan
ksullivan@postnet.net Ho

after the interview

ou did not laugh uncontrollably during any of your interviews. You did not misplace your identity. You were confident and authentic. We're talking home run.

Now come a few very important details. After each interview, write a thank-you note and then wait two weeks. If you still haven't heard from the company, call the interviewer to see if you're still under consideration. If so, request an appointment to see them again. If they don't grant you a second interview, ask nicely for a time frame on the decision process.

do they want you?

At this point you'll have some indication of whether you're in or out. If you're still in, one or more of the following could happen:

1. **You spend a day in the office or in the field** to get a feeling for the job firsthand. If the interviewer doesn't propose this, request it. Seeing where you will spend a significant portion of your waking hours will help you further discern whether this job is really for you. Be observant and try to get a "feel" for the work atmosphere. Do the employees seem enthusiastic and friendly? Is the work environment safe, healthy, and pleasant? Checking this out before you accept the position could mean the difference between a job you like and a job you hate.

2. **You're invited to a dinner or lunch** so the prospective employer can observe you in a social setting. Two quick tips: Don't order alcohol, and avoid smoking if they don't smoke. Also, plan ahead about how you want to come across. Are you friendly or abrasive? Are you well-mannered or boorish? Do you spill your beverage on your future boss' white divan? Do you listen to others, or do you dominate conversations? Be sure to exhibit your star qualities of enthusiasm and graciousness.

3. **You could meet again with the interviewer,** in which case you will probably be introduced to others in the company. Meeting employees is a golden opportunity to learn more about the

Brittany Zachritz, *former LifeBound intern*

Being raised in rural New York state, Brittany Zachritz felt she had a small town mentality. She decided to find the right college where she could "grow up and begin discovering a broader range of options for my future." Her decision led her to Syracuse University, a private school in a medium sized city. Although she wasn't entirely sure about her career interests, she applied and was accepted into the School of Information Studies.

Anxious about the prospect of studying in such a populated and fast-paced environment, Zachritz enrolled in the SummerStart Program. It turned out to be a great decision. The SummerStart program was designed to ensure a smooth transition from high school to college. The six-week program provided Zachritz exposure to academic, social, and cultural life at Syracuse. She lived with other participating students in the campus residence hall, took classes, and fully immersed herself in local leisure activities.

Through the SummerStart program, Zachritz experienced diversity first-hand, made a group of friends to start off freshmen year, and got a job on campus for the Office of Residence Life. She also determined that IT would be her focus of study over the next four years. In order to further explore her writing interests, Zachritz set a goal to gain admittance into the renowned S.I. Newhouse School of Public Communications as a newspaper major. She accomplished her goal before sophomore year. In fact, she took on a dual degree in newspaper journalism and information technology.

Zachritz then began researching careers where she could appropriately blend her communications and technology skills. The opportunities seemed endless, but Zachritz landed on a job working with the campus Literacy Corps Program in a local middle school. That experience was the perfect segway into an internship with LifeBound.

Zachritz spend the summer of 2006 serving as LifeBound's publishing intern. At the start of the internship she helped conceptualize two books: *Sophomore Guide to College and Career* and *Junior Guide to Senior Year Success*. Zachritz's research and ideas advanced these publications. After leaving Denver for her fall semester, she continued working on their development remotely, seeing them through to publication.

Regarding her internship in Denver, Zachritz says, "I was living alone at the

University of Denver and spending a lot of time with LifeBound's president, Carol Carter. The independence and responsibility allowed me to become more aware and focused on life. I was in town for an annual coaching seminar where I met inspiring mentors from across the country. Carol encouraged me throughout the summer to develop my assertiveness and professional communications skills which helped me to become more confident."

After her publishing internship experience, Zachritz had the background and courage to apply for an editorial position at the SU yearbook. She became editor-in-chief her senior year. For college credit, she served as a newsroom systems intern at *The Post-Standard* where she gained administrative and writing experience, and made connections with esteemed professionals.

Zachritz found work as a freelance publishing assistant. She handled manuscript development, interviewing, researching, writing, and editing. In addition, she is working toward a paralegal certificate. She plans to apply her experience and education working with the county youth court program.

organization, even if all you have the chance to do is observe. Don't count on the recruiter alone to provide you with a composite picture of the company.

4. **You're flown to the home office.** This is optimal since it's in your best interest to know the philosophy and daily workings of the company. You will be introduced to lots of different people. Hold fast to your energy! You need to be as sharp and enthusiastic in your final introduction as you were in your first one. (After it's over, you will be able to wilt and take a much-needed break.)

5. **You take a series of tests**—analytical, verbal, logical, and so on—during your continued interview process. You may also be requested to complete a personality inventory.

These extra steps vary from company to company. The bottom line, however, is to remain poised, inquisitive, and attentive. Act as though you want the job—even if you haven't decided. After each interview, send an additional follow-up letter or note.

do you want them?

Once you've finished the second interview and talked with your "contacts," you will probably know if the job is right for you. If it's your only job offer, you may have to take it. That's okay. Give the job your very best shot. In the process, you may grow to like it more than you thought you would. If not, there's nothing to stop you from seeking out other positions.

Once you've decided that you want the job, you will need to find out about the *employee package*, such as salary range and benefits. As stated in the previous chapter, you need to use discretion about when to discuss these matters. Usually, the interviewer will bring up the employee package during the second interview. If not, you can open the conversation yourself in this way: "I am wondering about the salary range and benefits. Is it all right if we talk about this now, or will this be covered another time?"

Here is a list of what you'll need to know:

- What is the starting salary?
- Is there a bonus?
- Is travel involved? If so, how much?
- Will you have the use of a company car?
- Is the job a "career track" position?
- Is there a profit-sharing program?
- Is there a retirement plan?
- What are the projected timetables for promotion?
- Does the benefit program include medical and dental benefits?
- Is there a tuition-reimbursement program?
- Does the company cover travel and moving expenses?
- What kind of formal training will you receive?
- When can you start?

If you have several job offers, list the pros and cons of the company in which you are most interested. Here's an example:

Company Evaluation Sheet: Acme

PROS	CONS
Company car	Relocation necessary
Bonus and salary	Too much travel
Interesting job	Will need to work overtime
Growth potential	Solitary job
Fortune 500 company	No formal training
Great co-workers	Six-month probation period

As I mentioned earlier, you'll meet more and more people as you progress through the interview process. Keeping up with so many names and faces can get confusing. To help you remember the important details, I suggest that you take notes. As soon as the introductions are over, and while the names are still fresh in your mind, write down what you want to remember about the people you've met. Below is a sample for you to follow.

People I've Met at the Company So Far:

Name	Date	What I Need to Remember About Him/Her
Henry Jones	2/16/10	Vice President of Operations; plays golf; 4-year-old daughter takes karate lessons.

Here's space for you to jot down the real thing.

People I've Met at the Company So Far: _____

_____

Name   Date   What I Need to Remember About Him/Her

_____

1. _____

_____

2. _____

_____

3. _____

_____

---

poising yourself for an offer

After you have all the answers to these questions, ask your interviewers if they have any more questions for you. If they do, answer the questions. If not, state that from all the information you have heard and all the information you've gathered, you would very much like to work for them. Personalize your closing conversation. Tell them what has impressed you about their company and be specific. Recount examples from the past few weeks or months that have led you to your conclusions. When you're finished, pause for a moment so that the interviewer has an opportunity to provide input. If the interviewer's comments seem vague and no job offer is forthcoming, then ask plainly, "What happens next?"

As the final stage of the interview process draws to a close, the interviewer may ask if you've interviewed with any other firms. Be honest, but be on your guard. Even if you're not as interested in the other

REAL WORK

IN THE REAL WORLD

Donald Trump, *real-estate mogul*

The words, "you're fired" are synonymous with Donald Trump and his hit show *The Apprentice.* On *The Apprentice,* Trump takes job seekers to the next level by giving them a set of responsibilities. Based on their performance they are retained or eliminated until the next show. Finally, one is selected to work for Trump.

Trump began as an apprentice himself, to his father, Fred Trump, in Brooklyn, New York. Trump has said, "My father was my mentor and I learned a tremendous amount about every aspect of the construction industry from him."

Trump's professional success in construction as well as other endeavors is undeniable. The Trump Hotel Collection has projects in development world-wide. In Manhattan alone, he has branded the Trump Tower, Trump Place, Trump World Tower at the United Nations Plaza, and Trump International Hotel and Tower. He has developed three casino chains, world-class golf courses, and written numerous best-selling books on attaining success and wealth.

With all that he has accomplished, Trump gives the following advice, "Friends of mine, they have such bad jobs. I say, 'Why don't you move?' They could move. They're afraid to move. They're afraid to do something." Trump further advises, "You know, I know people that love being in the mines. They love it. And then there are people that don't. They really should try to get out. I mean, there are a lot of great stories about that. But you have to try and do something that you love. That doesn't mean being an entrepreneur and building buildings all over. That means a job. Get a job that you love. Otherwise you're just not going to be good at it."

Sources: Trump, Donald. "Interview with Donald Trump." *Late Edition with Wolf Blitzer.* CNN News. 21 March 2004. Transcript. <http://transcripts.cnn.com/ TRANSCRIPTS/0403/21/le.00.html>.

My Two Cents

HOW DO I APPLY IT?

Lennee Mozia, Duke University

I am from Denver, Colorado, and come from a culturally diverse background. My father was born and raised in Lagos, Nigeria, and my mother is an African-American woman from Lexington, North Carolina. My family and I spend a lot of time discussing a variety of issues from politics and religion to social trends. As a result of my environment, and the way I am in general, I have a very analytical mind and have learned to apply it in many areas of study.

Although many people (including my family) have suggested that my knack for discussion and observing issues would be best utilized in a courtroom, I realized in my time away from school that I am much better suited as a literature major than a law student (then again, things can and do change). My writing classes at Duke University gave me a chance to creatively express my opinions about themes in literature and how they relate to each other and the world. These were a key factor in helping me decide what I want to do with my education.

Surprisingly enough, Duke University is not where I received an education on how to properly approach an interview. Nobody interviewed me during my college application process, but the activity is very important for school and life in general. My first real interview came over summer break after my freshman year in college. I interviewed for a job at Victoria's Secret in hopes of becoming a sales associate.

The first thing I was asked to do after turning in my job application was to come to my interview in the company dress code, which was a black suit, a nice shirt, and professional black shoes. Many times the interviewer will not ask the applicant to dress in any particular way, but it is important to look put-together and professional when going

companies, don't let them know that. You want to hold on to your bargaining power. If they think that they're the only company you are interested in or that is interested in you, they may make you a low offer.

If you're offered the position on the spot, don't accept. Tell the company you need some time to think it over, but make a commitment to call back with your answer. Then review the pros and cons list with your mentors, supervisors from your college jobs, professors, friends, parents, or other family members, such as your spouse or partner.

to an interview. I am a firm believer in not judging people by the way they look or dress, but I do realize that one should really make an effort to dress well at an interview—not necessarily to convey a certain image or status, but to show the interviewer that he or she cares about the position enough to look well-groomed and professional.

My interview for the sales job at Victoria's Secret was the best kind of interview for me to begin with because sales is all about dealing with people, and that is exactly what I think an interview is all about. In the first half of my interview, the store manager asked me to step out on the floor and try to sell some underwear (this was not what I was expecting). After I tried to sell underwear to complete strangers, I felt a little more at ease about the second half of the interview, which was a series of questions I had to answer about my job experience and what I wanted to bring to the company.

The best advice I could possibly give to anyone going through an interview (which may be a little clichéd) is to say whatever feels appropriate, but natural. We often think the scripted answers to questions are the best, but if one does not believe or know what he or she is talking about, it really shows. I found in my interviews, as well as in my sales experience, that if I give my honest opinion about everything in a very respectful manner, people are very willing to listen to me because I am being myself and that creates a confidence that is reassuring to whoever is asking the questions. With this confidence, I have also been able to advance in my job at Victoria's Secret and become a beauty lead for the store. I am not saying that one should walk into an interview and just say whatever is on his or her mind, but that one should never just say what he thinks the person wants to hear. This attitude toward an interview can put anybody at ease, and the confidence that comes from that ease is one of the best things to have in any environment.

negotiating salary

"When I accepted my first job out of college with the accounting firm of Touche Ross, I had two other offers from well-respected firms," says Donald Mason, who now works in Dallas for a private firm. "Because Touche Ross knew I was attractive to several employers, they offered me more money to start than the typical college grad."

In your first job out of college, you don't have tremendous bargaining power, but you do have some. So use it.

Employers never offer their highest or even their middle-range salary. They start low because they expect to negotiate with you. Push for a higher salary. Point out that you're more experienced than most people who have been out of college for two or three years because you gained four years of real-world experience during college. You're much more qualified and promising than the average college grad.

Don't push so hard that you alienate your new boss. But if you get $2,000 over the initial offer, terrific. If you haven't done anything in college to prove that you are better qualified than the rest of the pack of applicants, take what you're offered. On the job, you can prove that you're worth the best raises.

accepting the offer

When you accept an offer, do it gracefully. After you've ironed out the salary issue, accept with a positive, reaffirming statement, such as "I'm very pleased to be a part of your company."

This is your first official chance to bond with your new manager. You may want to take the initiative at the outset to ask about goals for your first year on the job. What defines minimum requirements? What sort of performance exceeds requirements? What do you have to do to be outstanding in your first year? Together, you and your manager may want to put some specific goals on paper so that you have something to refer to throughout the year. At salary review time, you will have something concrete with which to gauge your work, a contract of sorts between you and your manager.

tying up loose ends

Write thank-you letters to the companies you turned down. Thank them for their time. You may want to call those who gave you special attention. Expressing these courtesies leaves all doors open for the future.

You might also write thank-you notes to those who turned you down. You'll probably be qualified to work for them in the future. Maintain a favorable impression in their minds.

when to start

When should you start? That depends on how you're planning to celebrate finishing off college. If you've been waiting to backpack through Indonesia with your suitemates and have slept with a map of the South Seas above your pillow for three years running, don't forsake that for a briefcase and suit. The briefcase will be there when you get back, and student loans don't come due until six months following graduation. Take the time while you've got it. If, on the other hand, you can't wait to close in on that corner office, go for it. The job is yours. You can still see the world in two-week intervals during your paid vacations.

other incidentals

You'll have to fill out insurance and benefit forms. You may also have some training, either "soft" or formal. Even if you are hurried right into your job with the minimum of instruction, don't worry. Ask questions. Solicit advice. Work hard. Learn all you can.

Starting your new job may scare you as much as starting college. Be patient with yourself. This period of adjustment will be easier and shorter than that of your peers who are less prepared for the real world. In the meantime, keep using all the techniques you learned in your internships and other jobs. Within about six months, you should feel like an ace who's been with the organization for years!

MAJORING IN THE

CHAPTER FIFTEEN

It is as though I had lost my way and asked someone the way home. He says he will show me and walks with me along a smoother path which suddenly stops. And now my friend tells me: "All you have to do now is find your way home from here."

LUDWIG WITTGENSTEIN, *CULTURE AND VALUE*

I went to the woods because I wished ... to front only the essential facts of life, and see if I could not learn what it had to teach, and not, when I came to die, discover that I had not lived.

HENRY DAVID THOREAU, *WALDEN*

No matter what your first job after college happens to be, it marks a new beginning. It also marks a point of departure. If you started out with the company and got the job of your dreams, great. But if your job right out of college is less than terrific, remember that you have to start somewhere where you can build your skills, meet people, and develop work habits. That's a positive, exciting challenge.

You may go through any number of changes at the outset of your career: from your new job, to a string of promotions, to a better job with another company, to a smaller company, back to graduate school, or even to begin your own company. That first job is like a blank page. You fill it in as you go. And the possibilities can be limitless as long as you pursue them.

outlooks and insights

SUCCEEDING ON THE JOB AND IN LIFE

games people play

In the working world, people measure personal success by all kinds of things. How much money they make; what their job is; how many people they know; how many dates they have; what kind of clothes they wear; what kind of car they drive; and how they balance career and family responsibilities.

Many of these things have to do with appearances, not reality. They reflect what people want others to think not necessarily who they really are. Know the difference between the two and be true to yourself and your values. The best job in the world isn't worth much if you aren't happy. Similarly, no amount of money or possessions will make you any more satisfied with yourself if you aren't already content with who you are.

This book is about defining those things that are important to you and you alone. So resist comparing yourself to those around you. That's a game you'll never win. There will always be people who are better off and people who are worse off than you. In college and in life, it's essential to do what you believe is important, and what you feel is right.

People may not always agree with you, especially if they feel threatened by your abilities. The going will often seem hard. That's okay. Preserve your integrity, and don't let someone get the better of you. Your satisfaction will come from knowing that you took the high road.

President John F. Kennedy said it best in his 1961 inaugural address:

> For of those to whom much is given, much is required. And when at some future date the high court of history sits in judgment on each of us recording whether in our brief span of service we fulfilled our responsibilities to the state, our success or failure, in whatever office we hold, will be measured by four questions: First, were we truly people of courage? . . . Second, were we truly people of integrity? . . . Third, were we truly people of judgment? . . . Finally, were we truly people of dedication?

character and ethics

You are working very hard to prepare yourself for a rewarding career. You are diligently studying, you are accomplishing goals, and you are honing your people skills. Without a doubt, the time and energy you're spending developing these qualities will not be in vain. Nevertheless, the most easily overlooked quality required for success is character.

By character, I don't mean your personality type. You could have an open, endearing, and charming personality, or a closed and rigid personality, but still have a lot of character. Some of the best leaders in their fields are introverts.

What I do mean by character is the ability to be ethical. Although ethics is somewhat hard to define, it's a human quality that's easy to spot. Usually a sense of ethics is marked by concern for other individuals. Ethical people consistently exhibit a willingness to live up to the commitments they make, and they don't shrink from considering how their decisions affect those around them.

In your job, you'll face decisions that are difficult to make. When the answers aren't obvious, you can always seek wisdom by asking yourself the following questions:

Would others approve of my behavior if they knew about it?

Would I want someone else to behave similarly?

Is what I'm doing right for the organization? Is what the company doing right? If not, how will I handle it?

What are my own personal standards, and how do I define them?

Here's a prime example of ethics at work: It is the job of a journalist to report the truth on behalf of the public, but they must negotiate an ethical minefield when their sources decide they want something they said in an interview to not be printed. Therefore, an ethical journalist explains what tricky jargon like "off-the-record," "on background", and "for attribution" mean straight away, so they can be certain the story can go to press while respecting the interviewee's legal right to privacy.

Fairness is the cornerstone of ethics. Begin thinking now about your moral views, especially as they relate to work. Particularly if you aspire to be a leader, character is crucial.

taking risks

After graduate school, Bob Kinstle took a job with a consulting firm in Virginia. The company's main business was in defense contracts, but the group's charter was to develop computer information systems for the commercial market.

One of his first assignments was to manage a project for a large bank in New York City. Over the next several months, the project team grew in size as he designed and implemented the system. At the end of the first year, the project began to wrap up, and the number of people assigned to it dwindled until there was just Kinstle. The company began to doubt its desire to penetrate the commercial market and prepared to abandon all future work with the bank. Kinstle, however, stuck with the company—and was rewarded for his diligence.

"I began to consider leaving the company and pursuing the bank as an independent contractor," Bob says. "The choice was difficult. I had a promising career with the company—I was the youngest associate manager, having been promoted to that level faster than

Dr. Leslie Ruybal,
medical school student focusing on pediatrics

Leslie Ruybal grew up in a large family where there were always younger siblings and cousins to take care of. "I always liked being around children and babysitting," Leslie said. In high school, Leslie proved strong in math and science, and as a teenager she decided to become a pediatrician. "This career would incorporate everything I valued and what I was good at."

In college, Leslie's dad worked as the director of a Boys & Girls Club of America.

One day he received a flier from LifeBound about a "Successful Scholars" program, and he asked Leslie to investigate it. A short time later, Leslie began interning with LifeBound helping facilitate career exploration and study skills seminars for high school students. Leslie said, "I thought the LifeBound concept was brilliant."

During her internship, Leslie also facilitated CSAP (standardized tests for Colorado) preparation classes a few afternoons a week helping students practice their math, science and writing skills. But Leslie said it was the leadership and teamwork activities that made the most profound and most long-lasting impact on her, which would help her face the biggest challenge of her life: getting into medical school.

To prepare for the entrance exam, she took multiple practice tests and clocked in 18 months of study time. "Throughout this process I used the study and leadership skills I learned from my internship to help me persist with my goals," Leslie said. Her internship experiences at LifeBound also set Leslie apart from other applicants by

showcasing the maturity that medical schools are looking for. As of the writing of this book, Leslie was accepted into the Creighton University School of Medicine in Omaha, Nebraska.

If you could talk to the future Dr. Ruybal yourself, she would tell you that the skills you gain from internships can be applied to any situation. "There's not as much pressure to be a super star at an internship as there is in a professional job," explains Leslie. "Instead, you have the advantage of a guided experience where you can be successful in whatever field you choose. Internships are an audition for your future career."

anyone else in the company's history. Yet I longed for the freedom to set my own work schedule—to be my own boss," explained Bob.

"There really was no way to know the consequences of leaving the company," he continues. "Would they accuse me of stealing their client? Would the bank be willing to work with an independent consultant located in Virginia? What if the project really was over and no further work emerged? Could I find other contracts?

"After weighing the risks, I decided to make the change. I resigned from my position and notified the bank that I would be interested in continuing business with them. Largely because of the relationships I had developed over the previous year, the bank agreed to give me a small enhancement project related to our original work.

Kinstle started working in his home, where he could travel to New York and stay in contact with the bank's computers. "I am happy feeling free to pursue contracts that interest me, setting my own schedule for work, and designing systems that reflect my personality and preferences."

If you know yourself, your strengths and weaknesses and you've learned to think critically, you will be able to make decisions that fulfill your dreams. Taking calculated risks can mean the difference between an outstanding career and an average one, between a zestful life and an ordinary one.

Throughout this book, I have encouraged you to:

1. Apply yourself academically
2. Keep active in extracurricular activities
3. Gain work experience, both through part-time jobs and through internships

By following my suggestions, you should develop the inner resources to make these same kinds of critical career decisions when opportunities arise. Like Bob, you will be equipped to take risks that will lead you down a career path you'll love.

"All of us reach points in our lives when we can play it safe or walk into the unknown," says Bob Kinstle. "I'm not advising recklessness; however, after you've weighed the risks and rewards, you may still need to take a leap of faith to begin a new path."

calling it quits when it's time for a change

At some point in your career life, you will leave your job for another one. When the time comes for you to hand in your resignation letter, you'll want to make sure that you leave on good terms. Career coach Joyce Lain Kennedy advises: "At any job level, act like a manager and resign gracefully. Don't burn bridges when you quit your job."

The reasons for leaving on good terms are common sense ones. Making enemies could come back to haunt you in the form of poor references or a tainted industry reputation years later. To avoid these pitfalls, Kennedy offers some tips to help you bow out in style:

1. **Avoid quitter's remorse.** Be sure that you really want to leave your present job.
2. **Get the new offer in writing.** Make certain of your ground with the new organization before announcing your departure.
3. **Write a cordial resignation letter.** Always give at least two weeks notice, or whatever length of time your company requires. Never risk negative language in your letter. Simply note your new position, employer, and the date you'll be leaving.
4. **Meet with your boss.** Workplace courtesy requires that you let your boss know you are leaving before your co-workers, so set up a time to meet with him or her in private. Also, offer to help train your successor or otherwise ease the transition.
5. **Don't boast.** Bragging about your higher new pay could create discontent in the workplace.
6. **Don't bad-mouth the company or its employees.** Although you may have reason to complain, negative comments will get you nowhere. When pressed for the reason of your departure, simply point out that your new job is too good to pass up, which should be true.

being happy

It takes a strong commitment and hard work to maintain a healthy balance on the job and off. Being happy won't just happen. Like anything else, you have to work at it.

Once you've landed your job, take pride in what you do. Have concrete objectives that will guide and direct you. Concentrate not just on job success but on overall happiness. If there is any one point I want to make in this chapter, it's the importance of striking a balance between your personal life and your professional one. Remember, your job is only one aspect of your life.

Kenneth Olsen, former CEO of Digital Equipment Corporation, knows all about making things happen on the job and off. In a graduation speech to students at his alma mater, MIT, Olsen reflected on his thirty years of work since graduating from college: "Running a business is not the important thing. Making a commitment to do a good job, to improve things, to influence the world is where it's at. I would also suggest that one of the most satisfying things is to help others to be creative and take responsibility. These are the important things."

"Your most precious commodity is not material," says Charles S. Sanford, Jr., CEO of Bankers Trust New York Corporation. "It is and always will be your time." If you keep work in balance with other things in your life, Sanford urges, you can accomplish even more on the job. "Read a little poetry, enjoy friends and most of all, don't take yourself too seriously. In the final analysis, whatever you have accomplished won't be worth much unless you've had fun."

Okay, so the cynic in you cries: How much time did these CEOs spend working in their twenties and thirties? Good point. They probably spent a lot of time, but were they happy? How did all that time at the office affect their families? You have to ask yourself, "Do I want to be a CEO?" Some people would say "No thanks." I traded in the corporate life to run a small business that is part of a large corporation. That was right for me and my life goals. You have to carefully weigh the trade-offs of your long-term goals with what you are doing—and enjoying—in the short term. Most of the working population thrives quite happily in intermediate positions between entry level and the top of the heap. They find a balance between work they enjoy and spending time with their friends and family.

Maybe you won't have all the money in the world, but you will have time to enjoy those things that count the most when you're 90—a job you liked, a lifestyle you enjoyed, and the opportunity to contribute to your own growth as well as that of others.

REAL WORK

IN THE REAL WORLD

Dame Anita Roddick, *entrepreneur, human-rights and environmental activist*

You don't have to go too far to enjoy the delightful fragrances of The Body Shop's line of products. These days The Body Shop International can be found in 2,200 stores in 55 markets. It was founded by Dame Anita Roddick, the child of an Italian immigrant couple. As an adult with an education in teaching, Roddick began her work on a *kibbutz,*—a Hebrew community often based on farming—in Israel which became a launching point for her love of worldwide travel. During this time, Anita had exposure to the body and beauty rituals of women from all over the world.

From this exposure, and economic necessity, Roddick started The Body Shop in 1976, after marrying and having two children. Without having any formal training, Roddick relied on no-nonsense principles and old-fashioned "waste-not want not" teachings. Her commitment to recycling and resourcefulness was not a chic marketing campaign, but a sincere desire to do the right thing. That desire became the cornerstone of The Body Shop mission statement, "To dedicate our business to the pursuit of social and environmental change."

When Roddick's husband suggested a franchise concept, the reach of that mission expanded across the world. Examples of how Roddick used her business venture to do good in the world seem countless. Her spirit of activism was the momentum behind many movements including The Body Shop joining forces with the environmental group Greenpeace and the spear-heading of a Community Trade program that improved global economics by purchasing from disadvantaged geographic locations.

Despite the awards Roddick received for her pioneering business efforts in the earlier days of The Body Shop—which included being named Dame Commander of the British Empire in 2003—Roddick found great excitement as her life advanced. She published her own autobiography, *Business as Unusual,* and edited *Take it Personally.* She also started her own activist communications center, creating what she called "weapons of mass instruction".

A well-lived life is never one lived selfishly or too carefully. Before her death on September 10, 2007, Roddick took risks and focused on how she could benefit others. She left behind a legacy of responsibility and love. She practiced fairness, courage and confidence. This legacy is evident in the words of the suppliers of Community Trade cocoa butter in Ghana. In remembrance of Roddick, they say: "The seed she sowed is generating fruits of success and enlightenment."

Source: Dame Anita Roddick. TheBodyShop.com. 2008. <Http://www.thebodyshop.com/_en/_ww/services/aboutus_anita-roddick.aspx>.

thoughts for the journey

I began this book with a personal anecdote, so I'd like to end with one. It has to do with becoming discouraged. And it's a story without which this book truly would have no closure.

About three months before I finished the manuscript for this book, I was exhausted. My job was quite tedious—not because the work itself had changed, but because my approach to it had shifted. I had little time to see my friends, and at night I just wanted to go to sleep early. Boring. In short, I was doing all those things I've said throughout my book never to do. Realizing that I wasn't being myself, and knowing for a fact that I wasn't having a good time, I decided to take a break to get back the perspective I knew was missing.

Egypt was the place for perspective. Why Egypt? It was exotic, distant, and vastly different from life as I knew it. Also, one of my interests is travel, and after my junior year in Spain, I made a personal promise to visit as many countries as I could. So off I went for the first time on a vacation by myself, leaving my "normal" life and my work behind me.

When I saw the age-old pyramids at dusk, a renewed energy and inspiration filled me. The pyramids symbolize balance, perfection, human achievement, and teamwork. Seeing the achievements of an ancient culture that have survived for thousands of years left me with a feeling of great awe and real humility. I wondered how many monuments from America's civilization would survive four hundred years, let alone four thousand.

Clearly, the Egyptians saw no limits to what they could accomplish. They saw things not in terms of what they were in the moment, but of what they could become in time. They looked to the possibility instead of the limitation. They made dreams into realities.

"Well, bully for Tut," you say, "but what has this got to do with college and careers and human potential?" The answer is that the pyramids helped me to recover my "edge"—my own potential. The tensions loosened inside of me and confidence took over.

My perspective restored, I was free to concentrate on challenges—including work, the book, and my personal life—with confidence and energy.

Throughout your life, the inspirations that motivate you will ebb and flow. You won't always feel inspired, and you won't always perform at peak. The important thing to remember when you reach an impasse is not to panic. Remove yourself from the ordinary—through reading *Don Quixote* or going to a concert or exhibit or taking a day trip by yourself. Maybe your most relaxing time is spent watching a football game or a weekly sitcom. That's fine. Just allow yourself time to unwind and replenish your own central energy source.

David Glenn, a division manager for Chevron for thirty years, reflects: "Live in the now—in the moment. It is easy to get so focused on a goal or destination that you forget to enjoy the journey. Every day in our jobs and families we are challenged to be of the moment with someone rather than too busy. Perhaps one of the benefits of becoming established is that we can enjoy the journey more."

the blue sky ahead

You have a lot to be proud of. If you're reading this book for the first time as a freshman, you get credit for getting this far and for committing yourself to making college and your career pursuit everything they can be. Good for you.

If you are reviewing this chapter for the last time and you have a job and are wondering how four years could come and go so fast, take time to pat yourself on the back. Look back from where you are now, realize how far you've come, and be proud of your accomplishments. The next peak you scale—your first job—is very similar to the challenges you've had in the last few years. Accept the challenges that are before you. In addition to doing a good or great job, give to the world something of what it has given to you—through your family, your friends, your activities, and your actions. Don't be typical. You are unique. Show the world the special gifts and contributions that only you can offer.

And so, here's to your unique success story. Here's to the ability you have to dream the dream and make it real. Go change the world! Good-bye and good luck.

appendix A

FINANCIAL AID AND FAFSA

So, like many college students, you're probably feeling a little strapped for cash. In regards to paying for college, some of the best places to start searching are with federally funded scholarships, grants, loans, and work through the Free Application for Federal Student Aid. Apply for FAFSA money online at www.fafsa.ed.gov. If this is your first time using FAFSA, register for a PIN number first so that you can speed up your application process and return to a saved application to make changes. If you have used FAFSA before, fill out a renewal application because FAFSA saves much of your information from previous years.

This section will give you an overview of the financial aid system. If you wish to learn more go to http://studentaid.ed.gov.

aid eligibility

Eligibility for federal student aid is based on financial need and on several other factors. The financial aid administrator at the college or career school you plan to attend will determine your eligibility.

To receive aid from most programs, you must:

- Qualify for financial need (except for certain loans).
- Have a high school diploma or a General Education Development (GED) certificate, pass a test approved by the U.S. Department of Education, meet other standards your state establishes that the Department approves, or complete a high school education in a home school setting that is treated as such under state law.
- Be working toward a degree or certificate in an eligible program.
- Be a U.S. citizen or eligible noncitizen.

- Have a valid Social Security Number (unless you're from the Republic of the Marshall Islands, the Federated States of Micronesia, or the Republic of Palau).

- Register with the Selective Service if required (you can use the paper or electronic FAFSA to register, you can register at www.sss.gov, or you can call 1-888-665-1825 or 1-847-688-6888).

- Maintain satisfactory academic progress once in school.

- Certify that you are not in default on a federal student loan and do not owe money on a federal student grant.

- Certify that you will use federal student aid only for educational purposes.

The Higher Education Act of 1965 as amended (HEA) suspends aid eligibility for students who have been convicted under federal or state law of the sale or possession of drugs. If you have a conviction for these offenses, call the Federal Student Aid Information Center at 1-800-4-FED-AID (1-800-433-3243) or go to the FAFSA on the website, click on "Worksheets" in the left column, then click on "Drug Worksheet" to find out how this law applies to you.

Even if you are ineligible for federal aid, you should complete the FAFSA because you may be eligible for nonfederal aid from states and private institutions.

HOW WILL I KNOW WHAT I'M ELIGIBLE FOR?

The information you reported on your FAFSA is used to calculate your Expected Family Contribution (EFC). The formula used to calculate your EFC is established by law and is used to measure your family's financial strength on the basis of your family's income and assets. The EFC is used to determine your eligibility for federal student aid and indicates how much money you and your family are expected to contribute toward your cost of attendance for the school year. If your EFC is below a certain number, you'll be eligible for a federal Pell Grant, assuming you meet all other eligibility requirements (check out the website in the chart below for more information).

For other aid programs, the financial aid administrator at your college or career school takes your cost of attendance (COA) and then subtracts your EFC, the amount of a federal Pell Grant you are eligible for, and aid you will get from other sources. The result is your remaining financial need which breaks down like this:

Your Cost of Attendance
- – EFC
- – Federal Pell Grant Eligibility
- – Aid from Other Sources
- = Remaining Financial Need

Cost of Attendance- Assuming you're attending school at least half-time, it is the sum of your tuition, fees, room and board, books, supplies, transportation, dependent care, costs associated with a disability, and some costs from eligible study-abroad programs.

Costs unassociated with completing your education are not included. Remember to borrow only what you need: If you can reduce your expenses to an amount less than your school's estimated COA, you might not need to borrow as much as the school has awarded.

Expected Family Contribution   Your family's financial strength based on income and assets as well as their, and your, expected contribution towards your education. For a free EFC calculator, go to www.finaid. org and click on "Calculators", or you can get worksheets that show how the EFC is calculated by downloading them from the website at www.studentaid.ed.gov/pubs under "EFC Formula."

Federal Pell Grant   A type of federal grant given based on financial need and determined by your FAFSA status. For more info, check out www.ed.gov/programs/fpg.

loan entrance counseling

ABOUT DIRECT LOANS

Direct Loans are made to students attending school at least part time. The U.S. Department of Education is the lender, and you receive the loan money through your school. You may receive a Direct Subsidized Loan, a Direct Unsubsidized Loan, or both for the same academic year. A student qualifies for a Direct Subsidized Loan based on financial need, as determined under federal regulations. A student's need is not a factor in determining eligibility for a Direct Unsubsidized Loan.

Most of the provisions below apply to both the FFEL (Federal Family Education Loan) and Direct Loan programs.

Interest Rates   The interest rate you are charged for both Subsidized and Unsubsidized Loans is variable and is adjusted once a year, on July 1, according to the formula on your promissory note. The rate will never exceed 8.25 percent. The interest on a Subsidized Loan is paid by the federal government while you are enrolled in school at least half time, or during grace or deferment periods. If you have a Direct Unsubsidized Loan, you are responsible for the interest from the day the loan is paid to you until you pay off the loan.

Loan Fee The loan fee is another expense of borrowing a loan. The loan fee charged for Subsidized and Unsubsidized Loans is four percent of the amount you borrow. The loan fee is subtracted proportionately from each loan disbursement.

Promissory Note Before you receive your loan funds, you must sign a promissory note. In past years, borrowers completed a separate promissory note for each new loan borrowed. Now, if you attend a four-year school or graduate school, in most cases, you will sign only one promissory note that will be used for all of your loans at a single school. This new note is called a Master Promissory Note (MPN). Direct Loan borrowers can now complete the promissory note online at www.dlenote.ed.gov. FFEL borrowers should contact their private lender for promissory note guidance.

When you sign the Master Promissory Note, you are confirming your understanding that your school may make new loans for you for the duration of your education (up to 10 years) without having you sign another promissory note. You are also agreeing to repay your lender, the U.S. Department of Education, all loans made to you under the terms of the MPN. Therefore, it is very important that you completely read and understand all of the information on the MPN before you sign it.

You are not required to accept the amount that your school awards you. You should notify your school if you want to borrow a lower amount than the school has awarded you.

School Notification Your school must notify you in writing or electronically whenever it makes a loan disbursement. The notice must tell you the date and the amount of the loan disbursement, which loan funds are subsidized and which are unsubsidized, information about your right to cancel all or a portion of the loan, including the current loan disbursement, and procedures for canceling the loan.

Leaving School Early If you leave school, graduate, or drop below half-time enrollment, you will have a six-month "grace period" before you must begin repayment. During this period, you will receive repayment information, and you'll be notified of your first payment due date. You are responsible for beginning repayment on time, even if you don't receive this information. Payments are usually due monthly.

The law requires that, when you withdraw during a payment period or period of enrollment (your school can define these periods for you and tell you which one applies to you), the amount of FSA Program assistance that you have "earned" up to that point is determined by a specific formula. If you received (or your school received on your behalf) less assistance than the amount that you earned, you will be able to receive those additional funds. If you received more assistance than you earned, the excess funds must be returned.

The amount of assistance that you have earned is determined on a pro-rata basis. That is, if you completed 30 percent of the payment period or period of enrollment, you earn 30 percent of the assistance you were originally scheduled to receive. Once you have completed more than 60 percent of the payment period or period of enrollment, you earn all of your assistance.

If you received excess funds that must be returned, your school can explain what portion of those funds must be returned.

loan exit counseling

WHEN DO I BEGIN REPAYING MY LOANS?

After you graduate, leave school, or drop below half-time enrollment, you have six months before you must begin repaying your loans. This is called the "grace period." Your repayment period begins the day after your grace period ends. Your first payment will be due within 60 days after your repayment period begins.

If you have Direct Subsidized Loans, you won't be charged any interest during your grace period. If you have Direct Unsubsidized Loans, you'll be responsible for the interest charged during your grace period. You may either pay this interest as it accumulates or have it capitalized when you start repaying your loans.

WHAT IS THE INTEREST RATE ON MY LOANS?

The interest rate for both Direct Subsidized Loans and Direct Unsubsidized Loans is variable and is adjusted each year on July 1. The interest rate will be calculated differently depending on several circumstances.

The interest rate during the in-school, grace, and deferment periods is equal to the 91-day Treasury bill rate plus 3.1 percentage points (this applies to loans made on or after July 1, 1995).

For all Direct Subsidized and Unsubsidized Loans in repayment, regardless of the date the loans were made, the interest rate is equal to the 91-day Treasury bill rate plus 3.1 percentage points. By law, however, your interest rate can never exceed 8.25 percent.

REPAYMENT PLANS

Student Aid on the Web Four repayment plans are available. If you do not select one, you will be assigned the Standard Plan. Below are brief descriptions of each. If you would like more detail on any or all of the plans, visit www.direct.ed.gov/RepayCalc/dlindex2.html.

- **Standard Repayment Plan.** With the Standard Plan, you'll pay a fixed amount each month until your loans are paid in full. Your monthly payments will be at least $50, and you'll have up to 10 years to repay your loans. The Standard Plan is good for you if you can handle higher monthly payments because you'll repay your loans more quickly.

- **Extended Repayment Plan.** To be eligible for this plan, you must have at least $30,000 in Direct Loan debt. However, you will have 25 years to repay it. This plan features two payment options: the first is fixed, like the Standard plan above and the second is Graduated, like the plan below.

- **Graduated Repayment Plan.** With this plan, your payments start out low, then increase, generally every two years. The length of your repayment period will depend on the total amount you owe when your loans go into repayment. If you expect your income to increase steadily over time, this plan may be right for you.

- **Income Contingent Repayment (ICR) Plan.** This plan is directly related to your yearly Adjusted Gross Income (AGI), family size, and the total amount of your Direct Loans. To participate in the ICR Plan, you must sign a form that permits the Internal Revenue Service to provide information about your income to the U.S. Department of Education. This information will be used to recalculate your monthly payment, adjusted annually based on the updated information.

COMPANIES WITH INTERNSHIP OPPORTUNITIES

Below is an abbreviated directory of internships which separates internship opportunities by industry. This list will give you an idea of some of the companies that offer internships as well as some starting points for Internet research, but remember this is only a very small sampling of internship programs. In addition to requesting more detailed information about the programs listed below, don't forget to contact businesses in which you are interested that don't advertise formal internship programs. Some of them will allow you to create internships to suit your individual needs. Also, many large corporations, such as General Mills and Hallmark Cards, offer internships in different areas. For example, if you are interested in a specific company and have a background in marketing, check with that company to see if it has a marketing internship program.

Since this list is incomplete, be sure to investigate the many internship reference materials in your campus library and search sites online. Many of these references are updated monthly and yearly with the freshest opportunities, so check back often. To get you started, here are a few regularly updated sites and books:

BOOKS

The Vault Guide to Top Internships 2009 Edition, Vault Publishing, 2008.

The Quintessential Guide to Finding and Maximizing Internships, Quintessential Careers Press.

The Best 109 Internships, 9th Edition, The Princeton Review.

The Internship Bible, 10th Edition, The Princeton Review.

200 Best Jobs through Apprenticeships, JIST Works, 2009.

WEBSITES

www.internzoo.com

www.internshipprograms.com

www.summerinternships.com

www.internabroad.com

www.internships-usa.com

www.internships.com

ARCHITECTURE
American & International Designs
www.designamericanyc.com

ART/MUSEUM
The Andy Warhol Museum
www.warhol.org/get_involved/
index.html

The Drawing Center
www.drawingcenter.org

Franconia Sculpture Park
http://www.franconia.org/
callinterns.html

CONSTRUCTION
Betchel
http://www.bechtel.com/careers.html

Black & Veatch
www.bv.com/careers

Pulte Homes, Inc.
http://careers.pulte.com/

CONSULTING
A.E. Schwartz & Associates
http://www.aeschwartz.com/
internships.htm

Hewitt Associates
http://www.hewittassociates.com/
Intl/NA/en-US/WorkingHere/

History Factory
www.historyfactory.com

CONSUMER PRODUCTS AND RETAIL
Betsey Johnson
http://www.betseyjohnson.com/
opportunities.html

Campbell Soup Company
http://careers.campbellsoupcompany.
com/Interns.aspx

FAO Schwarz
http://www1.toysrus.com/fao/
fao-career.html

Procter & Gamble
http://www.pg.com/en_US/careers/
index.shtml

Nike
http://www.nikebiz.com/careers/
internships/

EDUCATION
American Federation of Teachers
http://www.aft.org/about/jobs/
intern.htm

Aspen Center for Environmental Studies
http://www.aspennature.org/work-aces

Center for Talented Youth
http://cty.jhu.edu/summer/employment/
index.html

ENERGY/UTILITIES
American Electric Power
http://www.aep.com/careers/
collegerelations/

Emerson
http://www.emerson.com/en-US/about_
emerson/Careers/Pages/Home.aspx

GE
http://www.ge.com/careers/students/
internships.html

ENGINEERING
BAE Systems
http://www.baesystems.jobs

CH2M Hill
http://www.careers.ch2m.com/na/
us/en-US/

Washington Internships for Students of Engineering
www.wise-intern.org

ENTERTAINMENT

MTV Networks
http://www.mtvnetworkscareers.com/
internships/

LucasFilm Ltd.
https://jobs.lucasfilm.com/internships.
html

NBC / Universal
http://www.nbcunicareers.com/

ENVIRONMENT

Chincoteague National Wildlife Refuge
http://www.fws.gov/northeast/chinco/
internvolunteer.html

Sierra Club
http://www.sierraclub.org/careers/

World Wildlife Fund
http://www.worldwildlife.org/who/
careers/internships.html

FINANCE

Aetna Inc.
http://www.aetna.com/about-aetna-
insurance/aetna-careers/students_
index.html

Northwestern Mutual Finance Network
www.nminternship.com

Charles Schwab & Company, Inc.
http://www.aboutschwab.com/careers/
college-recruiting/interns.html

GOVERNMENT

Federal Bureau of Investigation
http://www.fbijobs.gov/23.asp

United Nations Internship Programme
http://www.un.org/Depts/OHRM/sds/
internsh/

The White House Internship Program
http://www.whitehouse.gov/about/
internships/

HEALTH

The Hamner Institutes for Health Sciences
http://www.thehamner.org/careers/
current-openings/

International Planned Parenthood Association
http://www.plannedparenthood.org/
about-us/jobs-and-volunteer.asp

Physicians for Social Responsibility
http://www.psr.org/about/employment-
opportunities.html

HIGH TECH

Apple Incorporated
http://www.apple.com/jobs/us/
students.html

Motorola
www.motorolacareers.com

Dell
http://www.dell.com/content/topics/
global.aspx/corp/careers/welcome/
default?c=us&l=en&s=corp

LAW

American Bar Association
http://www.abanet.org/hr/interns/
home.html

American Civil Liberties Union
http://www.aclu.org/careers

Common Cause
www.commoncause.org/intern

LEISURE

American Hockey League
http://theahl.teamworkonline.com/
    teamwork/jobs/jobs.cfm/
    Internships?supcat=687

San Diego Zoo
http://www.sandiegozoo.org/jobs/
    general_info.html

SeaWorld
http://www.seaworld.org/career-
    resources/internship/index.htm

MANUFACTURING

Cummins, Inc.
http://www.cummins.com/cmi/content.
    jsp?siteId=1&langId=1033&menuId=
    5&menuIndex=0DuPont

DuPont Talent Acquisition
www.dupont.com/careers

United States Steel Corporation
http://www.uss.com/corp/people/
    careers/index.asp

MARKETING

American Association of Advertising
    Agencies
http://www2.aaaa.org/Portal/Pages/
    default.aspx

Fenton Communications
http://www.fenton.com/careers/

United Talent Agency
http://www.unitedtalent.com/internship/
    index.html

MEDIA

CBS News
http://www.cbscorporation.com/careers/
    index.php

The Boston Globe
http://bostonglobe.com/aboutus/career/
    coop.aspx?id=7104

The New York Times
http://www.nytco.com/careers/
    internships.html

National Public Radio
http://www.npr.org/about/jobs/intern/

Seventeen Magazine
http://www.seventeen.com/faq

NONPROFIT

Amnesty International
http://www.amnesty.org/en/jobs_all/
    internships

Habitat for Humanity International
http://www.habitat.org/getinv/
    default.aspx

Volunteers for Peace
http://vfp.org/about.html

PUBLISHING

The American Press
www.americanpress.com

Beacon Press
http://www.beacon.org/client/client_
    pages/about_openings.cfm

Random House, Inc.
http://careers.randomhouse.com/
    Interns.html

Penguin Group USA
http://us.penguingroup.com/static/
    pages/aboutus/employment/
    index.html

RELIGIOUS

Fellowship of Reconciliation
http://www.forusa.org/getinvolved/
    jobs.html

Hillel
http://www.hillel.org/careers/
    fellowships/default

Center for an Urban Future
www.nycfuture.org

SCIENCE/RESEARCH

Brookhaven National Laboratory
http://www.bnl.gov/esd/reserve/
    Intern%20Apply.htm

Lunar and Planetary Institute
www.lpi.usra.edu/lpiintern

National Aquarium in Baltimore
www.aqua.org

SPORTS

National Basketball Association
http://www.nba.com/careers/
    internship_program.html

United States Olympic Committee
http://www.teamusa.org/jobs/
    usoc-internships.html

NASCAR
http://www.nascardiversity.com/
    diversity_internships/default.aspx

THEATER/PERFORMING ARTS

American Conservatory Theater
http://www.act-sf.org/site/PageServer?
    pagename=about_opps_intern

Child's Play Touring Theatre
http://www.cptt.org/g-intern.htm

The Juilliard School
www.juilliard.edu/about/
    profintern.html

TRANSPORTATION

Boeing
http://www.boeing.com/employment/
    collegecareers/index.html

CSX Transportation
http://www.csx.com/?fuseaction=
    careers.main

Toyota Motor Sales USA, Inc.
http://www.toyota.com/talentlink/hr/

ALL INDUSTRIES

**International Internship & Volunteer
    Network**
www.iivnetwork.com

Internships in Francophone Europe
http://www.iiepassport.org/

Mountbatten Internship Programme
www.mountbatten.org

BOOKS FOR FURTHER REFERENCE

ACADEMIC ADVICE

College Majors and Careers, Checkmark Books, 2008.

What Color is Your Parachute? 2009, Ten Speed Press, 2008.

Graduate Admissions Essays, Ten Speed Press, 2008.

SCHOLARSHIPS

Scholarships, Grants & Prizes 2009, Peterson's Guides, 2008.

The Ultimate Scholarship Book 2009, Supercollege, 2008.

Get Real Money for College, AuthorHouse, 2008.

Money for College Consumer Guide, United Resource Media, 2008.

How to Write Scholarship Application Essays, Quick Easy Guides, 2008.

INTERVIEWS

Job Interviews for Dummies, Wiley, John and Sons, 2008.

60 Seconds & You're Hired, Viking Penguin, 2008.

RESUMES AND COVER LETTERS

The Resume Handbook, Adams Media Corporation, 2008.

Resumes That Knock 'Em Dead, Adams Media Corporation, 2008.

Cover Letters That Knock 'Em Dead, Adams Media Corporation, 2008.

CHOOSING A CAREER

What Color Is Your Parachute 2009, Ten Speed Press, 2008.

Guide to Internet Job Searching, 2008-2009, McGraw-Hill/Contemporary Books, 2008.

The Almanac of American Employers (2008 Edition), Plunkett, 2007.

Best Jobs for the 21st Century, Jist Works, 2008.

How the Real World Really Works: Graduating into the Rest of Your Life, Berkley Books, 1997.

College Career Bible 2009 Edition, Vault, 2008.

INTERNSHIPS

Vault Guide to Top Internships 2009 Edition, 2008.

The Intern Files: How to Get, Keep, and Make the Most of Your Internship, Simon Spotlight, 2006.

SUCCEEDING ON THE JOB

Vault Guide for Conquering Corporate America for Women and Minorities, Vault Reports Inc., 2003.

Cool Women, Hot Jobs, Free Spirit Publishing, 2002.

Job Search Handbook for People with Disabilities, Jist Works, 2004.

How to Sell Yourself: Using Leadership, Likeability, and Luck to Succeed, Career Press, 2008.

appendix D

GRADUATE SCHOOL: APPLYING AND GETTING IN

should you stay or should you go?

It may surprise you that the median age for graduate students in business and law is now 27. That means that with a graduate degree at 24, you'll be competing with people who have five years of work experience. To increase your odds, why not get some work experience after graduation before applying to graduate school? You can earn money, establish your independence, and then return to school with a new perspective. Besides, many companies pay for their employees' graduate work. You could take courses at night and earn your degree over four or five years.

EXCEPTION TO THE RULE

If you want to become a professor, go directly to graduate school. Do not pass Go; do not collect $200. Academia is competitive on terms of its own, and real-world working experience does little to improve your chances.

ENTRANCE EXAMS AND APPLICATIONS

If you've decided to seek another degree beyond your bachelor's degree, you might have to take one of a battery of tests: the GRE, GMAT, LSAT, or MCAT, to name a few. Your performance on these tests is just one factor weighed in the admissions process.

A good place to start is with the test itself, because your score will help you decide which schools you have a good chance of being admitted to.

A breakdown of the various tests follows.

- **GRE: Graduate Record Examination** This two-part test is designed to measure general analytical, quantitative, and verbal abilities, as well as knowledge and understanding of the subject matter of specific graduate fields. It is required for admission into many graduate and professional schools. Further information, practice tests, and registration forms can be obtained through the GRE website at www.gre.org, by writing to GRE-ETS, P.O. Box 6000, Princeton, NJ 08541-6000, or by calling GRE at (609) 771-7670.

- **GMAT: Graduate Management Admission Test** Required for students applying to business schools, the GMAT contains two 30-minute analytical writing sections and two 75-minute verbal and quantitative sections. Scores are usually mailed out about five weeks after the test date. For further information, practice tests, and registration forms, visit www.mba.com, contact ETS by mail at Educational Testing Service, Rosedale Road, Princeton, NJ 08541, or call (609) 921-9000.

- **LSAT: Law School Admissions Test** The LSAT consists of four 35-minute scored sections, as well as a 30-minute writing sample and two unscored experimental sections. One distinguishing feature of the LSAT is that no points are subtracted for errors, so lucky guesses can raise your score. Scores are reported within four to six weeks and are on a scale of 10 to 48. For more information or to apply, call (215) 968-1001 or visit www.lsac.org.

- **NTE: National Teachers' Exam** The NTE tests are standardized exams that measure the academic achievements of students who wish to join, or are already admitted to, teacher education programs. There are three types of exams: Core Battery Tests, the nationwide Specialty Area Tests, and the statewide Specialty Area Tests. Tests are given in a variety of subjects including art education, audiology, biology and general science, business education, chemistry and physics. For a complete list and further information, call ETS at (609) 771-7395 or visit the ETS website at www.ets.org/praxis/index.html.

- **MCAT: Medical College Admissions Test** The MCAT is designed to test a student's knowledge and understanding of the biology, chemistry, and physics designated as prerequisites to the study of medicine. This material is usually that covered in first-year college science courses. The test also evaluates basic analytical ability in solving medically relevant problems. Scores are generally given within 45 days. For registration information, write to MCAT Program Office, P.O. Box 4056, Iowa City, IA 52243, call (319) 337-1357, or email mcat_reg@act.org.

In addition to the MCAT, there are other medical tests, designed to measure general academic ability as well as science knowledge. These include the following:

- **OAT: Optometry Admissions Test.** Required for those seeking admission into schools and colleges of optometry. For further information, visit www.opted.org/info_oat.cfm#5 for an online application, write to Optometry Admissions Testing Program, 211 East Chicago Avenue, Suite 1846, Chicago, IL 60611-2678, or call (312) 440-2693.

- **AHPAT: Allied Health Professions Admissions Test.** Required for admission into allied health schools-those that offer programs in such fields as chiropractic, dental technology, midwifery, social work, physical therapy, and many other medical professions. Call The Psychological Corporation at 1-800-622-3231 or visit www.tpcweb.com/pse/index.htm for more information.

- **PCAT: Pharmacy College Admissions Test.** Required for admission to colleges of pharmacy.

- **VCAT: Veterinary College Admissions Test.** For those seeking admission into colleges of veterinary medicine.

For the PCAT and the VCAT, contact The Psychological Corporation using the information listed above.

TEST PREPARATION SERVICES

Whether you like them or not, standardized tests are an important part of the graduate school admissions game. They provide an efficient way for admissions officers to discriminate between hundreds of faceless applicants. Fortunately, studying for these tests can improve your scores tremendously.

Many organizations, on and off campus, offer courses that include subject reviews and practice tests as well as strategies to help students conquer each test. Some test-takers swear by these methods, while others hesitate to invest so much money in preparing for the exams. (The classes can run upwards of $500.) Below are descriptions of two of the most popular courses offered nationwide.

Stanley Kaplan The Kaplan course is for the student who thrives on self-paced study. Students are given review materials to study at home on their own time. Kaplan has also developed online courses and review materials for PDAs. Students also have the use of the Kaplan Study Center. The center is filled with people taking practice tests, listening to audiotapes, and questioning tutors. You can come and go as you please. For more information, go to the Kaplan website at www.kaplan.com.

Princeton Review How is Princeton Review different? First of all, the courses cater to the student who desires a structured classroom setting. Pupils who display similar weaknesses are grouped together. During weekly lectures, techniques and concepts are taught. Workshops may be attended for further practice. Private tutoring is available, as are online courses. Find out more about Princeton Review courses at www.review.com.

DECIDING WHERE TO APPLY

Once you know which field you'd like to do graduate work in, it's a good idea to consult the *Graduate School Guide* (School Guide Publications, 1-800-433-7771) or GraduateGuide.com (www.graduateguide.com). You can purchase this book, check it out at the library, or borrow it from your school's career services office. It contains a list of all the universities in the United States and indicates which degrees each offers.

There are other online services that can help you find a graduate school, depending on what your specific criteria are. These include www.gradschools.com, www.petersons.com, and http://grad.studentsreview.com. For other advice on graduate schools, read *Graduate Schools in the U.S. 2004* (Peterson's Guides, 2003) and *The College Board Index of Majors & Graduate Degrees 2004* (College Board, 2003).

As with your college search years ago, you'll need to make a list, contact the schools, find out their requirements, apply, and interview.

WHAT ELSE DETERMINES ADMISSION?

Test scores, college grade point average, activities, work experience, recommendations, and essays are all factors in the selection process.

Let's be realistic. No applicant is strong in all areas. As you complete your application packet, emphasize your strengths and minimize your weaknesses (don't deny them). Begin your applications early, and make sure that you give recommenders plenty of time (at least one month). Remember, things always take longer than planned, especially things of quality.

SCHOLARSHIPS

You may be eligible for local and national scholarships. Some highly competitive scholarships, like the Rhodes or the Fulbright, require recommendations, interviews, high grades, work experiences, and athletic achievement. But there are hundreds of other grants available through your school's scholarship office. Check them out.

In addition to applying for scholarships and federal money, you might also want to check out Appendix C for some great books with more ideas.

CONTINUING YOUR EDUCATION ONCE YOU GRADUATE

Graduated does not mean educated.

HARRY EDWARDS, *THE STRUGGLE THAT MUST BE*

The real university is a state of mind.

ROBERT M. PIRSIG, *ZEN AND THE ART OF MOTORCYCLE MAINTENANCE*

If a well-rounded college education is a combination of academic work and real-world experience, then the best education outside of college comes both on the job and off.

Chances are that once you graduate, you will, at one time or another, be transferred to another city. Keeping busy and meeting new people will become a primary concern. The following suggestions should help.

- **Taking Classes** Many people continue their education formally by enrolling in one class every semester. Some may even earn their master's degree through evening courses over a period of years. Others may take classes that don't apply to a degree. A class on Chaucer or immigrants in urban America will help you remember that there is a world outside your nine-to-five job. It will challenge your mind in ways that are different from your challenges on the job. The contrast is key.

- **Museum and Library Lectures** Most museums and libraries offer free or affordable lecture series on topics ranging from extraterrestrials to creative writing to the life cycle of vampire bats. Professionals in the field give the lectures. Usually the people in the audience are interesting too.

- **Weekend Seminars** There are seminars every weekend on topics ranging from wine tasting to finance and accounting. Some of the seminars are retreats, which can be both educational and recreational.

- **Book or Writing Clubs** In every city there are informal groups where books or writing are discussed. This is a great way to make friends. You may want to form your own reading/dinner clubs to discuss classics you never read or contemporary literature.

- **Outdoor Clubs** These clubs offer a variety of activities, such as hiking, canoeing, camping, sailing, and skiing. Sometimes weekend group trips are available to your favorite mountain or resort.

- **Computer Groups** If you have a computer and an Internet connection, you can hook it up and exchange information and play games with other computer buffs across the country. You may also want to try your hand at co-authoring a software program.

- **Free Concerts** Most cities feature free concerts or plays in the summer. You can pack a picnic and a blanket and relax while listening to Verdi's Aïda and gazing up at the stars. If your city doesn't have a series of park concerts, check the churches and synagogues. They often feature classical music concerts.

ORGANIZATIONS TO ENRICH YOUR LIFE

Below is a sample list of a variety of associations and organizations that are great for professionals and students alike. Many of these contacts were taken from Patrick Combs' *Major in Success,* which is another awesome reference. This is by no means an all-encompassing list but should provide a general smattering of possible areas that might be interesting to look into. For more options, we recommend typing your interests into a search engine and seeing what else pops up.

Organizations outside of school, like clubs, free concerts or museum lectures, can play a vital part in continuing your education. Additionally, they can provide meaningful and rewarding networking opportunities with others with similar interests. After all, the more people you know, the more people you can connect with and maybe even land that amazing job with.

AREA OF INTEREST	ORGANIZATION	CONTACT
ANIMALS		
Animal training	Animal Behavior Society	animalbehavior.org
Horses	American Quarter Horse Association	aqha.com
ARMED FORCES		
Military support	United Service Organizations	uso.org
Air Force	United States Air Force	airforce.com
U.S. Army	United States Army	army.mil
Marines	United States Military	marines.mil
BUSINESS		
Business consulting	Institute of Management Consultants	imcusa.org
Franchise ownership	International Franchise Association	franchise.org

AREA OF INTEREST	ORGANIZATION	CONTACT
EDUCATION		
History	American Historical Association	historians.org
Math	American Mathematical Society	ams.org
Teaching	American Association for Employment in Education	aaee.org
DESIGN		
Costume Design	Costume Designers Guild	costumedesignersguild.org
Clothing design	Industrial Designers Society of America	idsa.org
Bicycle design	USCF Mechanics Program	promechanics.com
Interior decorating	American Society of Interior Decorators	asid.org
FILM		
Movies	Motion Picture Association of America	mpaa.org
Camera operation	American Society of Cinematographers	theasc.org
Art direction	Art Directors Guild	artdirectors.org
Movie Critique	Online Film Critics Society	ofcs.org
Scriptwriting	Writers Guild of America	wga.org
FOOD AND DRINK		
Brewing	Association of Brewers	aob.org
Candy	National Confectioners Association	candyusa.org
Cooking	American Culinary Federation	acfchefs.org
FUN STUFF		
Ghost hunting	American Society of Psychical Research	aspr.com
Laser tag	International Laser Tag Association	lasertag.org
Magic	Society of American Magicians	magicsam.com
Theme parks	International Association of Amusement Parks and Attractions	iaapa.org
Video games	Entertainment Software Association	theesa.com
MEDIA		
Publishing	Direct Marketing Association	the-dma.org
Radio and broadcasting	National Association of Broadcasters	nab.org
MISCELLANEOUS		
Billboard making	Outdoor Advertising Association of America	oaaa.org
Book buying	American Booksellers Association	bookweb.org

AREA OF INTEREST	ORGANIZATION	CONTACT
Carpentry	United Brotherhood of Carpenters and Joiners of America	carpenters.org
Children's book Illustration	Society of Children's Book Writers and Illustrators	scbwi.org
Comic illustration	Society of Illustrators	societyillustrators.org
Corporate video direction	International Association of Business Communicators	iabc.org
Demolition	National Demolition Association	demolitionassociation.com
Event Planning	Meeting Professionals International	mpiweb.org
Fitness	American Fitness Professionals and Associates	afpafitness.com
Greeting cards	Greeting Card Association	greetingcard.org
Handwriting	Handwriting Analysis Group	handwirting.org
Photography	Photographic Society of America	psa-photo.org
Private Investigating	Private Eye International	pi-international.com
Speaking	Toastmasters International	toastmasters.org

MUSIC

Musicians	American Federation of Musicians	afm.org
Album promotion	National Association of Recording Merchandisers	narm.com
Drum Circles	Drum Circle Meetup Group	Drumcircle.meetup.com

OUTDOORS

Bicycle messenger	International Federation of Bicycle Messengers	messengers.org
Ecology	The Nature Conservatory	nature.org
Farming	National Farmers Union	nfu.org
Forestry service	Society of American Forests	safnet.org

PERFORMING ARTS

Screen acting	Screen Actors Guild	sag.org
Theater acting	International Thespian Society	itothespians.com
Stunt acting for men	Stuntmen's Association of Motion Pictures	stuntmen.com
Stunt acting for women	Stuntwomen's Association of Motion Pictures	stuntwomen.com
Performing Arts	Association of Performing Arts Presenters	artspresenters.org
Theater	American Theatre and Drama Society	athe.org

AREA OF INTEREST	ORGANIZATION	CONTACT

POLITICAL ORGANIZATIONS FOR STUDENTS

Republican Party	College Republican National Committee	crnc.org
Democrat Party	College Democrats of America	collegedems.com
Green Party	Campus Greens	campusgreens.org
Socialist Party	Young Democratic Socialists	ydsusa.org
Libertarian Party	College Libertarian Organizations	lp.org/campus-organizations
Independent Party	New American Independent Party	newamericanindependent.com

SPIRITUAL ORGANIZATIONS FOR COLLEGE STUDENTS

Christian	Campus Crusade for Christ International	ccci.org
Jewish	The Foundation for Jewish Campus Life	hillel.org
Muslim	Muslim Students Association	msanational.org
Pagan	Student Pagan Organizations	collegewicca.com
Catholic	Association of Students at Catholic Colleges	catholiccollegestudents.org
Mormon	Latter-Day Saints Student Organizations	lds.org/institutes/ organizations

VOLUNTEERING

Lion's Club	Lions Club International	lionsclub.org
Kiwanis	Kiwanis International	kiwanis.org
Awana	Awana Clubs International	awana.org
Rotary	Rotary International	rotary.org

appendix G

OCCUPATIONAL OUTLOOK AT-A-GLANCE

Below is list from CNN and Careerbuilder.com featuring 50 of the hottest jobs, their projected growth, and median annual salary. According to the Bureau of Labor Statistics (www.bls.gov/oco/), these jobs will experience serious growth over the next ten years. Obviously, this is not an all-inclusive list, and we encourage you to search out the growth possibilities in areas of interest to you. Besides using the internet in your search, we also recommend the *Occupational Outlook Handbook 2008-2009* that is put out by the U.S. Department of Labor.

1. Network systems and data communications analysts
   Projected growth by 2016: 53 percent
   Median annual salary: $64,600*

2. Home health aides
   Projected growth by 2016: 49 percent
   Median annual salary: $19,420

3. Computer applications software engineers
   Projected growth by 2016: 45 percent
   Median annual salary: $79,780

4. Personal financial advisors
   Projected growth by 2016: 41 percent
   Median annual salary: $66,120

5. Makeup artists, theatrical and performance
   Projected growth by 2016: 40 percent
   Median annual salary: $31,820

6. Veterinarians
   Projected growth by 2016: 35 percent
   Median annual salary: $71,990

7. Medical assistants
   Projected growth: 35 percent
   Median annual salary: $26,290

8. Skin care specialists
   Projected growth by 2016: 34 percent
   Median annual salary: $26,170

9. Financial analysts
   Projected growth by 2016: 34 percent
   Median annual salary: $66,590

10. Dental assistants
    Projected growth by 2016: 29 percent
    Median annual salary: $30,220

11. Database administrators
    Projected growth by 2016: 29 percent
    Median annual salary: $64,670

12. Computer systems software engineers
    Projected growth by 2016: 28 percent
    Median annual salary: $85,370

13. Network and computer systems administrators
Projected growth by 2016: 27 percent
Median annual salary: $62,130

14. Physical therapists
Projected growth by 2016: 27 percent
Median annual salary: $66,200

15. Physician assistants
Projected growth by 2016: 27 percent
Median annual salary: $74,980

16. Multimedia artists and animators
Projected growth by 2016: 26 percent
Median annual salary: $51,350

17. Preschool teachers, except special education
Projected growth by 2016: 26 percent
Median annual salary: $22,680

18. Radiation therapists
Projected growth by 2016: 25 percent
Median annual salary: $66,170

19. Securities, commodities and financial services sales agents
Projected growth by 2016: 25 percent
Median annual salary: $68,500

20. Customer service representatives
Projected growth by 2016: 25 percent
Median annual salary: $28,330

21. Registered nurses
Projected growth by 2016: 23 percent
Median annual salary: $57,280

22. Postsecondary teachers
Projected growth by 2016: 23 percent
Median annual salary: $56,120

23. Self-enrichment education teachers
Projected growth by 2016: 23 percent
Median annual salary: $33,440

24. Counter and rental clerks
Projected growth by 2016: 23 percent
Median annual salary: $19,570

25. Bill and account collectors
Projected growth by 2016: 23 percent
Median annual salary: $29,050

26. Medical equipment repairers
Projected growth by 2016: 22 percent
Median annual salary: $40,580

27. Management analysts
Projected growth by 2016: 22 percent
Median annual salary: $68,050

28. Instructional coordinators
Projected growth by 2016: 22 percent
Median annual salary: $52,790

29. Special education teachers, preschool, kindergarten and elementary school
Projected growth by 2016: 20 percent
Median annual salary: $46,360

30. Meeting and convention planners
Projected growth by 2016: 20 percent
Median annual salary: $42,180

31. Brokerage clerks
Projected growth by 2016: 20 percent
Median annual salary: $36,390

32. Advertising sales agents
Projected growth by 2016: 20 percent
Median annual salary: $42,750

33. Interior designers
Projected growth by 2016: 19 percent
Median annual salary: $42,260

34. Automotive glass installers and repairers
Projected growth by 2016: 19 percent
Median annual salary: $30,720

35. Motorboat mechanics
Projected growth by 2016: 19 percent
Median annual salary: $33,210

36. Cost estimators
Projected growth by 2016: 19 percent
Median annual salary: $52,940

37. Demonstrators and product promoters
Projected growth by 2016: 18 percent
Median annual salary: $22,150

38. Construction and building inspectors
Projected growth by 2016: 18 percent
Median annual salary: $46,570

39. Medical secretaries
Projected growth: 17 percent
Median annual salary: $28,090

40. Tile and marble setters
Projected growth by 2016: 15 percent
Median annual salary: $36,590

41. Executive secretaries and administrative assistants
Projected growth by 2016: 15 percent
Median annual salary: $37,240

42. Boilermakers
Projected growth by 2016: 14 percent
Median annual salary: $46,960

43. Roofers
Projected growth by 2016: 14 percent
Median annual salary: $32,260

44. Automotive service technicians and mechanics
Projected growth by 2016: 14 percent
Median annual salary: $33,780

45. Reinforcing iron and rebar workers
Projected growth by 2016: 12 percent
Median annual salary: $38,220

46. Mobile heavy equipment mechanics, except engines
Projected growth by 2016: 12 percent
Median annual salary: $40,440

47. Sales representatives, wholesale and manufacturing, technical and scientific products
Projected growth by 2016: 12 percent
Median annual salary: $64,440

48. Fine artists, including painters, sculptors and illustrators
Projected growth by 2016: 10 percent
Median annual salary: $41,970

49. Graphic designers
Projected growth by 2016: 10 percent
Median annual salary: $39,900

50. Art directors
Projected growth by 2016: 9 percent
Median annual salary: $39,900

appendix H

WHERE TO FIND HELP

T he strongest people are not the ones who never have trouble; they are the ones who seek out help when they encounter trouble. Remember that whatever you've experienced and whatever shame or guilt might be associated with it, the brave thing to do is to find ways to work through your fears. A great many resources exist for students and others who are facing these issues, so be sure you find the help you need. Above all, remember that you are not alone and that there are many people willing to help you.

Groups with local chapters have not been included (AA, Planned Parenthood, etc.), but check your phone book or any one of the referral numbers listed below for how to get in touch with these groups. Also remember that your school's counseling center is there to help you. Make an appointment with a counselor and start getting help.

EATING DISORDERS

National Eating Disorders Association (NEDA)

1-800-931-2237

www.nationaleatingdisorders.org

Anorexia Nervosa and Related Eating Disorders, Inc. (ANRED) Affiliated with NEDA

541-344-1144

Eating Disorder Referral and Information Center

858-481-1515

www.edreferral.com

Also look for these books:

Fighting the Freshman Fifteen, Three Rivers Press, 2002.

Bodylove: Learning to Like Our Looks and Ourselves, Gurze Books, 2002.

Over It: A Teen's Guide to Getting Beyond Obsessions with Food and Weight, New World Library, 2001.

Making Weight: Healing Men's Conflicts with Food, Weight, Shape, and Appearance, Gurze Books, 2000.

Binge No More: Your Guide to Overcoming Disordered Eating, New Harbinger Publications, 1999.

SUICIDE AND MENTAL HEALTH

Hope Line Network Provides listings, by state, of other help line numbers
1-800-SUICIDE (784-2433)

TeenLine Hotline Help Center
1-888-747-TEEN (8336)

The Trevor HelpLine Provides suicide prevention for gay and questioning youth
1-800-850-8078

Mental Health Referral Service
1-800-THERAPIST (843-7274)

National Mental Health Association Information Center
1-800-969-NMHA (6642)

Also look for these books:

College Student Suicide, Haworth Press, 1990.

Women and Anxiety: A Step-by-Step Program for Managing Anxiety and Depression, Haterleigh Press, 1998.

Unmasking Male Depression, Word Publishing, 2001.

ASSAULT, ABUSE, AND VIOLENCE

Rape, Abuse, and Incest National Network (RAINN)
1-800-656-HOPE (4673)
www.rainn.org

Sexual Assault Crisis Line
1-800-643-6250

National Center for Victims of Crime
1-800-394-2255
202-467-8700
www.ncvc.org

National Domestic Violence Hotline As well as helping victims of domestic violence, NDVH also provides information and help for those people who think they might be abusers.
1-800-799-SAFE (7233) (Spanish Available)
1-800-787-3224 TTY For the Deaf
www.ndvh.org

Also look for these books:

It Happened to Me: A Teen's Guide to Overcoming Sexual Abuse, New Harbinger Publications, 2002.

The Rape Recovery Handbook: Step-by-Step Help for Survivors of Sexual Assault, New Harbinger Publications, 2003.

DRUG AND ALCOHOL ABUSE

National Drug and Alcohol Line Provides information on alcohol and drug abuse, as well as advice on local treatment options
1-800-662-HELP (4357)

U.S. Department of Health and Human Services: Alcohol and Drug Information-Prevention Online
1-800-729-6686
www.health.org

Alcohol Treatment Referral Hotline
1-800-252-6465
www.adcare.com

Also look for these books:

Kill the Craving: How to Control the Impulse to Use Drugs and Alcohol, New Harbinger Publications, 2001.

Alcohol Abuse: Straight Talk Straight Answers, Ixia Publications, 1999.

STDS, HIV, AND AIDS HELP AND SERVICES

National Sexually Transmitted Disease Hotline
1-800-227-8922

National AIDS Hotline
1-800-CDC-INFO (232-4636)

HIV/AIDS National Resources Center
1-800-362-0071

AIDSinfo
1-800-HIV-0440 (448-0440)
www.aidsinfo.nih.gov

PREGNANCY COUNSELING

Planned Parenthood Hotline
1-800-230-PLAN (7526)

Teen Pregnancy Referral Hotline
1-800-522-5006

DEBT RECOVERY AND FINANCIAL HEALTH

Look for these books:

The Complete Idiot's Guide to Beating Debt, Alpha Books, 1999.

The Complete Idiot's Guide to Managing Your Money, Alpha Communications, 2002.

Cliff's Notes: Managing Your Money, Hungry Minds, 2001.

The Debt Free Graduate: How to Survive College without Going Broke, Career Press, 2000.

BEREAVEMENT COUNSELING

AARP Grief and Loss Toll-Free Support Line AARP offers grief support by trained volunteers who themselves have experienced the death of a loved one. Family members, friends, and co-workers who have lost a loved one are encouraged to call this line for support with their grief.
1-866-797-2277

UCLA Bereavement Hotline
1-800-445-4808

Try checking with your local hospitals to see if they offer community bereavement groups or personal bereavement sessions.

Also look for these books:

How to Go on Living When Someone You Love Dies, Bantam Books, 1991.

I Wasn't Ready to Say Goodbye: Surviving, Coping and Healing After the Sudden Death of a Loved One, Champion Press Limited, 2000.

TRAVEL ABROAD OPTIONS

Achieving your goal of traveling overseas might seem difficult if you don't think you have the financial resources to go as a tourist. All the information listed below is to help you achieve your dream with minimal expense to you. Not only do organizations try to help students find discounted travel opportunities, but many organizations, companies, and groups offer work and volunteer travel experiences for students and young people. While you might find that some of these opportunities cost something, usually your room and board are free and you receive financial compensation for your work.

Also in this appendix, you will find a list of funding and fellowship opportunities. While some of these opportunities, such as the Rhodes, the Fulbright, and the Rotary, have some specific requirements (e.g. applicants are beginning graduate work or are proficient in a language) don't let that discourage you from your funding search. Many scholarships are specifically for college students traveling overseas. For other funding opportunities and information, be sure to visit your school's study abroad office. If your school does not have one, larger schools welcome questions from people who are not students at their university, so check with them.

Search for student travel discounts:

www.studentuniverse.com

www.statravel.com

BEYOND THE PEACE CORPS: VOLUNTEER AND WORK ABROAD

Transitions Abroad
www.transitionsabroad.com

This magazine was "created as the antidote to tourism...with the specific goal of providing information that would enable travelers to actually meet the people of other countries, to learn about their culture, to speak their language, and to 'transition' to a new level of understanding and appreciation for our fascinating world" (www.transitionsabroad.com/information/media/history.shtml). *Transitions Abroad* also has a comprehensive website where you can investigate various ways to travel and do so cheaply.

International Student Travel Confederation   www.istc.org

ISTC, established in 1949, combines "more than 70 specialist student travel companies [who] work through the not-for-profit member associations of the ISTC" to make travel affordable for students through flight, insurance, ground transportation, work exchange program, and identity card benefits (www.aboutistc.org).

Council on International Educational Exchange   www.ciee.org

Search for opportunities to work, volunteer, and teach abroad; learn about global service projects and hosting opportunities; or join an international student exchange.

GoAbroad.com   www.goabroad.com

This site provides "comprehensive international education and alternative travel databases....In addition to some of the largest directories of their kind on the internet, GoAbroad.com provides extensive additional information...travel guides, currency converter, and embassy directories" (www.goabroad.com/about.cfm).

Service Civil International (SCI)
www.sciint.org

SCI "aims are to promote peace, international understanding and solidarity, social justice, sustainable development, and respect for the environment. SCI believes that all the people are capable of living together with mutual respect and without recourse to any form of violence to solve conflicts." SCI has U.S. and Canadian branches through which people can volunteer for various opportunities and workcamps around the world.

Global Volunteers
www.globalvolunteers.org

Global Volunteers is a private, non-profit, non-sectarian organization offering volunteer vacations worldwide. It mobilizes some 150 service-learning teams year-round to do volunteer work in 19 countries on six continents.

United Nations Volunteers
www.unv.org

The United Nations Volunteers (UNV) program is the volunteer division of the United Nations. The UN General Assembly created UNV in 1970 to serve as a partner in development cooperation as help is requested by UN member states. This organization supports human development globally by promoting volunteerism and by mobilizing volunteers.

BUNAC   www.bunac.com/usa

BUNAC offers U.S. students and youth work/travel programs to Britain, Ireland, Australia, New Zealand, and Canada and a volunteer program in South Africa. Each program offers a unique insight into life in a completely new culture and a chance to spend extended time working and traveling overseas.

Camp Counselors USA
www.campcounselors.com

CCUSA is a worldwide organization that provides youth with the opportunity to travel, work, and earn money. Over the past 16 years CCUSA has recruited and placed more than 95,000 participants from more than 60 countries in camps and with employers around the world.

Idealist   www.idealist.org

Idealist is a project of Action Without Borders, which is independent of governments, political ideology, or religion. Idealist's website will let visitors search or browse by name, location, or mission over 36,000 nonprofit and community organization in 165 countries. It lists thousands of volunteer opportunities in local communities and around the world and organizations that can help to get you abroad.

Cross-Cultural Solutions
www.crossculturalsolutions.org

Since 1995, Cross-Cultural Solutions has brought more than 2,500 participants to countries around the world. They are committed to international volunteer work and operate volunteer programs around the world in partnership with sustainable community initiatives. They are an international, not-for-profit organization, with no political or religious affiliations.

European Internships
www.europeaninternships.com

European Internships designs and delivers customized programs for those who want to learn about other cultures by studying or working abroad. It was born in the USA and created by bilingual people who have worked in the study-and-work-abroad industry for a long time. Their goal is to help participants fully immerse themselves in another culture, so each program is structured to help students learn about the language, customs, and lifestyles of the local people.

International Rescue Committee (IRC)
www.theirc.org

IRC is the leading non-sectarian, voluntary organization providing relief, protection, and resettlement services for refugees and victims of oppression or violent conflict. Employment and volunteer opportunities are listed for all over the world in all job areas.

Habitat for Humanity International
www.habitat.org

Habitat for Humanity International works with people who are committed to Habitat for Humanity's work of providing families with simple, decent shelter. Although assignment terms may vary, Global Assignee positions typically are for three-year periods. Positions in most countries require a willingness to communicate and affirm the Christian roots and principles of Habitat for Humanity.

NEED MONEY? FELLOWSHIP AND FUNDING OPPORTUNITIES

Fulbright Scholarships
www.cies.org

The U.S. Congress created the Fulbright Program to foster mutual understanding among nations through educational and cultural exchanges.

Rotary Ambassador of Goodwill Scholarships http://www.rotary.org/en/StudentsAndYouth/EducationalPrograms/AmbassadorialScholarships/Pages/ridefault.aspx

Some Rotary Clubs offer Ambassadorial Scholarship opportunities to increase international peace and understanding through graduate study abroad. Please refer to the club in your home district to find out whether it sponsors ambassadorial scholarships.

Rhodes Scholarships
www.rhodesscholar.org

Rhodes Scholarships enable outstanding students to pursue a degree from the University of Oxford.

Finding Funders
www.fdncenter.org/funders/

The Grantsmanship Center
www.tgci.com

The Ford Foundation
www.fordfound.org

The David and Lucile Packard Foundation www.packard.org

The Robert Wood Johnson Foundation
www.rwjf.org/index.jsp

W.K. Kellogg Foundation
www.wkkf.org

MacArthur Foundation
www.macfdn.org

The Andrew W. Mellon Foundation
www.mellon.org

The Starr Foundation
www.fdncenter.org/grantmaker/starr/

The Rockefeller Foundation
www.rockfound.org

The Annie E. Casey Foundation
www.aecf.org

Charles Stewart Mott Foundation
www.mott.org

The Robert W. Woodruff Foundation
www.woodruff.org

The Annenberg Foundation
www.whannenberg.org

Also look for these books to give you some travel abroad ideas:

Alternatives to the Peace Corps, Food First Books, 2008.

Volunteer Vacations: Short-term Adventures That Will Benefit You and Others, Chicago Review Press, 2009.

Work Your Way Around the World, Vacation Work Publications, 2009.

How to Live Your Dream of Volunteering Overseas, Penguin USA, 2003.

The International Dictionary of Voluntary Work, Globe Pequot Press, 2003.

Get Outside: A Guide to Volunteer Opportunities and Working Vacations in America's Great Outdoors, Falcon, 2002.

International Job Finder: Where Jobs Are Worldwide, Planning Communications, 2002.

Work Worldwide: International Career Strategies for the Adventurous Job Seeker, Avalon Travel Publishing, 2000.

Summer Jobs Abroad 2008, Crimson Publishing, 2008.

Taking Time Off, Princeton Review, 2003.

do you have advice?

If you would like to send me your comments on what you did and didn't like about the book, I would greatly appreciate it. Or, if you have a story of your own that you think would illustrate an important point, please write it down here or on a separate sheet of paper. I'll use your comments and suggestions as I revise the book for future editions.

1. This book gave me a clearer focus on my college goals and plans. Ⓨ Ⓝ

2. I like the various opinions and attitudes that the book reflects. Ⓨ Ⓝ

3. This book made me feel more comfortable about the future. Ⓨ Ⓝ

4. I would improve the book by (check one):
   ○ Adding more examples   ○ Having fewer examples   ○ Other

5. I would recommend this book to my friends.

6. How I found out about this book (check one):
   ○ I saw it in a bookstore.   ○ My teacher assigned it.   ○ It was a gift.

Thank you for your suggestions. Please mail or fax this form to:

Carol Carter   Fax: (303) 436-0938
LifeBound
1600 Broadway, Suite 2400
Denver, CO 80202

Your name: _____

Address: _____

_____

Phone: _____ *E-mail:* _____

Your comments/story: _____

_____

_____

_____

_____

_____

Do we have permission to quote you?   Ⓨ Ⓝ
Do we have permission to contact you?   Ⓨ Ⓝ

other success books
by carol carter

The books at right are available through LifeBound. Visit www.lifebound.com.

The books below are available through Prentice Hall Publishers. Visit www.prenhall.com (search by keywords "keys to").